DIPLOMACY

AND

DIAMONDS

DIPLOMACY
AND
DIAMONDS

*My Wars from the Ballroom
to the Battlefield*

JOANNE KING HERRING
with NANCY DORMAN-HICKSON

**CENTER
STREET**

New York Boston Nashville

Permissions information appears on pp. 321–25.

Center Street
Hachette Book Group
237 Park Avenue
New York, NY 10017

www.centerstreet.com

Center Street is a division of Hachette Book Group, Inc. The Center Street name and logo are trademarks of Hachette Book Group, Inc.

The publisher is not responsible for websites (or their content) that are not owned by the publisher.

Printed in the United States of America

First Edition: October 2011
10 9 8 7 6 5 4 3 2

Library of Congress Cataloging-in-Publication Data
King Herring, Joanne, 1929–
    Diplomacy and diamonds : my wars from the ballroom to the battlefield / Joanne King Herring with Nancy Dorman-Hickson. — 1st ed.
      p. cm.
    ISBN 978-1-59995-322-9
    1. King Herring, Joanne, 1929–   2. Celebrities—Texas—Houston—Biography.   3. Political activists—Texas—Houston—Biography.   4. Socialites—Texas—Houston—Biography.   5. Houston (Tex.)—Biography.   I. Dorman-Hickson, Nancy.   II. Title.
    F394.H853K566 2011
    305.5'24092—dc23
    [B]
                                        2011018133

My Heart Part
To Beau King and Robin King, my beloved sons; and precious
Stanisse, Beau, and Beckett, my family

My Soul Mate
Desiree Lyon Howe, beautiful and talented. She taught me
the true meaning of love and friendship by her unceasing loyalty
and support at all times in all things. She is my blessing and
a blessing to every life she touches.

My Super Agent and Friend
Lacy Lynch — her rare abilities, endless efforts, and unceasing
loyalty made this book.

My Champions
Larry Brookshire, Susan Krohn, and Posey Parker, who never stop
fighting for me

My Muses
Katrin Debakey and Rosemary Howck

My Front Line
Kelly Mask and Alexis Lockwood (my assistants), Paul Erickson
(my warrior), Christina and Michael Bednorz (my guardians) —
they took the bullets and never complained about the blood.

I am also grateful to Ali Velshi of CNN, whose belief in
our project fueled our success.

Without all of them, forget it!

Acknowledgments

Now I understand why acknowledgments are so long — it takes an army! To publisher Hachette, Rolf Zettersten, Harry Helm, the tireless, dedicated, handsome, and charismatic Adlai Yeomans, and my editors, the far-seeing Christina Boys and super talented Adrienne Ingrum — for their patience, charm, efficiency, and ability. You have touched the manuscript with magic.

To my fantastic agency, Dupree/Miller, and specifically, my agent, Lacy Lynch — few agents, if any, have the knowledge and ability to comprehend world affairs and the leaders that make them like you do. You have been a gift from God, and the book would absolutely not be possible without your inventive thinking and skillful engagement from the idea to the page to the publicity and beyond. More than an agent, you are a trusted friend. Huge thanks also to CEO Jan Miller, Vice President Shannon Marven, and the precious Nena Madonia.

To darling Nancy Dorman-Hickson, my coauthor, for your talent and sweetness — you went above and beyond with your dedication, resilience, and prowess.

Thanks also to Ellen Vaughn for her keen editorial insights, which helped shape the direction of the book in the early stages, and to Paul Erickson, who helped every part of the process. Also to Kyle Ryan Kiker, Fred Courtwright at the Permissions Company, Michelle Watson, and Heather Klausmeyer for helping the book across the finish line.

To Jann Lynch, a true southern lady with a keen aesthetic eye. Thank you for your prayers, support, hospitality, intelligence, and charm.

I can't go without thanking my assistant, Kelly Mask, for her absolute and total dedication and for keeping me organized and sane in times of stress, and super achiever Alexis Lockwood for working into the night and endlessly stepping up in a time of need and carrying the book to the end. My gratitude also goes to Posey Parker, the ultimate friend and champion on my behalf.

Thank you, Marina Escobar, for allowing me to lean on you, and to Leonora Gaudin — more than anyone, you are responsible for the success in the later part of my life, infusing it with sunshine.

Last, above all, I want to thank Desiree Lyon Howe, author and foundation head, who, no matter how busy, how burdened, or how sick, dropped everything to change my life and in doing so made this book possible.

Contents

DIPLOMACY
AND
DIAMONDS

CHAPTER 1

Houston Chronicle
Section D ★★
Monday, Oct. 13, 2003

Shelby Hodge

Dinner abuzz over film role

OVER dinner at River Oaks Country Club Thursday night, discussion percolated around who would play **Joanne Herring Davis** in the film version of *Charlie Wilson's War*. **George Crile**, the *60 Minutes* producer who wrote the book on the East Texas congressman, said he favored **Sharon Stone**. **Lollie** and **Richard Jack** felt **Nicole Kidman** was right for the role.

Davis, who worked behind the scenes in the adventure that became Crile's "extraordinary story of the largest covert operation in history," could only demure at the suggestions. (**Tom Hanks** and Universal Studios have bought film rights to the book.)

Joanne and **Lloyd Davis** hosted Crile, in from New York, and two dozen friends at the dinner.

Rice University president **Malcolm Gillis**, businessman **Leo Linbeck**, former Iranian Ambassador to the United States **Hushang Ansary**, developer **Jenard Gross** and cardiologist Dr. **Lance Gould** were among those invited to share their wisdom at the 40-foot-long table. Education, preventive medicine, freedom and **Mel Gibson**'s controversial film *The Passion* were among the topics that ricocheted around the table.

Crile was in Houston to speak to the World Presidents Organization at the invitation of **John "Scotty" Arnoldy**.

Look for more words on Joanne Davis. Screenwriter **Ann Guest Moore** is interviewing the popular hostess for a biography.

Julia Roberts Played Me . . . the Bipolar Tart

WIDESCREEN

A MIKE NICHOLS FILM

TOM HANKS **JULIA ROBERTS** **PHILIP SEYMOUR HOFFMAN**

CHARLIE WILSON'S WAR

Based on the outrageous true story.

Joanne Herring

A TEXAS BOMBSHELL

Years later, as he tried to explain how it all happened, how the CIA ended up with a billion dollars a year to kill Russian soldiers in Afghanistan, Avrakotos would offer a curious explanation. "It began with a Texas woman, one of Wilson's contributors. She's the one who got him interested."

Joanne Herring was a glamorous and exotic figure out of the oil-rich world of Texas in the 1970s and '80s. At the time nobody imagined that, in addition to her role as a social lioness and hostess to the powerful, she was simultaneously responsible for setting in motion a process that would profoundly impact the outcome of the Afghan war. When almost everyone had written off the Afghans as a lost cause, she saw potential for greatness in the most unlikely characters. In the pivotal first years of the jihad, she became both matchmaker and muse to Pakistan's Muslim fundamentalist military dictator, Zia ul-Haq, as well as to the scandal-prone Charlie Wilson.

Most of the women Charlie was seeing in those days—and there were many—were half Herring's age. But Joanne Herring was a woman of extraordinary resources who knew how to mesmerize a man on many levels—not the least of which was her ability to sweep this congressman from the Bible Belt into her dazzling world of black-tie dinners, movie stars, countesses, Saudi princes, and big-time Republican oil magnates. Invariably, when reporters wrote features about Joanne Herring, they invoked Scarlett O'Hara. The comparisons are found in clips from the

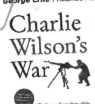
*H*ow does it feel to have a film made about you? Awful! CIA agent Gust Avrakotos (played in the movie by Philip Seymour Hoffman) said in George Crile's book, *Charlie Wilson's War,* "It began with a Texas woman…She's the one who got him interested." That was true, but I almost choked when I read the original script for the movie *Charlie Wilson's War.* What if a movie showed Charlie arriving at *your* party with his administrative assistant and you imperiously ordered her to retrieve a martini with two olives before you even said hello? My mother would have died of embarrassment!

My southern style would be, "Come on in, honey. What would you like to drink? This is my son Beau. He'll introduce you to the other guests. Charlie and I need to talk."

This script had Charlie's aide sitting on the stairs, drunk, between two trained greyhounds. Trained for *what*? To guard the stairs! They were to prevent interruptions during "hot-tub parties." No, sir, that is not me. My role in the script was horrible. I was a Christian who was sleeping with every unidentified man in sight and using "Jesus" as an exclamation point. This caricature of me was terrible. I was portrayed as the worst pseudo-Christian in history, spouting the F-word like the guy who prays loudest at church on Sunday and cheats you at the office on Monday. If it was bad — it was me! In my spare time I caused 9/11. The last scene was the Pentagon shooting up in flames. The script *actually said,* "Joanne and her conservative Christians caused 9/11."

I knew that whatever they said about me in this film was going to follow me for life. The script would be a record of what people remembered — even my sons, my grandchildren, and their children's grandchildren. Imagine having your grandmother immortalized on film, wildly swilling martinis (with two olives), wallowing in bed with strangers, and spouting "F*%k!" while dancing on the flames of the Twin Towers!

I was very happy with the book that George Crile wrote, and I was thrilled about the movie — until I read a purloined copy of the script. I was also distressed about the script because it was about the manipulation of Congress and the worst side of American politics.

The filmmakers had never met me. Christian conservative Republicans have no place in the Hollywood realm. We are valued only as targets for fun, for spoofs, and for playing corrupt businessmen or villains. I don't mind the politics because I welcome other opinions, but I knew none of those customarily assigned roles were accurate in this case. I knew it because I lived it.

I kept asking the studio people, "Don't you want to talk to me?"

No!

"You're paying Julia Roberts a lot to play me. She doesn't want to talk to me?"

No!

"Julia likes to play her roles the way she sees them," I was told.

I got the script by a miracle achieved by my childhood friend Anne Baker Horton, the cousin of James Baker, former secretary of state. She asked her daughter-in-law, June Horton, who was vice president of the William Morris Agency, to try to get it. Though it could have cost her her job, June, who was very powerful and very clever, went out on a seriously frail limb to obtain it for me.

When I first read the script, I wept, wailed, gnashed my teeth, and said, "I am going to sue."

"No, you are not," said June. "You are a public figure. You have no rights."

"No rights?" I said. "This is America! What do you mean I have *no rights?*"

"Do you know a big-time famous lawyer who has a reputation for winning cases against the odds?" she asked.

"Do I know a big-time lawyer? You bet your bippy! He just won a case for a guy who killed his neighbor and cut him into pieces; he got a 'not guilty' verdict. That's my man!" Dick DeGuerin charged sixteen million dollars a case. A bit beyond my pocketbook.

"I'll write the letter," June said. "All we need is his letterhead, his signature, and his reputation."

I dressed in my "go see the best lawyer in the world" outfit and waltzed into Dick's office, hoping he would help me. After hearing my story, he said, "Joanne, you are a southern lady. I shall not only handle this letter for you with pleasure, but I would never dream of charging you. Southern women must be protected."

Shades of Rhett Butler and Ashley Wilkes combined. I was overwhelmed! Southern customs had never seemed so beautiful as they did now, when I needed a Sir Galahad on a white horse. Well, I got 'im. But that's not all I got!

June wrote a very diplomatic letter, as planned. It was faxed to Dick with the admonition that he did not have to do a thing but okay it for his secretary to type, then sign and send it. Saturday morning I got a call from his secretary asking if I wanted to read the letter before Mr. DeGuerin sent it. "No," I cooed. "I know what is in the letter. Just send it with my deepest gratitude."

Monday morning I received a copy. This was not the same letter. To my horror, Sir Galahad had crafted a letter that threatened Tom

Hanks and Universal Studios with hanging, burning, and disembowelment! "Farewell, cruel world," I thought, envisioning the jail in which I would spend my life after Tom Hanks and Universal Studios got through suing *me*. I waited for my summons to court.

In the interim, June had lunch with the head of Universal Studios, who said, "I don't know what we are going to do with that crazy woman in Texas who is threatening us with hanging, burning, and disembowelment." (He, of course, didn't actually use those words. He used the F-word.) But then he said, "I guess we'll have to do something about it."

Gary Goetzman, Tom Hanks's production partner, called me and asked, "Why are you unhappy?"

"Because," I answered, "you have turned me into a hypocritical, bipolar tart."

He laughed, as I had hoped he would, and then I proceeded to tell him the true reasons I was so unhappy.

"One minute, I am spouting Christian values in Jesus's name," I explained. "The next, I'm rolling in bed with some man, drinking martinis with two olives. I say I am a Christian, then shout 'f^#k' when I'm mad and say 'Jesus' when I'm surprised. The tart part needs no explanation — who are all those men I'm in bed with anyway?"

Gary listened and backed me. The F-word came out. It didn't fix everything in the script, but it was a step.

Later I got another call from Gary inviting my son Robin King and me to the set of the movie in Morocco so that we could all "get to know each other." Then he invited us to Hollywood, where he had planned all kinds of exciting things, such as a dinner in our honor with Tom, Julia, Philip Seymour Hoffman, director Mike Nichols, and screenwriter Aaron Sorkin. So my next Sir Galahad/Rhett Butler in this adventure was named Gary. He was a darling, very charming, and made the difference for me.

It was the documentary my son Robin and Charles Fawcett, the director, made in Afghanistan during the Russian invasion that was the reason Charlie Wilson and the world originally got interested in the war. When George Crile was writing *Charlie Wilson's War* in the 1990s, he had called Robin endlessly to get his views for the book. It was a difficult time, as Charlie had been indicted by a grand jury for alleged corruption. In truth, he was a patriot who gained nothing but pain for trying to stop communists in various parts of the world. But in the strange political world of Washington, bad things sometimes happen to good people. Robin refused to talk to Crile because he feared I might be drawn into the controversy surrounding Charlie. (Indeed, I was questioned by the grand jury.) Charlie was ultimately never charged, and returned to full service in Congress.

In 2007, the movie people begged for scenes from Robin's film, which Robin refused to release. The first script had been so damning of me, he was afraid of how they might use the footage. It always saddened me that he did not get the credit he deserved for the important part he played in documenting the war between Afghanistan and the Soviet Union.

No one believed the Russians were invading and that the atrocities were taking place. Robin's film, made in 1981, long before the 2003 book release and the 2007 movie release of *Charlie Wilson's War*, proved these attacks and showed world leaders and all those who saw it the truth. Nothing could have been done in the 1980s without his film. He stayed in the war zone for a year helping these beleaguered people. Even though he got some media recognition in the early days and was interviewed by the networks recently, I was still happy when he was finally recognized for his work by the Motion Picture Association of America in a ceremony in 2008.

When we arrived on location in Morocco, Tom was there to greet us. "I've been in love with you for six months," he said. "I have your picture pasted all over my office. Let me give you a kiss." I was happy to comply. Tom, who was as charming, beguiling, and endearing as he appears on screen, went out of his way to make us feel special. For instance, it was very muddy there on location, so he said, "The queen can't get her feet wet"...as he scooped me up and carried me to the car!

The trip to Morocco changed everything because the filmmakers got to know me.

One day I noticed a man in the distance on top of a hill. "Oh, there's Charlie," I said.

"No, that's Tom," someone replied.

I was amazed. Charlie had back problems and an unusual way of holding himself. Tom had so fine-tuned the impersonation that he had even learned to stand like him. He had obviously studied Charlie very closely. But no one seemed interested in studying me. They were all so nice, which made it hard to understand why portraying my real personality did not seem to matter.

When I met Julia, she was absolutely charming, and even more beautiful than she is on-screen. She introduced me to her husband and showed me pictures of her children, who were enchanting replicas of their mother. Her husband was young, good-looking, and terrific. Julia had turned the tables on Hollywood men by marrying a younger, attractive, intelligent "trophy husband," who obviously adores her.

In the end, I did matter to the movie's star. I found out when I watched the movie's DVD extras that Julia was interested more than I thought. Joanne's "just so enigmatic and energetic....She walks into a room; she's a very bright light, so it's intriguing to be that person and to try to pull that off as a complete, true human being. I think she likes keeping people on their toes and having people go, 'She does what? She accomplished what?'"

But despite all this kindness shown to me by the filmmakers, the script remained unchanged except for the deletion of the F-word.

So I went to the most caring person I know who loves God — Ed Young, the minister of the Second Baptist Church of Houston, with forty-three thousand members. If prayer would help, there was plenty of it here. We bowed our heads and prayed.

During my Hollywood visit, I had said to Tom, "You are the most loved actor in America. Why would you make a movie that makes America feel bad? The script depicts Washington as a corrupt, manipulative place and the folks that run it as pretty awful. [I wasn't the only one who got socked in the script.] Our country needs to feel good about itself. You need to buy *Benjamin Franklin*, by Walter Isaacson, and *John Adams* and *1776*, by David McCullough — books about our founding fathers — and make movies that make Americans proud, just as they are proud of you."

Six months later he called me from Hungary and said, "Joanne, we've changed the whole script. It cost us a million dollars. We like it and you're going to like it."

I gasped.

"We have done a really intelligent adult movie," he said.

"Who am I sleeping with now?" I asked dryly.

"Your husband."

"Is that *obvious*?"

"Yes," he said.

"*How* is that obvious?"

"He has on a wedding ring." He paused. "*But* there *is* still a little hanky-panky with Charlie. Joanne, remember, this is Hollywood."

(Little did I know that *his* idea of "little" involved hot-tub scenes and greyhounds.)

"And, by the way," he continued, "Gary and I *did* buy *John Adams*, *Benjamin Franklin*, and *1776*, *and* we're going to produce them."

"Thank you, Tom," I said, breathing again, oh so happy, and deeply grateful to both Tom and Gary and to God.

Prayer *had* made the difference.

John Adams was made as a fascinating, historically correct miniseries. If you haven't seen it, buy it, keep it, show it to your children, and give it to their schools. It is an enthralling way to learn history. The story of our founding fathers' struggle to establish our republic will be just as relevant tomorrow as it is today.

When the movie was released in December of 2007, it was a thrill to attend the premiere in Hollywood. Tom proved to be the great American that we all love, and I'll never forget Gary Goetzman either. Those who serve silently, serve best! He, too, is a great American.

Let's not forget writer Aaron Sorkin, either, who wrote *The Social Network* and many others. He is a brilliant writer but a screaming liberal. I love him to pieces anyway. He is a sugarplum.

I was touched by these talented and caring men. My views were not their views. Their politics were not my politics. But we came together to tell a story important to our country, and it made a difference. It's what I did with Charlie, and it's what I am doing today. We've got to work together. We all win when we do!

And the new script? I had no idea what was in it. I thought positively and held my breath...

Cross-century garb highlights sixth annual Plantation Ball

THE blending of centuries at the sixth annual Old South Plantation Ball Tuesday at River Oaks Country Club provided a kaleidoscope of fashions that kept guests moving through historical eras at a dizzying pace.

There was chairwoman Kathleen

Shelby Hodge

Janick in her deep emerald-green ball gown, skirt billowing to the horizon thanks to a most effective hoop petticoat. Her fashion nod was to the 19th-century antebellum era.

Co-chair Joella Morris donned a lavender Martha Washington ensemble, complete with antique tatting and a suite of dazzling amethysts. She and honoree Joanne Davis both wore wigs of white finger-curls, popular among the wealthy of the 18th century.

Davis opted for a stunning French costume from her historic film *Thirst for Glory*, which focused on the French role in the American Revolution. Davis reported that the feature, filmed during the Bicentennial, is being revived for possible distribution.

Coco Blaffer Mallard arrived in a sophisticated, slinky black evening gown clearly of the 20th century. She was accompanied by her husband, Herbert, who wore a Confederate uniform. Baroness Sandra di Portanova wore a red sherbert-colored contemporary gown with flowing skirt, reminiscent of Scarlett O'Hara.

Inspiration for the cross-century attire was the Plantation Ball, which traditionally honors the families of one of the great old homes of the South. The Davis family estate Mount Vernon on the Brazos was the honored structure Tuesday, and Davis and her son, Robin King, who lives there, were special guests at the event.

With the Mount Vernon connection, a number of guests such as Richard and Charlotte Howe fell

Steve Campbell / Chronic

Dressed in period attire for the Old South Plantation Ball Tuesda were, from left, co-chair Joella Morris, chair Kathleen Janick, "Georg Washington" (a k a William Sommerfield of Philadelphia) and Joanr Davis.

into the Colonial dress routine. Adding to the aura of the era was a convincing George Washington played by William Sommerfield of Philadelphia's American Historical Theater.

Those preferring the ruffled femininity of antebellum gowns included Janice McNair, Melissa McNair, Janie Price and Odean McKenzie.

Special guest was James Rees, associate director of the Mount Vernon Ladies Association of the original Mount Vernon. Rees said he seldom makes these appearances outside the Washington, D.C., area because of his heavy workload. Mount Vernon is open 365 days a year and is the most visited historical site in the United States, with some 1 million visitors pouring through each year. Rees came to Houston at the invitation of Stewart and Joella Morris.

Another special guest was Alexander Ivanenko, first deputy chair-

man of the Russian Federation State Property Management. A guest of the city of Houston, Ivanenko and his wife, Ludmilla, attended the ball at the invitatio of Stewart Title and the Morrise

The Morris family made available their historical carriages for the ball. Guests attending the pr ball cocktail reception at the hon of Baron Rick and Baroness San dra di Portanova were transport to River Oaks Country Club via the horse-drawn vehicles.

Those attending the reception included Harvey and Sharon Zin I.W. and Diane Marks, Maumus Claverie, Walter and Barbara Je ferson, retired Judge Neil McKa and Ann McKay, Richard Hibber and Rose Mary Malone, Michel and Billye Halbouty, Bob McNai Cal McNair, and Christian and Viviane Escudie.

The gala benefits the Confeder ate Museum on the Old South Plantation in Richmond.

Trotter great-great-granddaughter returns to ancestoral

Was it chance or fate which caused Houstonite Joanne Davis to notice an advertisement in *The Old House Journal* for a home that she thought to be "the old home place" in Quitman, Mississippi?

Joanne, the great-great-granddaughter of the Trotters, and her son Robin King were intrigued enough by family history to come to Quitman this past week, where there was a lot of searching, reading and speculation going on at the Courthouse.

One of the interesting discoveries was that Mrs. Davis' great-grandmother Fannie Lewis Trotter married William Henry Dunlap the same date that Mary Elizabeth Trotter married John H. Ayers - December 8, 1873. No doubt a double wedding, possibly taking place at their home that now stands so stately at 419 East Franklin.

The home was built by their father, William B. Trotter, originally of Tennessee, who at the time was an attorney in Quitman. In 1845 William Trotter was a candidate for fourth district attorney and colonel of the 31st Regiment of the Mississippi Militia; later (1847) elected Brigadier General. Trotter married Elizabeth Lee Terrell of Virginia in 1846. Her mother, Frances Lewis Terrell, was the granddaughter of Fielding Lewis and Catherine Washington, first cousin of George Washington.

Mrs. Davis was also able to document that there was a plantation and plantation house. Stories handed down to her through generations of the family had originally come from the Mississippi plantation home.

Was there some jealousy between the sisters and their husbands after the Ayers

purchased the Quitman home that made the Dunlaps ride off to Texas, never to live again in Mississippi?

This home has a very colorful history - one that Mrs. Davis and her son Robin would like to help

Mrs. Joannie Davis and son Robin King

Uncle George, Me, and Revolutions

My family was full of raconteurs whose personal stories came tumbling out of the past as if from a cornucopia rich with history. Bedtime stories were always about the family. Here are a few.

My great-great-grandmother (the great-niece of George Washington) possessed courage. She bravely faced General Ulysses S. Grant, who burned, robbed, and destroyed everything in his path. When

15

Grant arrived at her door, and announced he was going to make her home his official headquarters, she greeted him by saying, "You're welcome in this house — as long as you conduct yourself like a gentleman. I expect you to return the house to me as you found it. Under no circumstances are you to come into my bedroom."

This was an invading army, yet Grant actually complied! He burned every other building in the town (and even stole her husband's tombstone) but never set foot in Great-Great-Grandmother's bedroom. Good thing too. That's where she hid the family's treasures!

When the newspapers first started writing about me, believe me, they checked out whether I really was related to George Washington. I was, through his cousin Catherine and his sister Betty. My favorite story involves Betty.

In 1776, the Marquis de Lafayette was coming to her house for dinner, and Betty knew he would be expecting spirits. The war's embargoes had caused shortages of everything, though, including liquor. Betty considered the tiny amounts of liquor left in her remaining bottles. She combined them and poured the mixture into a cut-crystal glass, to which she tied iridescent cock feathers, to make it more festive.

"A cocktail!" cried the delighted marquis.

Legend has it that Betty's fancy creation was the first cocktail ever served.

"Uncle George" Washington was used mercilessly by my family to teach me how to behave properly. I constantly heard "Uncle George did this" and "Uncle George did that." I *tried* to measure up to his high standards. There were many — too many — but I did my best... until the day my grandmother handed me a scrub brush and said, "Uncle George *always* washed out his own bathtub."

Her credibility crumbled. The maid had just quit.

There were many lessons I did learn from the legend of George Washington — a sense of duty and the necessity for sacrifice, for instance. Over and over I've made choices between my children, my family, my job, and what I felt called to do. People considered only the public side of my life and what was written about me in the society pages. But fun has often played only a small part in my life. I have always had a sense of responsibility, and even amid the seeming frivolity, when I'm using often underrated or dismissed social tools, such as good manners, I usually have a serious goal in mind.

George Washington could charm anyone, but it frustrates me that no one ever writes that about him. Instead, he is always painted as a dignified, rather boring figure. History records that, in reality, he loved music, parties, and dancing. He was the best dancer and the best horseman in Virginia. He loved having fun. He was not the stiff, dull man that is often portrayed. How could a bore be twice elected unanimously to serve as the army's commander in chief *and* the president of the United States?

Washington had important help from the French in winning America's independence. Perhaps the French did it for political reasons — every country does — but without them, America could not have won. They provided troops and money at a crucial time, when Washington's army had not been paid in more than a year and his men were deserting daily. The French fought the naval Battle of the Chesapeake — no American ships were even in that battle — without which there would have been no victory at Yorktown. Yorktown was *the* decisive battle of the American Revolution.

Washington convinced three important Frenchmen — the Marquis de Lafayette, Admiral Joseph de Grasse, and General de Rochambeau — to help our fledgling country, a treasonable offense! But he got these French men to support his *American* Revolution. They risked their reputations, fortunes, and lives because of Washington's magnetism and his dream of freedom, equality, and opportunity. Ten years later, in the French Revolution, they lost everything except their heads.

I have become involved in Afghanistan again, a nation not too dissimilar to what our own was when George Washington was alive. The war machine of the Soviet Union was defeated by this small nation the size of Texas. We helped the Afghans then by supplying weapons and support, but not one American soldier died in that war. Though we owed the Afghan people a huge debt afterward, we left them a war-torn country, wounded and dying. That's when the terrorists (the Taliban and Al-Qaeda) moved in. And that's why I am now working to rebuild Afghanistan — to win the peace that that country, twice torn by war, so richly deserves. I want to help revive that country's strength so that its people can stand up — and defend themselves so our American soldiers can come home.

CHAPTER 3

Duckling with Dyslexia

This is my house on Kirby Drive, which was first named Buffalo Drive.

MEMORIAL PARK

RIVER OAKS C

PROPER

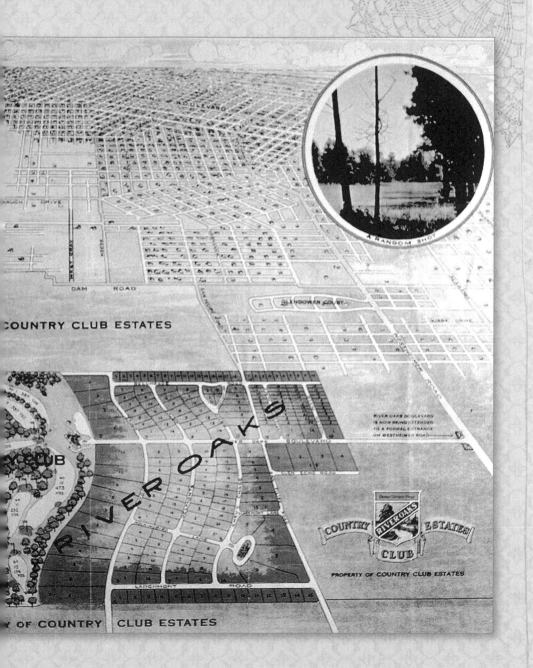

COUNTRY CLUB ESTATES

A RANDOM SHOT

GLENDOWER COURT

RIVER OAKS

COUNTRY CLUB ESTATES

CLUB

PROPERTY OF COUNTRY CLUB ESTATES

RIVER OAKS BOULEVARD
IS NOW BEING EXTENDED
TO A FORMAL ENTRANCE
ON WESTHEIMER ROAD

COUNTRY RIVEROAKS ESTATES
CLUB

PROPERTY OF COUNTRY CLUB ESTATES

Y OF COUNTRY CLUB ESTATES

*M*y parents always taught me that money doesn't matter. "What matters," they said, "is who and what you are." There was always *enough* money. But many of those with whom I grew up were people of enormous wealth. My parents, William Dunlap Johnson and Maelan McGill, came from nice families, but both were orphaned and adopted by aunts and uncles with no children. One uncle was the founder of Gulf Oil, and the other owned hundreds of acres in Houston, which became Memorial Drive — so nobody starved. Isn't it interesting that two orphaned children each had a childless aunt and uncle longing for children? See how God provides? And God provided me with a wonderful family.

Our house was on three and one-half acres on Kirby Drive in River Oaks, an elegant neighborhood. Ultimately, an Arab prince bought it.

There were no sidewalks because nobody walked anywhere. Nobody but me, that is! I *had* to walk to school. My family thought it was good for me. Other kids had chauffeurs and maids to drive them to school. Our family had a chauffeur and a maid too. But they never treated me in the style to which I thought I should become accustomed. It didn't really matter how I arrived at school, though. No one paid me any attention, anyway.

I was tall — the tallest child, male or female, in the class. I had black hair, slanted brown eyes, and high cheekbones, which would serve me well later. But on a young child, such bones were not pretty. My mother, a ravishing redhead with aqua eyes, tried to make me feel good about my drab coloring. "Oh, I always wanted a child with black hair and brown eyes," she'd say. She was kind, but I knew the truth: I was a little mouse.

Eventually, I grew into my bone structure and looked better. After my first divorce, I wanted a new look and a new life. I experimented with every color and finally decided to see whether blondes have more fun. Miss Clairol and I settled on blonde as my "natural" hair color. When people said I looked enough like my friend Eva Gabor to be her sister, I was flattered beyond belief. The sister of Zsa Zsa, Eva was the Hungarian actress who was known for her role as Lisa Douglas on the television show *Green Acres*.

But that was many years in the future. As a kid, I was quite plain. I was also skinny at a time when women had to be plump to be considered pretty, like Jane Russell, the icon of my generation.

And I was dyslexic. There are a thousand ways to be dyslexic, but, basically, it means your eyes play tricks. You read letters backwards. Numbers jump from column to column, changing the line of figures completely. You can't read or add what you can't see. Even today I often have to dial a phone number several times because the numbers keep jumping. When I type the word "had," it comes out "dha."

When I was a child, teachers and parents knew nothing about dyslexia. Undiagnosed children with dyslexia often become shy, defeated, or class problems. They are punished for "not trying." When I was baffled in class, it was scary and humiliating. I'd try so hard but would almost always get the wrong answer. Before I went to school, my mother had read the *Encyclopedia Britannica* and the Bible to me. She *knew* that I had understood what she was reading. So when I did poorly in school, she realized that I was not dumb and kept right on challenging me. My mother's belief in me helped me succeed despite this handicap — which prepared me to wage war against conventional thinking in my future.

When I was ten, we sold our house in town and moved to five hundred acres about ten miles from Houston. It was our family's "country home," and it was a copy of Mount Vernon, with a ballroom and a beautiful stable, replicas of those belonging to the governor's palace in Williamsburg, Virginia. Five generations of us lived in that house near Houston.

One morning while getting ready to ride my horse, I felt something hard hit my leg. "Daddy!" I shrieked. "A snake!"

John, the stable manager, began to run toward me, but, to my horror, my father stopped him. "Kick it off!" he told me.

I felt betrayed. I could not believe my indulgent father was not coming to my rescue. I kicked it off, expecting a hug.

Then he said, "Kill it!"

"How?" I wailed.

"That hoe against the tree," he directed. I grabbed it and brought it down hard on the snake, my heart pounding. The snake was dead.

"Rattlesnake," my father commented. "Good work." Then he calmly walked off.

Only later did I realize that it was a harmless king snake — and he knew it, too. Daddy upgraded it to give me confidence. He always said, "Children need to experience success or they won't realize their full potential."

It was a harsh lesson, but it worked. From my ten-year-old perspective, I had just single-handedly killed the most poisonous reptile on the face of the earth. I really needed that feeling because my classroom humiliation left me with no confidence. My father was teaching me that whatever happened, I could handle it.

"Never give in to fear — it interferes with winning," he often said.

Winning came naturally to William Dunlap Johnson. He lettered in every sport, was first pick for pro football one year (over future Olympian Jim Thorpe), was the first All-American in the Southwest Conference, was elected to the honor society, and was voted "most popular man" and "most likely to succeed." As captain of the football team at Texas A&M University, to inspire his teammates he refused to wear a helmet. In the 1922 Cotton Bowl Classic (which in those days was as big as any one of today's New Year's Day bowl games), he scored the winning touchdown — barefoot! Fear and failure were (and are) just not done in our family.

Loneliness helped me overcome dyslexia by making me a voracious reader; many people who have dyslexia often have difficulty and discomfort reading, but practice makes perfect. As a young girl, I taught myself the joy of constantly learning new things. I gobbled up all kinds of books in the family's formidable library. Then my uncle sent me a state-of-the-art record player along with his classical music collection. The music helped me appreciate the great composers, while the reading awakened an interest in history. Mine was a self-education in the classics at the ripe old age of ten! I thought that was quite sufficient.

But my father and mother obviously decided that if I wasn't pretty I should be educated. My father taught me when, where, and why. My mother taught me how. Later in life, my parents' lessons helped me in ways I couldn't have predicted: first in the building business with my husband, next in my television career, and finally when I visited the great palaces in England, France, Spain, and Italy. At the time I desperately needed to fit in.

My father's sessions on art, architecture, and design were relentless and thorough. His tutorial continued for two years . . . and I hated every minute of it. (There was a difference between teaching myself and having my father *force* me to learn.) Without realizing it, however, I was acquiring knowledge and experience that I would return to again and again in the future when I had little else and needed those lessons. Another tool in my toolbox!

My mother instilled in me manners and the social graces to dress, talk, and dine appropriately. She even taught me the proper way to eat fruit with a knife and fork. She seemed to know everything that I would need to know as an adult when I was in lofty surroundings, however, not quite everything.

Years later, in the shah of Iran's palace, when I looked around for the small knife traditionally used to put caviar on toast, it was nowhere to be seen. Neither was the toast. So I looked around and thought the only utensil that seemed appropriate was a fork, only to notice belatedly that the other guests were eating their caviar with a small spoon that I had only seen used for demitasse coffee. When they saw me use a fork, however, they immediately picked up their forks and joined me, making no issue at all of my ignorance. Their silent support was the most genuine example of manners and hospitality I have ever seen. But that was far in the future.

My first death knell came the year I was ten.

For a month my mother suffered a fever of 106 degrees caused by a strep infection of the blood. At that time, nobody survived this illness, let alone survived a month with a fever of 106. The only hope was to find a survivor who carried the blood cells that could cure her. The family sent out urgent newspaper and radio messages. Hospital records were searched. At last, a donor was found. By God's miracle, Carlton Speed lived in Houston! His blood saved her life. I was to become wary every time a new decade arrives. Every ten years, without fail, my life has been marred by eminent tragedy.

At the time, the family sheltered me from knowing how serious her situation was. When I learned the details later, I shuddered. If my mother had died, you would not be reading this book. She never gave up on her little ugly dyslexic duckling. In fact, her recovery from that strep infection may have been inspired by the loss of her own mother when my mother was only twelve. She was a child of wealth and privilege in Dallas, a student at "the" Highland Park Academy, but life as she knew it ended when her mother contracted tuberculosis in an age with no cure. She died slowly, horribly — in front of my mother's eyes. My mother's father, a spoiled playboy, sold their house and left with all of the family money, abandoning his son and daughter.

My mother's brother (twenty at the time) quit college to raise her until she was eventually adopted by her aforementioned aunt and uncle, and he later became editor of the Associated Press.

This experience led my mother to vow that she would never abandon her children. Not even disease could force her to break her vow. Without her, the ugly duckling in the story might never have had a chance to become a swan.

CHAPTER 4

Swan with Swain

At age twelve my looks began to change. "I love her bone structure," Paul Gittings, a renowned photographer, told my parents. His close-up of my face won an international contest. Suddenly, people thought I was okay.

With the ensuing attention my confidence grew and my life changed. Stories emerged that are still told today.

Lloyd Hand, who became chief of protocol for President Lyndon B. Johnson, loves to tell the story of "One-Step" Joanne as a teenager. He says he remembers stepping onto the dance floor where the boys were lined up to dance with me. As soon as one boy danced one step with me, another would cut in for his turn. After each cut-in, I'd squeeze the boy's hand and whisper, "Come back." And he would!

Today, it's hard to imagine life in the late 1940s. Kids then accepted and followed the rules, which were strictly enforced. Parents were very protective. For example, each generation had a dance club to which you had to belong, or you were out. In Houston, members were carefully vetted by the parents, who were some of the city's most influential people. The club I belonged to, Merrymakers, existed solely to introduce children to each other in the hopes that the "right" marriage into the proper family would materialize. The children dated from among this group or not at all. That's just the way it was back then. Parents wanted to give their offspring the world with a fence around it. It isn't possible, of course, but they tried.

At dances, the chaperones sat in stolid elegance against the wall. They resembled Mount Rushmore — never uttering a word but never taking their eyes off of us either. My mother insisted that I introduce myself to the chaperones like a "lady" should. I was the only child at the parties whose mother demanded this. I dreaded it, since the "cool kids" never talked to the adults, but I did it.

Over the next forty years, these parents (there were different ones at each dance) never forgot my good manners whenever I saw them. This tiny courtesy opened many doors for me and taught me the value of having the support of older people of position and power. They often act like a machete, cutting away brambles from your path.

My father told me to befriend everyone, not just the popular kids. That's how I found many smart and interesting friends — it isn't always the football heroes and glamour girls who stand by you. I learned never to judge a book by its current cover. Many "ordinary" kids go on to have extraordinary careers and lives.

I always remembered my own unattractive, unpopular years. My changed appearance didn't eliminate the memories. But that time of my life helped me become a better, more compassionate person. To this day I enjoy helping the underdog.

But before I grew into that understanding, I sometimes handled my newfound gifts from God poorly. My new life was a gift from God, but I didn't bother to consult Him on anything. I now turn to God first. "If it is Your will, please help me to accomplish this. If not, close the door," I pray.

I have faced many closed doors.

We wonder why babies die. We wonder why we have wars. We wonder about the unexplained, the tragic, the incomprehensible. I know that God is not the source of these things. I also know we can't control what happens to us. But we *can* control how we react. I so admire those who, by faith, have turned tragedy around and used it for good, changing the lives of others by their example.

When overwhelmed, we simply must walk on in faith, knowing that somehow this too will pass and that Jesus is there to walk with us into a better tomorrow. Time and again in my life, God has turned my tragedies into strengths that I would need in the tomorrows to come. Sometimes it takes years to see that, though.

World War II was raging during my junior high school years, but our little corner of Texas was largely untouched by the privations of war. My family did what our country asked. We moved into town to save gas. We tried to grow a victory garden, but nothing seemed to come up. We canned but couldn't do anything with the canned vegetables because they were awful.

My father, an engineer, was working with McCloskey shipyards to develop the first all concrete boats. The Liberty ships were a success and were built, launched, and used toward the end of the war.

Another government edict was to invite servicemen for lunch. I did, to my mother's surprise. Those eighteen-year-olds were bored to death with a thirty-seven-year-old woman and a twelve-year-old girl.

The summer after my first year in high school, my father, an engineer, had a contract to build an airport, roads, and housing in the jungles of Colombia as part of the war effort. What a marvelous opportunity to experience an exciting new world, right? Wrong. Fifteen-year-olds are not looking for adventure. I wanted to be with my peers. In Colombia, I feared my only social life would be with howler monkeys.

In most of the world today, you can just walk up to someone and start a conversation. But in Colombia in 1945, you had to be introduced. Lacking the proper introductions, young men began following me around as an American novelty. The most ingenious and attractive was Fernando Quintana, age nineteen at the time. He and his mother just "happened" to be in the hotel elevator at the same time as my parents and me.

"Señor," his mother said to my father, "my son was so determined to meet your daughter that I agreed to accompany him in the hope of seeing you. I want to invite you to our home for dinner." My parents were enchanted by this elegant lady and her wonderful invitation. Through Fernando's family we met the most important people and saw a Bogotá that few Americans ever see. For me, interacting with influential foreigners on their own territory would become essential in my future. Another tool in the box.

There was a problem, however. Fernando did not know that I was only fifteen . . .

Oops! Time to go to the jungle!

By then my father had already left, and Mother and I missed the plane that was to take us inland to the jungle. To meet him, we had to ride a paddle-wheel boat pushing a barge up the Magdalena River. The cabins were not air-conditioned. The cow on the barge disappeared, and that night we had steak. My new puppy enjoyed what I could not swallow. This was another world.

The jungle was different from anything I'd known before. My parents spent every night at parties with an international group of engineers, scientists, doctors, and military people in our luxurious camp. For them this really *was* an adventure, but all I had was a wild horse and scorpions the size of lobsters.

Never one to suffer silently, I launched my campaign to go home.

I wept. I wailed. "I am not going to spend the best years of my life in this jungle!" I protested. It had been all of three months so far. "No! No! No! I want to go home and now!"

"Where do you want to go? Hockaday?" asked my bewildered parents.

"Heavens no, I'm not that dumb!" An all-girl school was not what I had in mind.

Before making this announcement, I had reviewed all my relatives and where they lived. Bryan, Texas, had Allen Military Academy, Texas A&M University, and, of course, the high school, which meant there would be lots of men there. Cool!

"I want to go to Bryan and live with Great-Aunt Hettie," I told my parents, never giving a thought to what Great-Aunt Hettie might think. The whole family almost fainted. "Oh, no, you're not taking on Joanne," they told Hettie. "You're too old and she's a handful. She'll kill you."

Despite the protests, Aunt Hettie agreed to take me in. Southern families are like that.

My great-uncle Charles Gainer, Hettie's husband, was a former state senator and speaker of the Texas House of Representatives. He and Hettie were wonderful examples of the gracious society in which Texas was rooted. So I snagged one of my scorpion/lobster friends, put him in a jar of alcohol, and transported my jungle trophy to Texas.

Before I moved to Bryan, parties, clothes, and boys were all I thought about. Because of my dyslexia, I thought I wasn't smart. I thought attractiveness was all that mattered because that was all I had. But Bryan High School changed my life. There, kids were not interested in society as I knew it. They took education and being part of a church seriously. After arriving, I realized that my values and priorities had to change.

One of the students who epitomized Bryan High School values was Bill Powers. He was student body president and the football team captain. He became a naval fighter pilot, one of the men who inspired the Tom Cruise character in the movie *Top Gun*. (He even *looked* like Tom Cruise.) Bill was always very kind and complimentary. He once told my son Beau, "The day Joanne walked in, I was smitten. She won contests, the leads in plays, and the offices of many clubs. She really didn't seem to care about grades."

But Bill, I did care about grades. Every kid wants to do well. I just didn't make them. Although I knew that Bryan students were serious about their studies, I aimed my own efforts toward excellence at activities I was comfortable with, such as plays, operettas, and contests. I never thought I could do better than Bs and Cs — until the day the principal called me into her office. "Joanne," she said, opening a file in front of her, "I've been looking over your grades."

My heart plummeted and my smile faltered. I sat frozen, unsure of what to say.

She glanced up and gave me an appraising look. Then she said something that caused this mediocre student's heart to leap: "You can do better. In fact," she added in a voice filled with conviction, "you can make the National Honor Society. All you have to do is try."

No one had ever said I could make good grades. The only praise I'd ever had was for extracurricular activities. But Miss Weddington saw beyond my facade to what was locked inside. If I hadn't had the extracurricular activities to build on I could never have been able to believe what Miss Weddington said. After that, my grades improved dramatically. Her belief in me made the difference. I learned then that how people perceive you and how you perceive yourself can be very different. Often what we need is encouragement and success at something whether it be knitting or calf roping, just something.

From the dyslexia I developed a retentive memory. In the beginning I learned to memorize what the teacher said.

Johnie McAdams, my speech instructor, also saw something in me that might never have surfaced without her guidance. In fact, she made my eventual television career possible. "Joanne was a piece of work," Ms. McAdams later told a friend of mine. "She could memorize a script in one night. I hate to tell you this, but I saved the best parts for her.

"Joanne did one thing none of us will ever forget. There was a thin, frail child named Emma Jane who came from a poor family. She was the subject of painful adolescent laughter when she was noticed at all. People thought she was 'slow.' Joanne began speaking to her," Ms. McAdams recalled. "She hung her head and did not answer, but Joanne kept talking to her every day and walking her to the door and down the hall. Slowly Emma Jane began to change. She sat up straight in class. She no longer crept down the halls. She began to hold up her head. Then she started talking. Her grades improved and she began to behave like the other students." Mrs. McAdams said that people can make a big difference in others' lives when they try.

I remember that shy girl very well. All it took for her to gain confidence was for someone to pay attention to her. I had been there. I understood how she felt. I paid attention.

As I gained confidence, I started debating, and to my surprise I won most of the debates. This became an important tool for my television show.

When I made the National Honor Society, my mother cried. Success is a gift from *God*. If God had not given me successes to build my confidence, I could never have faced the failures life was to bring me, not to mention rebounding from those every-ten-year downfalls.

In my last year of high school, my mother returned from South America. She wanted to make my senior year memorable. For my high school graduation tea, the dining room glistened with family silver brought from Houston. Breathtaking flowers added color and aroma, and a grand table groaned with food displayed on an embroidered linen tablecloth.

Girls from the city's finest families arrived. And there, to their surprise, standing in the receiving line with them, was Emma Jane, wearing a beautiful organza dress. Her presence added the perfect closing to my high school days. I never returned to Bryan, though I loved every minute I was there and owed everyone so much. But a page had turned. I was ready to take on the world — or at least Texas.

CHAPTER 5

HOUSTON SOCIETY

By SHELIA FORTUNE, Society Editor

The goal for the campaign is 150,000 dollars for purchasing new animals for the Houston Zoological gardens. **Mrs. Horace T. Robbins,** fund drive chairman, is convinced that the old animals are not exotic enough and wouldn't be even if they did have new hearts, and therefore **Dr. Cooley** has made initial preparation for the drive. She says "Animals are universally appealing and we anticipate the society's ability to make a significant contribution to the zoo's collection at the conclusion of the drive. **"Mrs. C. G. Johnson** and **Mrs. Neill T. Masterson III** are fund drive co-chairman assisted by honorary chairmen: **Mrs. Gus Wortham, Mrs. Oscar Wyatt,** and **Mr. Eddy Scurlock. Mrs. Robert King** is the publicity chairman. The society is involved with new zoo specimens, zoo facilities, and zoo-related entertainment. Future plans include provisions for adding a Safari zoo in the Addicks Dam vicinity adjacent to the existing zoo grounds.

Operational and managerial responsibility for the Hermann Park Zoo is vested in the City Parks and Recreation Department, but no funds are available in the municipal budget for the purchase of new animals. Giraffes, for example, cost about $4,000, and the going price for baby African elephants is $6,000. Animals for the new children's zoo scheduled for completion this summer range in price from $75 for capybaras to $700 for baby chimpanzees and $1,200 for antelopes.

Contributions to The Zoological Society Fund Drive will help purchase the animals for the children's zoo, which will feature a contact area where children may play with tame animals.

For members, the Society is planning a periodical publication, speakers bureau, educational programs and a lecture series. Assisting President **Dr. Cooley** are **Curtis Hankamer, Duncan MacFarlan** and **Robert Maurice;** vice-presidents; **Richard A. Beutel,** secretary; **Bland McReynolds,**

treasurer; and **Harold C. Geis,** executive director.

Mrs. Thomas P. F. Hoving visited Houston to attend a dinner at the **Jean De Menils** for Houston collectors. After setting the "Fun City" program into motion, **Mr. Hoving** resigned as the Director of Parks and Recrea-

tion of New York City to become the of the Metropolitan Art Museum. O most novel projects has been to est art authorization service sponsored museum. Before the dinner he was of honor at a cocktail party hoste **Lester J. Rutledge.** Mr. Hoving

Mrs. Horace Robbins, Dr. Denton Cooley, President of the Houston Zoological Society, and Mrs. Robert V. King pose with a few very tame creatures who attended Mrs. King's party for the Houston Zoological Society's introduction of the "Help Noah" campaign which will increase the society's membership and raise funds for the purchase of animals for the zoo.

What Southern Girls Do: We Get Married

The picture that got the attention of the Hollywood agent.

When I left for the University of Texas at Austin, in 1947, my grandfather said, "Don't worry about grades; just get to know people." Translated, that meant land a rich, socially prominent husband. Girls were discouraged from even considering medicine or law or any remunerative position.

My family did not care what I studied since my having a career never entered their minds. But it entered mine. Since I had played the leads in high school plays, I studied music and drama to prepare myself to sing in musical comedies on Broadway. Most hopefuls who failed to make the big time ended up teaching in a second-rate school. That was probably my destination until God took a hand.

Scarlett O'Hara always asked men for advice. So naturally I did too. One senior economics major suggested I take a class in his field. I signed up but I didn't like it, so he gallantly agreed to attend the class and even to take the exam for me. I'm ashamed to say I accepted his offer. There were one hundred students in the class, so he thought he could get away with it. To our horror, he discovered that my final exam coincided with his most important test. Disaster! I had been to only two classes all semester!

Furious, scared, and guilt ridden, I asked, "What am I going to do?"

My friend replied, "I will not be able to graduate if I miss my exam. But I know how your professor thinks. I'll coach you. You should at least pass." To overcome dyslexia, I had developed an excellent memory, another tool. I used it now.

I walked into the exam room, took out my pencil, and wrote. Instead of answering the questions, I had written twenty-seven pages on his theory of economics. I made an A and got an accolade from my professor. He asked the class to vote for me for the University of Texas "Sweetheart" title. From that experience I learned to focus on the big picture and learned not to cheat.

My family suggested that I get a summer job. They thought it was important that I "learn to earn" so that I could appreciate the efforts made to support us "helpless women." This was the beginning of my full-time focus on my dream career, singing in a Broadway show, dating, and marriage. I never returned to the University of Texas because of some totally unexpected opportunities.

Around this time, Bill Roberts, a popular Houston journalist, asked to photograph me for his column. This was the first and only time I was photographed in a bathing suit. (My family gasped and asked, "How crass can you be!") In the article, Roberts mentioned my contest titles. Word got out and a modeling agency called. Modeling was *not* the summer job my mother had in mind. It wasn't what I had in mind either. I wanted to sing in a Broadway musical. But photographs are seen and forgotten.

At about the same time, Houston's top law firm, Baker Botts, called. They always hired a receptionist from a good family. All the girl did was sit at the front desk and smile. It was a good display case. She quickly got an appropriate husband and quit, because, of course, married women typically did not work. Thus, the job was regularly open and much sought after. I was offered this coveted position and I accepted because my mom told me to.

Meanwhile, my father's brother heard that the Summertime Opera Company was seeking a girl to sing the second lead in the next local production. This was a fabulous opportunity for me and my theater aspirations. The leads were always imported accomplished professionals. To snare a second lead would give me the opportunity to pursue my dream of singing in a Broadway musical. I auditioned and got the role. I felt like seventy-six trombones had just led the big parade down my street.

"You cannot sing at night and work in the daytime," said my mother. Thus, I bid adieu to the receptionist job at Baker Botts.

I remember the newspaper review of the show well: "Joanne Johnson can neither sing, dance, or act, but no one since Hedy Lamarr or Liz Taylor has needed to less."

The left-handed complimentary review bothered me, but my family was delighted. Bye-bye, Broadway. They never intended to let me go to New York. They played along because they thought I would never get the chance. They were right. I didn't. I just wasn't good enough! And, frankly, I wasn't willing to put in the time and practice required to develop what talent I did have. I just wanted to open my mouth and sing! That's what they do today, but back then you had to be Julie Andrews. My unwillingness to practice warred with my desire to be a singing star. I wasn't listening to God or anybody else. I was listening to my own rather unrealistic dreams about a singing career.

Without my knowledge, the modeling agency had sent my photograph to MGM Studios. MGM was having a talent/beauty contest to find a new star. The prize was a role opposite *Clark Gable*. An MGM representative came to Houston to interview me.

"I have years of acting experience in school plays," I gushed.

He rolled his eyes and said, "Honey, you have a terrible southern accent, but we are only interested in how you look. You would play an Indian and all you would have to say is 'Ugh!'" The role was that of Kamiah, a Blackfoot princess and the wife of Clark Gable's character, Flint Mitchell, in the movie *Across the Wide Missouri*.

I sat there wondering what to do and how to act, intimidated by this important man. But my mother was very much on her high horse. She looked down her nose at this common theatrical person who did not even speak English correctly. Her disapproving demeanor amused this tough character immensely. He must have thought, "That dumb woman has no reason to act so lofty. There are a million like her snotty little daughter who would sell their souls for this chance." I really expected him to get up and simply walk away. He did not walk away — but he was not very encouraging either. He simply said, "We will see."

I did not long mourn my dream of a career on Broadway. I turned my attentions to something *really* important: the debutante season was in full swing. I was a year younger than the big-time glamour girls who were the queens of the season, but I was also invited to debut parties around the state — Dallas, Fort Worth, San Antonio — and I basked in their glow. Amon G. Carter Jr., the biggest husband-catch in Fort Worth, invited me to a house party and skiing at an elegant resort in New Mexico. But my parents had financial limits: they had provided fabulous ball gowns, but ski clothes were definitely *not* in the budget.

Actually no one in the group, including Amon Jr., had any ski clothes — but he didn't have a budget! It was not a problem for him or any of the rest of his crowd to spend thousands on ski outfits as it was for me.

Joan Farish, daughter of one of Houston's most distinguished families, heard that I needed ski clothes. She hardly knew me but offered me all of her wonderfully appropriate clothes, which she'd worn at her school in Switzerland. In life, you always get paid back, one way or another. This time *I* was Emma Jane.

Girls usually did not "go steady" with just one guy in the 1940s and early 1950s. We dated a lot of people — so we had to learn to control racing hormones. When you control the situation, you win. If he can convince you to succumb, he wins. Even today I believe that. The world changes, but people don't. Men in history and men today like a conquest but don't value an easy one. I believe if a woman jumps in bed easily tonight, tomorrow the man will be bragging. If today she makes him wait, tomorrow he will be begging. Making men wait only whets their appetite.

In the end, sex is not what keeps men hanging around anyway; it's the intrigue, the interest, and the intellect. That's why it's important for women to develop their minds and obtain knowledge.

My virtue intact, I spent a glorious year meeting the right people and lining up suitors for parental approval. This was objective number one to a family intent on protecting their daughter from the evils of show business and the infamous studio couch. Why risk it when everything that careers could buy was available in Texas on the magic carpet of marriage?

In the forties and fifties, I really did not know what love was. I just did what I was told. Dating whomever I pleased was just not possible. I dated only those considered appropriate by my parents.

Charles Henry "Pete" Coffield was one of the richest boys in Texas. His father was wealthy and powerful, both in Texas and nationally, and Mr. Coffield had big plans for his only son — which did not include me. He wanted a merger, not a marriage. I had nothing to merge. His son, however, for perhaps the first time in his life, stood up to his father and said, "I am going to marry Joanne. She comes from a good family and has everything except money. Why do we need money? I love her."

His papa called on me and said I was "beautiful and good with people." He then said, "Pete is determined to marry you, so I won't stand in the way."

Stand in the way? I was aghast. No one had ever even implied that I was inappropriate as a suitable marriage choice. Even Pete's mother had been calling me her daughter-in-law proudly ever since I met the family. I had had many suitors, and their families had all approved. I did not like Mr. Coffield's comments one bit.

Enter Bob King. Bob was twenty-seven, older than my group. He had served in World War II, was out of college, and already had a successful business. His rich, innovative father, C.E. King, cleverly taught his two sons, Bob and Buck, how to become millionaires themselves. They did so almost overnight due to the elder King's progressive thinking. He bought three hundred acres of land, put in streets, water, electricity, and lights; hired an experienced foreman; and told the boys to build and sell houses to returning servicemen on the GI Bill.

Subdivisions like this sprang up all over the country and not only provided low-cost housing, but created thousands of jobs for carpenters, plumbers, electricians, painters, and so on. Bob and Buck built ten subdivisions all over Houston. This was hard work. They had to know subcontracting, banking, design, salesmanship, and, most importantly, how to choose land in the path of development.

Bob liked high living and enjoyed his well-earned money. He told everyone who would listen that he was in love with me. "I am the man who is in love with Joanne Johnson," he once introduced himself to a large group, "and my objective in life is to marry her."

Bob knew about Pete, so he decided to court my parents and

grandparents. He sent them flowers, did errands, and drove them places. They adored him. They thought it was wonderful for me to have someone who loved me and would take care of me forever. "Marry me," Bob said. "I will build you the house of your dreams."

I liked a twelve-acre piece of land in Houston's Rivercrest neighborhood. Bob bought it in anticipation of our inevitable (in his mind) nuptials.

I was still dating Pete and other boys, so Bob asked my mother if he could *move in with us*. To my horror, my mother said yes. He was told he could never come upstairs where I stayed, though. "That would not be proper," my mother said primly.

So he moved into the family room, and for six months he watched as I came and went with other boys!

Every weekend I flew to Dallas to see Pete and his family. "Why go on the plane?" Bob asked. "I will drive you up and bring you back. It takes the same amount of time." I accepted. Pete said nothing, but his father teased his son mercilessly about the "King fish."

My family was devoted to Bob. He was movie-star handsome, he was rich, and he was always promising me the world. I began to fall in love, so soon it was good-bye, Pete.

The wedding invitations were in the mail. The day my wedding pictures were made, MGM called about the Clark Gable movie for which I had auditioned. My father, who answered the phone, was told, "We want to give Joanne a chance because she has something very rare…star quality. She glows."

"We are not interested," he tersely replied. He did not tell me about the offer until *after* I was married. The part went to María Elena Marqués, a beautiful Mexican actress.

Now I had a new dream. My marriage would be a fairy tale. I would work to make it as "happily ever after" as possible.

I was so inexperienced, I thought life was like the movies or a novel and I could play the roles I fancied. I was tired of Scarlett O'Hara. I had played her for years and would be haunted by her for the rest of my life. Daphne du Maurier had written a best-selling book called *Rebecca*. I now wanted to be Rebecca. This mythical creation with a stately and regal home called Manderley was beautiful, witty, and charming. She was also *dead*! In the movie, Joan Fontaine and Laurence Olivier played the characters.

In my immature imagination, I resurrected Rebecca as me. It may be difficult for young women today to relate to that notion because so much has changed. But in the 1950s, the emphasis for women was strictly on home and family. That was our lives!

I read books and magazines on how to be a good wife. Like Rebecca, I even kept my stationery in an embroidered box. Everything had to match. When I had a tea for fifty ladies, all fifty of the china, silver, and lace-trimmed napkins were matched. Now *no one* does that! It was ridiculous.

With my father's help, I had designed the house Bob and I built for our home. Our Xanadu was built on the land that Bob had purchased. Bob was amazed at the results. "Design the houses I'm building," he requested. My life of luxurious indulgence was about to end.

I began handling the design and decoration of Bob's houses. This was *hard* work. I had to use the same sofas, drapes, and bedspreads over and over yet make each house look different. I also did the landscaping with laborers who had never worked with plants.

I started designing the floor plans for Bob's small houses, carefully drawing the plans to scale. Every inch costs money, thus these plans had to be properly done and fit the lots, which were smallish too. I had had no training for this other than what my father had taught me, but I became good enough so that the draftsmen we hired eventually began to respect me. It was tough for the boss's wife to tell guys with degrees in architecture how to draw floor plans, though.

Also, I'd drive up to the construction sites in my convertible wearing my frilly dresses. The workmen were offended at taking orders from the boss's wife. They did not like it when I asked them to correct mistakes or to be careful with the equipment. Gradually I learned to work with tough guys who had no respect for a woman "out of her place," that is, the home.

I had to check on the work done by the plumbers, painters, air-conditioning subcontractors, and so on. They were all men. There were no women contractors and few, if any, women architects. So I, in my frilly dress, had to tell the men when things were done wrong, a difficult and awkward task. The subcontractors never liked me, but because I learned their trade and knew what I was doing, they accepted me. And, of course, my husband paid them.

This was my first battle in a man's world. Now I use humor, and tough guys do not always like me, but they do not faze me. Then, I just did the best I could and hated every moment. The glass ceiling may not be as thick today as it was in the 1950s, but it's still there. Every woman will tell you that, and back then I was always bumping my head against it, as so many women have. Now, instead of making demands, I make suggestions. When you don't push, men will ultimately give you what you want. In my case it seemed they always gave me more.

I worked side by side with Bob King. He covered the financial side, buying the land and calculating and watching costs to keep the company functioning. I got the houses built, decorated, and landscaped, and that helped to sell them. In all we built five thousand houses, and our houses always won in the home shows.

I was running our big house in Rivercrest, being the social butterfly I thought I was supposed to be, and trying to run half of Bob's business, all at the same time. I trained my mind to anesthetize myself so that I wouldn't feel pain from being so tired, a tool I have used often to get me through tough times. In 1952, though, I felt twinges after straightening up. I thought it was from lifting too many heavy objects. I should have noted that the ten-year mark was approaching. This time, the joy of my teenage years and my fairy-tale marriage was leading up to a *death* ... mine.

CHAPTER 6

A Brush with Death and New Life

I was only twenty-one years old and the mayor had named me Houston's official hostess. I had it all, but it meant nothing, because I wanted to die.

A steadily increasing pain in my back had me considering death as a blessed deliverance. I had seen many doctors, yet the pain only grew worse until nothing in my body functioned. I could not walk. Dr. George Ehni admitted he did not know what was wrong. "You must have a myelogram to find out," he said. I was put facedown on a gurney, increasing the already unbearable pain, then fluid was injected into my spine for X-rays. At the time, the brutal process was in its infancy. The attending nurse fainted.

After almost unendurable pain, they found the problem: a thick, dark, ominous blockage in the spine. Dr. Ehni surmised it was a tumor growing within my spinal column. It had to be removed. One night before the surgery the nuns who worked at St. Joseph Hospital came to me and prayed. "You should know how serious this really is," they told me. "We think you should be prepared. No one has ever walked away from this surgery. You will either die on the operating table or be in a wheelchair for life."

I was stunned. Nothing in my gilded life had prepared me for this, and the doctor had failed to mention it. I had never felt so alone in my life. In the wee hours of the morning, I learned to walk with God.

I did not tell my husband or my parents what the nuns had told me. It was just me and God. It finally comes to that in all of our lives. We are completely alone unless we have Jesus, who will never leave us, no matter how often we leave Him. I talked to Him about many things during this ghastly time, and I stopped asking, "Why me?" Other people had plenty of their own problems too. As I was to see so often, I would not want to trade mine for theirs.

I made my peace with God. "Lord, I have led a charmed life," I said. "You have given me everything. I am not afraid to die." I really did not fear death. I accepted it.

But I could not accept living the rest of my life in a wheelchair. Yet the morning they rolled me into the operating room, I said, "Okay, Lord. If You want me to live in a wheelchair, I accept it. Your will, not my will, be done." I gave God my life at the entrance to the operating room — to die, which I was not afraid to do, or to live in a wheelchair if He chose. The choice I made that day changed my life. I understood faith at that moment as I never had before.

I came out of the operating room a medical miracle. The tumor had been wound around the fragile nerves inside my spinal column. Dr. Ehni untwisted the nerves, removed the tumor, and put the nerves back in their proper place without lasting damage. Until that time, no one had ever done that. At thirty-four, Dr. Ehni would became world famous, while color photos of my back went into medical books.

I never had another moment of pain. The tumor was gone. I could ride horseback, ski, climb, dance, and do everything I had feared losing. I felt unbound gratitude toward Dr. Ehni and to God.

Little did I know that disasters come in threes. At twenty-four, I encountered my second.

I began to ache when I saw other friends' children. That was all they talked about. They were completely occupied with these enchanting new lives. I had nothing to add. I felt lost in that world. It hurt. I could not understand why I was not getting pregnant. "What is wrong with me? Why no baby?" I asked my doctor.

The doctor couldn't understand either. "I don't know," he said. "Wait and see." Then, after months of tests, the doctor said, "I occasionally have an unmarried girl from a good family who gives up a child for adoption. They would be comforted for their child to go to someone like you who could care for it well."

I raced home and said, "Bob, the doctor will find us a baby from a nice family that we can adopt!"

"Never," he refused. "I will never accept anyone else's baby... forget that."

I burst into tears, which I rarely did. Tears had no effect. My life seemed meaningless. I ran to my car to get away from the hurt. As I drove toward the sunset, great swatches of color — magenta, pink, blue, purple, orange — spread across the evening sky, all mingled by the Master's hand. No artist has ever matched His work. Was God speaking to me, as He often does, through His beautiful world? I felt His power and mastery over all things — nature, illness, and even the pain of being childless.

"All right, Lord. You say that if we have faith the size of a tiny, almost impossible-to-see mustard seed, you will move mountains. I shall take that mustard seed and believe against all unbelief that you will give me a child," I promised.

Weeks, months, a year went by... nothing. God does not keep a schedule. It was tough to understand for a woman wanting a child.

One afternoon I was filled with misery and wanted to dissolve into tears. "No," I said to myself. "If I give in to this sadness, I do not have the mustard seed. I believe staunchly. I will not fail in my faith. I will go forward smiling."

Please understand: God did not help me through this moment of doubt. I had to make that decision myself. He gives us free choice to take the path to happiness or the path to fear and destruction. He does not lead us there. That's what makes having and keeping faith so difficult. Faith is a choice we make, with no promises ahead that we can see. Faith is the things hoped for, the things not seen. There are no guarantees. We must accept what comes, no matter what dangers we see in the darkness around us — which can seem black indeed. It is hard to keep believing.

But I left the quiet womb of the car, comforted and assured. I felt flooded with peace.

Several months later, my surprised doctor said, "I would never have believed it possible. It is a miracle... you are pregnant."

Sometimes dreams really do come true — the right dreams. The Lord never fails. He keeps His promises. Though it is sometimes difficult to keep going on against all odds, if it is His will, our faith will be rewarded. Beau King was born — a special gift from God, the most wonderful gift of my life. A baby, a new life! He was perfect.

It was not easy, though. We both almost died in the birth process. My cervix would not dilate, and the anesthetic stopped dilation, so the doctors were unable to give me anything to stop the pain. I didn't scream or moan, though. In my family, tears and signs of pain, fear, or sadness were considered signs of weakness. We endure and do not inflict our struggles upon others. When Beau was finally born, his head was pointed from the forceps that finally released him. He was huge. The nurses called him "the cowboy" because he was the tallest baby in the nursery. His difficult birth never slowed him one moment of his life, though. He was a cowboy then and, at six foot three, is a movie-star-handsome cowboy now.

The family rejoiced and the whole of Memorial Hermann Hospital rejoiced with us. My room, even the floor, was full of flowers. I had nightgowns and bed jackets worthy of Rebecca de Winter, the fictional character I still was trying to emulate. Beau's grandmothers ordered clothes from Paris. Mrs. King handmade exquisite baby dresses. A young prince had been born. Life was perfect.

My third disaster was about to occur.

I woke up two days later feeling wonderful. I leaped out of bed and ran to the bathroom to get ready for my constant stream of visitors.

When I looked in the mirror, something looked odd. I tried to smile. One side of my face smiled; the other didn't. Again and again, I tried to make my mouth move, but the mirror reflected only a horrid lopsided grin. All thoughts of normalcy vanished in the strong revealing light of the morning. This crooked face belonged to a travesty of a woman. I called my mother, who came rushing to my side, as did the doctor.

"You have Bell's palsy," he said. "You had a hard delivery...this is sometimes the aftermath." To cheer me, he added, "It might go away in a few days. It sometimes leaves no sign at all." But I noticed that he shook his head sadly as he left.

Throughout the next few days, the agony continued. The first time the nurses brought in a tray of food, I picked up a fork and took a bite without thinking. I will never forget the sheer horror of seeing scrambled eggs fall from my mouth onto my bed jacket. I dribbled food! My mouth had no muscle strength. I had to carefully hold my mouth to keep food from falling out. I cleared the room first. I did not want anyone to see me.

Fearful thoughts raced through my mind. I would never again be able to even eat in public. Would my husband leave me? How could I raise a child looking like this? He would be ashamed to acknowledge me as his mother. I was sure people would turn their heads away, unwilling to even look at me. I felt like a caricature, a virtual monster. A desolate future spread before me. In the fifties, self-worth was dependent on how you behaved and how you looked. All of my life, that's what I had been told was important in a woman. Now to have it swept away in a moment...I was left with very little in myself to value.

This was the beginning of another crucial walk with the Lord. My unattractiveness as a child had made me understand and care for the underdog. My successful girlhood gave me courage to face the possibility of being in a wheelchair at a young age. My deliverance from that illness had taught me that surrendering my will to His could work miracles. My baby confirmed that belief was the answer to all obstacles. The miracle of my baby, Beau, strengthened my faith and helped me to understand how easily we can lose the things we value too much. We sacrifice to achieve meaningless goals. In the face of real misfortunes, their importance disappears like raindrops.

I had valued the wrong thing — my looks; now they were gone. I had made an idol of everything valued by the world. I listened to the siren song without asking or consulting God and followed like a hungry goat gobbling up everything. I took my tiny seeds of faith and He moved mountains to deliver me from all evil. I barely thanked Him before I went right out and became as worldly and grasping as before.

I sought God's forgiveness. "I have my child, my family, my life, and even the riches I wanted," I thought. "I will survive the Bell's palsy. I will be grateful, not greedy. I will praise God all the days of my life."

Three days later, the Bell's palsy was gone.

CHAPTER 7

That Was
The Party That Was

A ROMAN ORGY CIRCA 1959
by Bill Roberts

Fifteen caesars ran around the marble halls, togas flying, chasing vestal virgins, drinking love potion and dancing a ballet of love.

Vestal virgins?

The virgins dreamily eyed the lusty caesars and applauded their feats of derring-do. Later, one virgin swooned as the caesars carried her outdoors to be burned at the stake. She had hoped for a fate worse than death.

It was the last Age of Innocence in America and one of the best private parties of the century. At least below the Mason-Dixon Line. It was the grandest private party ever held in Houston. It was a Farewell to the Fifties and none other than Joanne King Herring Davis (minus the Herring and Davis) reigned supreme.

Joanne knows how to throw a party. This most adored of Houston hostesses gives parties in London, Paris, Madrid, Washington and Houston attended by enough royalty to make anyone without a title seem an absolute misfit. Many real kings

(including the crowned heads of Sweden, Jordan, Morocco, and the Shah of Iran), five princes and princesses, twenty-four ambassadors, and God knows how many prime ministers and other heads of state—Sadat!—have come when Joanne has said, "Let's party!" Once, she entertained Princess Grace and Prince Rainier at her home.

She is the honorary consul general of Pakistan and Morocco, the first and only woman ever chosen by the King of Morocco to be his ambassador. She is one of the great beauties of the Western world. She is very, very rich. She does things. Properly.

This gorgeous woman was queen of Houston television during the sixties and early seventies. She has done a few TV specials since those days, one a year or so ago on General Maurice Hirsch, a "Texas Hero." She chairs a gala ball or two each year.

But her most famous role will always be as hostess of the legendary 1959 Roman Bacchanal at her marble mansion on Rivercrest Drive in Houston. Some called it a Roman Orgy.

A Roman Orgy

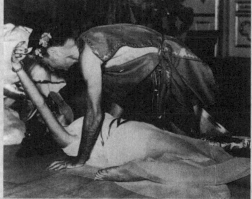

Houston's own legendary Cleopatra and her caesar, Joanne and Bob King, OPPOSITE PAGE, lounging together in their Grecian alcove, are served a potent Love Potion by a young Nubian slave.
CLOCKWISE FROM LEFT: Humble Oil heir John Blaffer loses to Eddie Black in the first rounds of a wine-drinking contest; Henry Taub and Camilla Blaffer enjoying the reposing life of Romans; the party crowd gathered in the grand banquet hall to watch the love ballets and "The Dance of the Gladiators"; and Henry and Carol Taub in their very own "Dance of Love."

Dark-haired Cynthia Colt, the chosen vestal virgin, is carried to her destiny, FAR RIGHT, and tied to a stake among the garden trees by a group of Bacchanalian revelers, ABOVE, in preparation for her ritual "burning." A throng of Romans, headed by Joanne King, watches the ritual with boisterous anticipation from the stairwell of the King Mansion, RIGHT.

Joanne has been quoted as saying a party must have a purpose—her guests must learn something. On this night in 1959, on the cusp of the Serious Sixties, there were macho caesars, in garlands and togas, arm wrestling and splattering vino over smug Mussolini faces as they held squirt contests from tricky wine flagons. *Life* magazine was on hand—but so was I—and this is the real story....

At Joanne's command her guests quaff love potion. Long, deep, happy draughts. They perform a ballet of love. They draw lots to see which vestal virgin will be burned at the stake.

The huge marbled grand reception hall of the magnificent Robert V. King home on Rivercrest Drive is the centerpiece of the action. You've seen such homes in the movies or on Robin Leach's "Lifestyles of the Rich and Famous." In fact, Joanne was one of the first Houstonians to be featured on "Lifestyles," which became the eighties popular show about the UBP—the Utterly Beautiful People. And in 1959, her home would have qualified—tall Grecian columns, big white fountains on the terrace and throughout the estate, shooting streams of glistening water over Roman statues of olden days when gods mingled with mortal men....

The host and hostess, Bob and Joanne King, sit in a Grecian alcove, presiding over a big silver smoking punch bowl filled with Love Potion. The guests, dressed as Roman senators, gladiators, star-crossed lovers, lie at ease on covered mattresses around the marble room, drinking from silver goblets. Small Nubian slaves stand at their elbow, ready to do the Romans' bidding. The "Nubians" are children of servants from that posh Rivercrest Drive neighborhood. They were generously paid for their performances.

Action begins! Claude Williams, the Kress heir, strides around the room lifting a sign. The Slave Auction—real girls for sale! Two stunning social beauties run into the room, onto the auction block—gorgeous Jane Mosbacher, wife of international sailing sportsman Bob Mosbacher; and lovely Charlotte Williams, wife of Jake Williams, the other Kress heir. These dolls bring $20,000—in Roman money, printed just for this night.

The long white beard is on Dr. Horace Robbins, dressed to his Roman teeth. He carries a skull that proclaims he is a doctor of Roman medicine.

Music from the band Samson and Delilah fills the marble halls. Five beautiful "slave girls" glide onto the floor and do a tantalizing love ballet. They are Julie Johnson, Bunkie Bowman, Nancy Robbins, Kay Johnson and Joan Fleming, and are so sensational the crowd makes them do it again. The girls rehearsed three weeks for this moment. The sound is that of gladiators, breathing heavily.

Now the men do their dance: Henry J.N. Taub, nephew of the powerful Houston businessman and philanthropist Ben Taub; Jake Williams, brother of Claude; and host Bob King. These macho gladiators call their gyrations "The Dance of the Gladiators." They, too, win an encore.

Then—can they stand it!—the boys and girls combine to do "The Dance of Love." (Oooops! Jake Williams drops Julie Johnson on the cold, hard marble—but she's OK. The dance ends successfully....)

A wine-drinking contest breaks out. The Romans use those Spanish bottles that squirt the wine in a long thin stream. It is a contest of skill, not capacity (since capacity runneth over). Bunty McLean beats businessman Frank Nelms. John Blaffer, scion of a few hundred million from the Humble Oil fortunes, challenges big Eddie Black, a young insurance mogul. Blaffer squirts wine in his own eye.

"I have but one stomach to give to my country," says Blaffer, irreverently and irrelevantly. Alfred Glassell, the international fishing sportsman, defeats Black. He, in turn, is defeated by Tom Peckinpaugh, the socialite and insurance man.

A gal gets into the act. Suzanne Nelms challenges Carol Taub and wins. Suzanne faces hubby Frank Nelms. She routs Frank with her flagon skill. The contest ends.

Notable sights:

Camilla Blaffer brings Joanne King a "death's head" she made herself. It covers a bottle of wine....

Motorists in the area are startled to see the usually sedate Pat Nicholson, who lives just across the way from the Kings, riding to the party aboard his bicycle—toga streaming in the wind....

That gorgeous blonde in blue, reclining leisurely on the floor, is Joan Fleming from New York....

Bunty McLean, dressed as Bacchus, stuffs two cigarettes into his mouth and lights them one at a time in a parody of Bob Hope's parody of Paul Henreid in *Casablanca* or some movie....

Sandra Payson Meyer and husband Bill Meyer, the New York real estate tycoon, are happily mesmerized.

Hostess Joanne King suddenly decrees that nobody will be allowed to leave the festivities until dawn!

At midnight the Romans play "Roman Roulette." Joanne King makes apprehensive vestal virgins take pips from a small jewel box. The black pip means "death—burning at the stake." Cynthia Colt draws the unlucky pip.

Stalwart Romans grab dark-haired, beautiful, screaming Cynthia. They carry her out of the marble hall, down the long marble steps to a stake in the green trees. She swoons on the stake, arms outstretched. There is an explosion and smoke hides Cynthia from view.

Actually the smoke lets Cynthia get away, because now Bob King sets off fireworks. Rockets and starbursts light up the midnight sky. Cynthia joins Joanne on the terrace to watch the fireworks. She wins applause and congratulations for her acting. "Thank you," Cynthia says. "I think I'm ready for Joan of Arc."

Ready or not, it has been said that the practice of burning vestal virgins at the stake was discontinued in Houston after this party, giving wags an opportunity to resurrect the old joke that the rite was abandoned because of a severe shortage of certifiable candidates.

A combo plays. The noble Romans and their ladies do a twentieth-century fox-trot. Nubian slaves parade through the room, holding aloft a roast suckling pig with a red apple in its mouth. Steaks are served on flaming swords.

It is the greatest private party in Houston history.

As I leave, I can't think of what noble lesson has enriched my mind, but I hear Joanne King giving an order to one of her slaves that makes a great deal of sense.

"Quick!" she commands. "More love potion!" A statue of Bacchus looks on the scene with happy approval.

EPILOGUE

Joanne King married Bob Herring, head of Houston Natural Gas, some years after her divorce from Bob King. After Bob Herring's death, she married Lloyd Davis, an investor who formerly owned Fisk Electric and Fisk Telephone, in the summer of 1985.

Bob King also remarried. He lives in Brenham with his wife and two children, dabbling in real estate and ranching.

Claude Williams retired after thirty years as chairman of Williams Bros. Construction Co., which builds freeway spaghetti bowls.

Bob Mosbacher, enormously wealthy, is a friend of Vice President George Bush. He became a world-champion sailor; and in 1959, he was on the cover of *Sports Illustrated* magazine. He married Georgette Barrie in 1985, ending years of bachelorhood after Jane's death.

Julie Johnson married insurance consultant Robert Harrison and they live in Columbus and Wimberley.

A member of the prominent Otto family, Bunkie Bowman, now deceased, was married to Rodney Bowman.

Nancy Robbins lives in Clear Lake with her husband, Dr. Horace Robbins, a general surgeon.

Kay Johnson married Navy Commander Gordon Roberts and they live in New Mexico.

Joan Fleming was married to William Fleming. She is now married to George W. Aldridge Jr.

Since the death of Ben Taub, his nephew, Henry J.N. Taub, has run the empire. A widower for years, Henry is famous as a civic leader, bon vivant, and the escort of beautiful women.

Jake and Charlotte Williams divorced. Charlotte married Leif Gran; they live in

River Oaks. Jake (now deceased), his brother Claude, architect Fernando Segura (once married to Josephine Abercrombie), Bob Abercrombie Jr. of the oil millions, and Jack Valenti, now the president of the Motion Picture Association of America, were among the young men of the fifties who made the girls of Houston dream great dreams.

Bunty McLean, from an old, old Texas family, married Mary Lovett, daughter of Malcom Lovett, another famous old-family name, noted in society, Rice University circles, and Lovett Boulevard. Bunty has since passed away.

The Nelms name also is one long in the social annals of Houston. Frank and Suzanne Nelms remain happily married and active. She is a cutting horse champion, and you find them at their ranch in Brenham or at their vacation home in Ruidoso.

John Blaffer, now deceased, was the son of Robert Lee Blaffer, one of the founders of Humble Oil, now Exxon Company USA. John married Camilla Davis, of the great Dallas fortune. After John Blaffer's death, Camilla married W.B. "Tex" Trammell, possessor of another great fortune; all giving rise to their friends' tease that Camilla could give lessons in "How To Marry A Millionaire (not that she needs to)." The Blaffer Family has given prodigiously to the arts and great institutions in Texas and across the nation.

Alfred Glassell gained international fame as a fisher of giant fish. Those action scenes in the movie of Ernest Hemingway's *The Old Man and the Sea* are really from scenes made of Alfred Glassell playing his world-record black marlin. Alfred and Clare live in Houston.

Tom Peckinpaugh, now deceased, came from old family lines in Houston: Peckinpaughs, Carters, Neuhauses. His wife, Budine, has remarried.

Nicholson became Dr. Pat Nicholson, director of development for the University of Houston, now retired. He wrote *In Time,* a book about the creation of the university. His last book is *Mr. Jim,* an engaging biography of Jim Abercrombie, oilman and founder of the Pin Oak Charity Horse Show and the Texas Children's Hospital.

After her divorce from Bill Meyer, Sandra Payson Meyer married an English lord. Sandra was the daughter of Joan Whitney Payson, the New York socialite and multimillionaire who started the New York Mets baseball team. ▬

Bill Roberts is a former daily columnist for *The Houston Press* and *The Houston Post.*

It was the last Age of Innocence in America and one of the best private parties in the country.

*U*mp ahead a few years to the end of the decade. It was the late 1950s, World War II and Korea were behind us, and everybody thought anything was possible. Our country was on top. It felt good to be alive in America. I had a glorious, fun-filled life.

In July 1959, we threw a party considered so scandalous it has people talking even today. Some called it a Roman orgy...We called it a Bacchanal.

Planning for the authentically themed Roman party meant researching everything Romans did, wore, and ate. We showed a keenness for Roman history that our classroom professors never witnessed. Everybody wanted to distinguish themselves from the next run-of-the-mill Roman slave or Caesar.

We were thinking of deep debauchery...or what looked like it...

Our "slaves" were recruited from a local Boy Scout troop and were well paid. They went to sleep on Caesar's couches at 9 p.m., so they didn't do much, but they looked adorable. Remember, Romans supped lying down. This was somewhat difficult with slumbering Boy Scouts everywhere. None of the guests minded, however. They were too busy performing, laughing, and admiring themselves. Every minute of the party centered on the stars — the guests! The secret of a good party is to involve the people invited.

Bill Roberts of *Ultra* magazine called it "the greatest private party in Houston history." It's the party that seems to last longer than the Roman Empire! Decades later, I am *still* trying to clarify what really happened that evening. Let me say once and for all, the whole thing was more a choreographed pageant than a Roman bacchanal. Not one person got drunk. They were too busy. Besides, it would have been dangerous with all that dancing on the marble floor. This was a party with no purpose except that of amusement. I learned from the bacchanal that for a party to become legendary, the guests must become active participants in the fantasy and merriment. There are no bystanders at a bacchanal.

I soon became known as a hostess. Later, my parties became a means to get serious, meaningful things done, but at the time, I rarely had a serious thought.

Once in a Great While, A Fairy Tale Comes True

Joanne King's Home Is a Palace . . . Her Wardrobe Is a Royal Collection

BY BEVERLY MAURICE
Fashion Editor

"Her lips shall be red as the rose,"
said the fairy godmother, "and her
face as fair as the snow, her hair as
black as ebony. . . ."

Once in a great while, a fairy tale comes true, and there is someone of extraordinary beauty, and someone who lives up to it with a flair, like Mrs. Robert Vernon King.

It is doubtful if even legendary princesses like Snow White and Rose Red enjoyed a more imaginative life.

Built a Palace

Joanne wed a t a l l, handsome "King" named Robert, and the couple built an 18th century palace just off Westheimer.

All of which is conventional enough for a storybook character, but there the similarity ends.

As far as we know, Rose Red never gave a charity ball in her grand salon, or entertained 2000 guests at tea for the Women's Christian Mission. If so, Life Magazine didn't cover it.

And while Snow White may have appeared on television occasionally, could she have managed the job of Women's Editor, with a noonday program on KHOU?

Joanne does all this with scarcely a curl awry.

"This house is a gay, Viennese waltz," says Joanne. "I'm never sad or blue in here."

Neither is anybody else, probably because the charm of the hostess is as dazzling as the architecture.

On a French theme, the white mansion brings the past up to date. The gold leaf is gleaming, the marble statues polished white, and the hi-fi is disguised in a magnificent armoire.

"I wanted everything to look just as it did in the day of Louis XV," says Joanne. She feels that period styling doesn't necessarily call for faded colors and tarnished gold.

With fantastic attention to detail she coordinated the floor plan, the construction and the motifs with her builder husband.

"We didn't use any steel in the ceiling, because they built grand ballrooms without it in those days."

Posing for the camera in a red sequined sheath in her grand salon, she told the story of the chandelier.

Weighs a Ton

"We were a little worried about whether the ceiling would hold it. The chandelier weighs a ton, and it belonged to Madame de Pompadour. It's such a beautiful piece that really, we built the house around it."

Seven feet tall, it is all Bacarrat crystal and gold leaf, and some of the prisms are as big as pineapples.

Once upon a time the chandelier graced a chateau for the famous French historical

CHAPTER 8

The Fairy Tale Becomes Untrue

By the piano in the grand salon, she wears Maurice Rentner's pink pique, with a shrug jacket edged in Tom Jones ruffles. Robin, her 2-year-old, shows his Gainsborough suit, made

On the terrace overlooking the pool, she wears a blouse made of layered silk scarves, red over blue, silk stretch pants and glove-soft boots to match.

*M*any copies of this 1964 *Houston Chronicle* article have been sent to me over the years. I remain astonished that a newspaper clipping about somebody else would be kept for so long. I guess people love to believe in fairy tales. In reality, they are just that — fairy tales! Real life is quite different. That was especially true around the time this article was published. Bob and I were suddenly broke — or what seemed awfully close to it. Once again the ten-year bell tolled and changed my life as I knew it.

Our economic problems were not from lack of trying. My husband worked with a vengeance. The market took a downturn, and there were no customers for his five hundred houses littering the suburban prairies.

In our own home, the heater and air conditioner stopped working and we could not replace them. It was tough going. Despite our economic problems I yearned for another child. I heard the same old story: "Forget it. You will not have another child." Still, I continued my mustard-seed praying and finally made an appointment at a fertility clinic.

Even in our darkest days God never leaves us completely bereft. On the day of my examination, the doctor said, "I do not know why you are here. You are two months pregnant!" Several months later Robin was born amid great joy. He was gorgeous! People stopped me on the street to tell me how beautiful he was.

Our family struggled, but we managed to keep afloat. The work involved was beyond my strength. I wanted to keep up appearances, so I rarely slept — there was no time. To the world, Rebecca still lived, but in reality she was a slave to her family while pretending the grandeur still existed. With hard work and innovative thinking, Bob pulled us up and things got better, the sacrifices easier.

One day my grandmother Laura Dunlap Sampson, said, "I need help, Joanne. By myself, I have been supporting what I call the Women's Christian Mission. But I can't do it anymore. There are so many battered women. I don't have enough money to help them all." She was one of those marvelous people who were always thinking of others. I never met anyone whose face didn't light up when they talked about her.

The Women's Christian Mission was created because a woman named Mary Brown came in to the Seaman's Mission with her five children. My grandmother was on the mission's board. "I can't live at home anymore," Mary Brown said. "My husband beats me and now he is beating the children." She was penniless and had nowhere to go. At the time, there were several missions for men, but nothing for women and certainly nothing for a woman with children. My grandmother was horrified when Mary was turned away. She took Mary home and kept her and her children until my grandmother could start the Women's Christian Mission.

She bought a two-story house with her own money and filled that little house to the rafters with abused women and their children. She even had them staying in the garage. The mission soon grew so much that more money was needed.

"Can you help me?" she asked me.

My heart broke for those women and for her struggle to help them. However, I had a conflict. I had just been made chair of the Opera Ball. This was *the* social pinnacle in Houston. Now that I was faced with a real problem that could change lives, it didn't seem important at all — except to my inflated ego. I went to war with myself: do God's work or work for myself? I knew in my heart that the Lord wanted me to work on the Women's Christian Mission. God seemed to be saying, "Joanne, you have had everything. Now you must help those who have nothing."

I would learn only later that having your picture in the newspaper is interesting only to you. Tomorrow it's going to wrap up somebody's garbage. At the time I was young and full of myself, and so I said, "Okay, I am going to do them both." I now call such nonsense "idiot's delight" or "a fool and her vanity are soon parted."

I told my grandmother, "I don't know anything about running a mission. But I know how to raise money. I will help you."

Being the Opera Ball chair required a full year of commitment. And that was before the board decided to add a fourth opera. "You can do it, Joanne," the board members cooed. I purred with pleasure and agreed to raise more money than any ball chairman in the organization's history.

Meanwhile, back at the mission, I needed to tell people about what the mission did, making it interesting enough to support financially. I took the worst-looking battered alarm clock I could find, a little old-fashioned one with bells on top. I carried it to the newspapers and the television and radio stations and said to the CEOs, "See this alarm clock? Give me five minutes. When it goes off, I'll leave." They were amused, but my gimmick piqued their interest enough to have me interviewed by their reporters and TV hosts. I told them hair-raising, salacious stories about women having their hair cut off, then being locked in rooms and forced into "slavery" (a polite word for "prostitution") at the hands of avaricious men, all true stories from the women who needed help.

I was a sensation. Afterward, one station manager asked if I would come back for another show.

"I'll do anything for Jesus," I said.

His reply: "We ain't doing this for Jesus, babe."

At the time, no one had ever read or heard such stories in the family-friendly media, especially coming from a nice young woman from a good family. This raised the mission money. The mission celebrated its fiftieth anniversary in 2007 and continues to be a well-known sanctuary for desperate women in need.

The Opera Ball was a huge success, also. We raised the money for the fourth opera and more. It has continued in all its glory without me. The Opera Ball did not need me, but helping battered women find new lives helped me find a new life as well.

CHAPTER 9

Dining on Dead Deer

fresh

Today-the four stages of marriage
part II, things you don't
know about each other after 10 years.

The Joanne King Show
12 noon on KPRC-TV

Joanne King, right, interviews Mrs. Braxton Thompson, director of docents at the Museum of Fine Arts, who talks about past civilizations and what they contributed in the way of arts and science.

Live from Houston

BY NORA KRISCH SHIRE

JOANNE KING is not just another pretty face. That agile, analytical mind beneath those chestnut brown curls is what has kept her on Houston television for 10 consecutive years.

"Mother always told me I could not take credit for my looks," the hostess of Channel 2's noon shows says, "but I could take credit for what I knew and the kind of person I was inside." So learning became important as did reaching out for people and putting herself in her viewers' chairs.

Beginning her eleventh year on television, Joanne King today is a svelte 5 feet 5, small-boned and undeniably glamorous.

On-camera she is warm and comfortable, questioning and commenting. Off-camera, she is relaxed and exuberant, unconsciously touching her table companions on the arm, on the hand. On-camera or off, she is reaching out, communicating.

Her fans, and they are legion, have followed her career—and watched her life unfold—on two Houston television channels: Problems with small children, how to entertain several hundred guests, divorce, being single again and remarriage.

Ten years ago Joanne King was the wife of a prominent businessman, a socialite who traveled extensively and the mother of two small boys. That year she also was chairman of the Opera Ball. Meanwhile, her grandmother, Mrs. W. E. Sampson, was having difficulty with her own project, the Woman's Christian Mission. The home for women was having financial difficulties and was about to close its doors.

Mrs. Sampson asked her granddaughter what could be done. "I told Grandmother I did not know how to run a mission," Joanne recalls, "but I knew how to raise money."

She presented her case to Channel 11 which invited her to be a guest on the noon show co-hosted by Al Bell and Ron Stone. She made her pitch for the mission (which, thanks to the efforts of many volunteers, was saved).

AND SOON JOANNE was asked back to do another show. Then came the opportunity to co-host the noon show.

"I was really bad in the beginning," Joanne admits, "and it took months before I overcame my fears."

Being her father's daughter, she conquered them. William Dunlap Johnson had always encouraged her not to be afraid to tackle anything.

"When I was 7 years old I told Father I wanted a pet tiger. He said that would be all right and that he would help me get one. We found out the zoo had one which needed a home, but he made me call the zoo and explain why I wanted it and how I would go about feeding it. The zoo agreed. Unfortunately the baby died before the transaction took place."

Joanne also credits her father with broadening her horizons. "He thought a girl should be knowledgeable on a variety of subjects. He believed it was necessary for a girl to know about music, wines, art and furniture styles.

"This is an interesting attitude for a man who went to Texas A&M University and was the first All-American in the Southwest Conference," she says proudly.

Joanne's noon show became an information show 10 years ago and its format is unchanged. "It is meant to be informative. I ask the guests the questions I think the viewers would ask if they were given the chance."

Her show became the first on Houston television to invite newspaper reporters to be interviewed. It also was the first local show to offer mailouts ranging from recipes to cosmetic instructions to furniture care. "I was the first woman on Houston television to wear slacks," she grins, "and my stage set was the first designed to resemble a living room."

TV feature PAGE

BY ANN HODGES
TV-Radio Editor

To show you the kind of memory Jack Benny has—at age 39 plus 33—he remembers Texas all too well.

"I played a couple of towns there that I've never forgotten, and this, believe me, was before World War I," Jack reminisced over the long-distance line from Hollywood. "The towns were Waxahachie and Corsicana. Come to think of it, how could ANYBODY forget a pair of names like that?"

But he really hadn't called to discuss old times. Benny, for all his chronological years, doesn't dwell on the past. He's too busy looking ahead to the future.

"I tell you, I've never been busier, and I've never felt better," declared the man who, for the first time in 33 years, is relieved of the responsibility of doing a weekly radio or TV series.

"I'm getting a real bang out of it, because I'm doing a lot of work, but the kind of work I like to do best," he said happily.

"My hour-long special (his first of several for NBC this season, set for 8 p.m. tonight on Ch. 2) was a real pleasure. I think it's going to be one of the best things I've done. I've got Bob Hope, Elke Sommer and the Beach Boys—something for everybody.

"Bob and I kinda mix in with the Beach Boys, ham it up a little," he laughed. "You know, Bob'll do anything if he can wear a wig. That's what I told him."

"And by just doing specials, I have plenty of time to do what I really like to do best—concerts," Benny continued. "I'll be playing all over this year—including Fort Worth, San Antonio and Austin. We had hoped to come to Houston, too," he added regretfully, "but that fell through. I don't know what happened. I'd still love to come."

And that isn't all Benny has on his crowded agenda. He's also planning to play fairs and nightclubs, to check into the possibility of doing a Broadway play and to take his wife, Mary Livingstone, to London on vacation.

Meanwhile, he's moving.

He and Mary, after 28 years at the same address, are selling their Beverly Hills home.

"It's just too big," Jack explained. "With only the two of us, we rattle around. We'll move into an apartment, but we'll spend most of the time at our place in Palm Springs.

"Only thing that bothers me," Jack chuckled, "is when the house goes, what'll I do with the vault?"

Come to think of it, maybe Jack is losing his Midas touch. He forgot to reverse the charges on the call.

Venice Revisited

Ch. 11's Joanne King—about as lovely a TV hostess as you'll find on a screen anywhere — took a leisurely stroll through the city of Venice Tuesday night, and the result was an eye-filling 30 minutes of old-world beauty. The program, a TV salute to Foley's Splendida Italia celebration, w a s photographed by Ch. 11's Bob Wolfe last May, and his cameras caught that unique Italian city in all its springtime glory. What a pity, though, that it wasn't in color. Guiding Joanne through the city was an expert—Italian Count Paolo Barozzi, member of one of the founding families of the Venetian state, and his presence was an added bonus, since his hometown itinerary included some off-the-beaten-path attractions. The background music was a lively echo of Italy, and the script, charmingly narrated by Joanne, was an asset, too. It was written by Bob Levy, who also produced the show. . . . Ch. 2 will present its Splendida Italia salute, a prize-win-

IN VENICE AT THE BRIDGE OF SIGHS
Count Paolo Barozzi and Joanne King; 9 PM

11 Joanne King's Venice [SPECIAL] Channel 11's women's director toured Venice last spring in company of cameraman Bob Wolfe and Count Paolo Barozzi, descendant of one of the founders of the Venetian Republic. The results of that tour are displayed in this 30-minute travelogue which looks not only at Venice's more famous spots, but some of its lesser known corners, too. Stops on the way include the **Bridge of Sighs,** Saint Mark's Basilica, the Palace of the Doges, the throne of Attila the Hun, a glass blowing f a c t o r y, the gambling casino on the Lido, and, of course, a gondola trip on the Grand Canal.

*I*n 1963, I received a letter from KHOU-TV, asking, "Would you like to do our noon show?" I almost fainted. I had never even *thought* of doing television. I was so astonished that I put the letter in my desk and left it for about a month, telling no one. At the time, married women of means did not work outside of the home. We were struggling financially, so I wasn't really a "woman of means" at the moment, but the mind-set remained even if the money wasn't there to back it up.

Finally a man from the station called: "What about it?" He said the station wanted to do things never done on TV before, such as having a sports hero for a sportscaster.

Now that's the *expected*, but in the early 1960s it was revolutionary. "We want to do a woman's show and we think it should be hosted by a woman." There were few women on the air at the time. "We want a woman who is not a typical TV personality but someone the audience admires, a society queen named *King*. Are you interested?"

My family gasped in horror at the offer. "Oh, heavens no! You on television?" they said. "No, no!" It was fine for me to go on television to help the Women's Christian Mission, but not as a job. It was considered outrageous.

Bob's mother said, "Horrors."

My mother said, "Ladies don't do that."

My father said, "Do you mean they're actually going to pay you?"

I said, "Please pray about it." The family prayed and decided it was not God's will or theirs. I was conflicted because God was telling me something different. I was convinced that my family's heavenly hearing was off. Why else in heaven's name would the people from the TV station have asked me? An offer that out of the ordinary, to an unqualified college dropout, had to be from God.

Despite my family's objections, I took the job at the CBS affiliate, hosting *News at Noon with Joanne King* beginning in 1963 and continuing until 1972. I moved to the NBC affiliate with the *The Joanne King Show* in 1973 and kept this daily noon show until 1975. Then I continued with a weekly talk show for the same station until 1976.

What no one but God and I knew was the main motivation that made me accept the job. I did it to save my marriage to Bob King. At the beginning of my TV career, I was starting to realize that there was a huge gap between what I wanted and what Bob wanted. Bob King, the man my family chose for me and the father of my children, was a wonderful man. But his idea of heaven was literally to move to a desert island with no people around, while I loved being around people all of the time. I thought working in television might help me satisfy my need for people.

The TV manager had said, "The only thing that worries us is whether you will walk with the people."

"Walk with the people?" I repeated. "What do you mean 'walk with the people'?"

He explained what he meant, saying, "The audience has the mentality of twelve-year-olds."

"I don't believe that." I thought he was underestimating the viewers, but what kind of TV show could I do? No one helped or advised me. I asked myself, "What do you like to do?" "I like to learn," I thought; "doesn't everybody? I have access to the best minds in the world. Why not share them to teach the viewers — and me." I needed to prepare like crazy. This then became my education, and it was thorough. It also became another tool in my toolbox.

But before earning any praise, I had to go through a rough learning period.

My first show was terrible. I quickly realized the difference between being interviewed and interviewing. When I'd been on TV before, it had been so easy. I just told my sensational stories and the interviewer made me look good. I was shocked to discover that I was a terrible interviewer. For my first show I asked my friends Robert Mosbacher, who later became U.S. secretary of commerce, and Denton Cooley, the famous surgeon who performed the first successful artificial heart transplant in the United States. They were handsome; "women will like that," I thought. It did not occur to me that they had to talk too. I didn't ask Bob about oil and I didn't ask Denton about medicine, which they would have been very good at discussing. Instead, I posed this absurd question: What do you first notice about a woman?

Nobody advised me or gave me a single tip about how to get better. They just threw me on the air. Those first shows were some of the worst moments of my life. I was bad. And on top of that, I was working without a contract. I was told I had a year if I was good, and no more than thirty days if I was bad. "One day out of thirty down," I thought. But my family doesn't quit or complain...they just keep going.

When that first show was over, the men in the newsroom were shocked speechless. They could not believe that the station would actually pay someone to be that bad! Once they got over their shock, I amused the men at the station. They flirted, calling me "the goddess," even on the air. Yet they resented that I was there. They thought I didn't need the job and said so. If only they'd known — our family really *did* need the money at that time. But the world at large was unaware of our dire straits.

Then the men I worked with began enjoying how bad I was.

To be honest, I *had* strolled in thinking I would be a great interviewer and that I was going to knock them dead. I knocked them dead all right — deadly bored. People would watch only to see what mistakes I would make next.

Three or four months into my TV career, the station was asked to film an international art exhibit coming to Houston. The exhibit featured works by Michelangelo, Renoir, Leonardo da Vinci, and other renowned artists. If the program was good enough, it would air on PBS. A young, very promising director at the station was given the show and allowed to choose the host.

"I want Joanne," he told them.

People at the station were horrified. "Joanne? She's the worst person you could choose!"

He said, "I think she'll add a lot to the show."

The director did not tell me he was using me until the night before the show filmed. I stayed up all night refreshing my memory and studying the art exhibit catalog. I was terrified until I realized that this was a subject I knew in spades. The valuable teaching sessions ten years earlier had not been in vain. I was grateful when the art my father had made me study in all its forms paid off. I knew the artists enough to make educated remarks and to ask the correct questions. The program was filmed instead of being shot live like my daily show was, so the director could shoot until he got it right. We started early in the morning and finished at about seven o'clock that night.

Wonder of wonders, the program was good. It was shown on PBS *and* all over the world. The young director was immediately given a job at ABC in New York. I got job offers too.

At first, I thought my success was a fluke. But then I began to call on the training I already had. I realized that remembering lessons of the past can solve the problems of today. When we are desperate, we often find we have more abilities than we realize. We must only look into ourselves and into our lives and find what we already have that is useful.

I wasn't afraid anymore. The men at the station who had snickered at me weren't snickering anymore. They didn't like having me as competition. But I smiled and I ignored them. "You can do this," I told myself.

I knew I couldn't do a really good show without intense study and effort. Audience members want to hear only what they can retain, not copious details. To help brilliant guests "edit" all of their learning into a few minutes for TV is hard. I began to think concisely so that I could help these erudite people speak in bullet points. For me, it was like getting a college education five days a week, one on one, with some of the smartest people on — and off — the planet! I interviewed John Glenn, the first American astronaut to orbit the earth.

That type of show seems commonplace today, but nobody else did then what is now called "a newsmagazine." Dinah Shore, who had a long-running television show, told me that she copied my program.

Developing interview skills is an art. Sitting next to visiting tycoons at dinners when I was a young woman, I'd learned to ask questions to draw them out: "What do you do? How do you do it? Why is it significant? What lasting effects does it have on the world? Why did you develop it? How does it make our lives better?" If I'd realized earlier that I could apply these skills to my TV interviews, I might have avoided a trimester on my way to birthing a television career.

But now I thought deeply about the TV audience: "How does this subject help them? How can I make their lives easier and more fun?" People are always interested in things that apply to them. My father used to say, "The sweetest sound in the world is a person's own voice." (Once I sat next to a man on a plane who insisted on telling me about rowing at Harvard. I was annihilated with boredom. The next week my husband had an important client for dinner. He *had* to sell this deal. Guess what this man liked most in the world? Rowing at Harvard. My husband made the deal.)

The ability to listen and to ask the right questions was in my toolbox the entire time. When I looked there, I realized I had been interviewing for years.

In the sixties and seventies, Houston was considered a "glamour" market, so stars included Houston as a tour stop when they were publicizing their movies or television shows. As guests on my TV show, I had Julie Andrews, Jack Benny, Candice Bergen, Jacqueline Bisset, Bing Crosby, Sammy Davis Jr., Dom DeLuise, Clint Eastwood, Henry Fonda, Buddy Hackett, Audrey Hepburn, Bob Hope, Steve McQueen, George Peppard, Jimmy Stewart, Robert Wagner, John Wayne — you name it, I had them all.

I expected Steve McQueen to be difficult. But when I think of him, I think of sunshine because he was so nice. Sammy Davis Jr. was also a darling. He gave a lot of himself, not only during interviews but with charities as well.

Houston was not just a tour stop. It was a shooting location as well. Ryan O'Neal and Jacqueline Bisset made the movie *The Thief Who Came to Dinner* in Houston — and I was in it! I ended up on the cutting room floor. (I still get paid when it plays on TV — $1.68 per broadcast.)

Among the luminaries I met was Sean Connery. He is very intelligent and has a quick wit and a firm grip on world affairs. And once, he had a firm grip on me. What do you do when Sir Sean puts his hand on your thigh while sitting down for dinner? I thought, "There are twelve people sitting at this table. Do I make an issue of this by removing his hand or do I ignore it and hope it goes away?" I hoped for it to go away. It did not go anywhere. "Well," I thought, "if it doesn't move, I won't either." It didn't move all during dinner. I spent an agonizing evening, but Sean only did it as a joke. He just wanted to see how I would react. Not very well, obviously.

Another off-color moment: I remember Lee Marvin walking down the hallway behind me at the station discussing my backside. He liked it and said so in blush-worthy language. I learned to ignore these things, smile, and go on.

One star I saw often was Frank Sinatra. I liked him. I liked his wife, Barbara, even better. When Frank and I were introduced, I asked, "How do you feel about being part of everyone's love story?"

He smiled with pleasure and said, "Nobody's ever said that to me before. That means so much to me." Then he kissed me on the cheek.

People always linked the song "My Way" with Frank, thinking it reflected the way he lived his life. Actually, he told me, "I hate that song, every word of it, more than any song I've sung. People always want me to sing it. Everybody thinks that's me. But it isn't."

Over the years, I dined with the Sinatras, Elizabeth Taylor, and Ava Gardner several times at private dinners. Liz, whose Oscars were on display in her living room, was indeed lovely, charming, and welcoming, and though she tried hard when she married handsome John Warner, senator from Virginia, politics just weren't her scene. Ava, who came from humble beginnings, had learned to fit in with jet-set society, and while she entered into conversations, she always seemed somewhere else…until she saw my jewels. When we dined together, I wore a real fifty-carat emerald ring, a gift from Bob King — in fact, a parting gift from Bob, upon his realization that we were separating, a testimony to his character. Plus, I sported a marvelous fake ring. It was so marvelous, in fact, that everyone commented on my "jools." Ava recognized immediately that the fake was a better color.

"Yes," she said, "both are lovely, but I prefer this one," indicating the false stone.

Hmm! Did she know the difference? Maybe this was her way of telling me.

Another star, John Wayne, I liked immensely. After the show, he invited me to dinner. There wasn't a flicker of romance, just dinner. As we tried to talk, fawning people kept coming up to him for autographs. Finally, he got tired of it, and when a woman approached, he said, "Lady, my hair comes off and my teeth come out. Now, get lost."

John Wayne was a real patriot in a world of pacifists, and through his movies he tried to convey the imminent threat of communism, an act of courage in the Hollywood of the sixties and seventies.

Then there was David Niven, the dapper, elegant actor who played the jewel thief Sir Charles Lytton in the first *Pink Panther*. We were at the Mount Kenya Safari Club in Africa, and his daughter had broken her leg riding one of the club's horses. As we stood at the railing, looking at the horses, he said, "Her broken leg is ruining my vacation. I think I'm going to shoot her. That's what they do with horses." He always had some funny quip. He and Tom Hanks shared the same qualities. They both put themselves out to make others happy.

Clint Eastwood is intelligent and, like John Wayne, saw the communist threat and tried to show the communists' intentions in the movie *Firefox*. People were not ready to hear his message, however. The movie, though great, bombed at the box office. Eastwood himself was exactly like he is on-screen: laid back, laconic, and a trifle bored.

A lot of the stars I met were good-looking guys, but George Peppard from *Breakfast at Tiffany's*...Whoa, Nellie! Even Audrey Hepburn looked a little dazed by him.

Actors think with their emotions because that's what they're called upon to do every day. They react emotionally rather than basing their opinions on the in-depth study needed to fully understand the complex forces behind the real horrors unfolding around us daily. They look at the world and judge it emotionally. Real knowledge comes from those who go out and get involved.

Being on television and later being portrayed in *Charlie Wilson's War* has occasionally led to some rather strange encounters. Once, artist Andy Warhol invited me as his special guest to a "happening" at his house. He picked me up himself in his stretch limousine — white, to match his hair. When we arrived, a crowd waited in anticipation.

Guess what "happened" at the happening?

Andy went to the top of the stairs, hoisted a box of blocks...then tossed them down the steps.

"Ooh!"

Men clutched their chests.

Women swooned.

"Such *art*!"

"Such *spirituality*."

I still have an actual Campbell's soup can that he autographed for me.

On another occasion, Ahmet Ertegun, founder and president of Atlantic Records, invited me to dine with members of a band he had signed.

"Who in the world are these strange people? Why am I here?" I thought. I had never heard of these funny young guys. The long-haired, curly-headed blond one looked just like a sheep who needed shearing. Later I told my son Robin about this bizarre dinner I had had.

"Who were they?" he asked.

"Something Zeppelin," I replied.

"Mother, that's Led Zeppelin! They're the most popular rock group of all time. They *never* give interviews! You had probably the best dinner invitation in the United States that night!"

That wasn't the only time I had a mix-up with musicians. In 2008, I asked my dear friend Posey Parker to help me remember the name of a group I was supposed to meet that night. "It's some kind of bird."

Posey paused. "You don't mean...the Eagles?"

"That's it!" I cried. I left an event where I was the honoree to meet the charming Glenn Frey, who had asked me to meet him backstage when he performed in Houston. I learned he lives down the street from Tom Hanks. At one time, their kids carpooled together.

When I met Margaret Thatcher, I had carefully thought out my opening sentence. After all, it had worked for Sinatra. I confidently waltzed up to her.

"Mrs. Thatcher, how does it feel to have changed the world?" I asked.

She gave me the most *withering* look, then said, "*Mr.* Reagan, *Mr.* Gorbachev, and *I* changed the world." She then turned her back on me in front of everybody. I dissolved into a puddle.

What I *should* have said was, "Mrs. Thatcher, you have stood tall, no matter how rough the seas, and your country's fortunes reflect it." *That*, she would have liked.

Later I was with her in Gstaad and we had a marvelous time. Thank goodness she didn't remember our first encounter! She is kind, and she really listens with interest when you say meaningful things.

I continued to have movie stars on my show for fun. It was the professors, historians, writers, scientists, and smart, dedicated politicians who expanded the minds of the audience as well as my own.

My ratings soared! This type of show had a place, and people really liked it. Even though it was local, it had the ratings of a national show. It became the sixth-highest-rated show in the United States, attracting attention throughout the country and even internationally.

While my TV career was getting better, my home life remained mired in financial difficulty. Despite the income from my television show, we struggled.

In the Rivercrest neighborhood, our ballrooms still glowed. Everybody knew we were "broke" by their standards but no one knew what to do to help. So they avoided mentioning our financial troubles and kept right on inviting us to their gatherings and pretending nothing was wrong. I was and remain touched at this show of friendship. Really, at the time, that was the best thing they could have done for us.

I called my old beau's father, H.H. Coffield, in Dallas, who long before had decided he had made a mistake in not wanting his son Pete to marry me. (Mr. Coffield flew me in his plane to all his parties, paid for some of mine, and invited me to sit next to President Lyndon B. Johnson at an event.)

Mr. Coffield had a storybook ranch with outrageous hunting accommodations. The enclosed glass deer blinds were carpeted and included a hidden bar, La-Z-Boy seats, cognac, and copies of the *Wall Street Journal.*

Later, many of my European aristocratic friends came to Texas as my guests and "hunted" there at one of the private shoots that Mr. Coffield allowed me to have. Fashion icon Hubert Guerrand-Hermès of Paris came out, covered from chest to ankle in a natty suit of shining aluminum. Hubert had heard about coyotes, wolves, scorpions, and other denizens of the desert. Fearful of rattlesnakes, he had the designers at Hermès create a proper Wild West shooting costume.

"Hubert, you look just like the Tin Woodman of Oz," I said. "What on earth are you going to do in that?"

A known wit, he replied, "I am going to shoot. When the rest of you are writhing in pain, dying from the venom of those infamous snakes, I shall not mourn you!"

But these light moments came later. At the moment, the problem was lack of money. I thought, "How can we save on groceries?" I called on Mr. Coffield to help me with my cost-cutting measures, although he did not know my reasons. Meat was expensive, and I said, "Mr. Coffield, I just love venison. Do you think I might have a deer from the ranch?"

"Certainly, honey," he responded. "Would you like some doves and quail too?"

My mouth watered (I love quail), but I did not want to expose our lowly state so I refused. One must keep one's pride.

"No, I just have a yearning for some venison," I replied. "It is such a delicacy." In Texas, at the time, venison was considered trash.

Nobody would serve it except made into sausage, which is *no* delicacy. I shall never forget the look on my Beau's face when he first tasted the venison I received from Mr. Coffield. Head bowed, aqua eyes brimming, he asked, "Mommy, you really want me to eat this?"

"Yes!" I said. And he did. The year before we had flown around the world first-class. But venison was all we ate that winter. We had it grilled, stewed, ground, and baked — and it always tasted like gamey dead deer! I hate venison.

Years later, the French deputy minister of foreign affairs had a dinner in my honor at Maxim's in Paris. He proudly announced that he had managed, at great expense and effort, to get the chef to procure venison! "How marvelous," I murmured. I almost threw up in memoriam.

Our financial reality continued to be bleak. We couldn't pay the bills. I even had the boys brushing their teeth with soda powder. But reality set in. The house, my dream come true, had to be sold. I realized that I had done many things to satisfy my own desires, but we could no longer afford to keep it. So I gave it to God willingly.

One day, I walked outside and looked at my dream house, the house where my husband had indulged my every whim. It was beautiful and I loved it. But it had become a great burden. We didn't own it. It owned us. It cost a fortune to maintain. The roof had begun to leak. The huge hundred-thousand-gallon swimming pool was cracking.

The house was almost like a metaphor for our lives during this time. On the surface, we seemed to have it all. And that's what readers of the "Fairy Tale" article and my television viewers thought. But underneath, our once privileged existence was in dire need of repair.

"Lord," I said, referring to the house, "I give it up. I regret the sacrifices we have made trying to keep it. We have had great happiness here," I continued, "but take it. I give You this idol and any others I might not be aware of; I give You my life totally. Thank You for my family and for keeping them safe, and take the house, Lord. I give it up unreservedly."

I walked inside, enjoying the rainbow of light cast by prisms from the door transom made of antique diamond-cut crystal. I looked at Madame de Pompadour's eight-foot Baccarat crystal chandelier. I thought of the Sèvres dining services, usually seen only in the cabinets of the vastly rich or in museums. I remembered the three men who came to apply gold leaf to the many carvings of the master carver who spent three years working eight hours a day, seven days a week. I recalled acquiring the furniture and treasures I had coveted. Now the famous auction house Sotheby's coveted them.

After my rededication to the Lord, all of this materialistic wealth seemed unimportant. I looked at it all and laughed. I walked dry-eyed into the future, prepared to begin a more modest way of coping beyond even the steps we had taken so far. I was ready to give up even the outward appearance of our "glamorous" life that the "Fairy Tale" reporter Beverly Maurice had written about.

The glitter and the gold of my former life held no meaning for me now. I should have been scared, but I wasn't. I had given God my promise and I meant to keep it. I had no regrets.

Sometimes in life we can be crumpled like worn socks. But when we put on shoes, no one sees the holes. I had been walking in the worn socks of my life, struggling over money. But now I was willing to give up the privileges and anything else He wanted me to do. I waited for God's guidance into my new, simplified life. I was a new person — and completely ready to be one!

God laughed. He had other plans for me. He always does, and they are always good. He threw me almost daily into the company of some of the most sought-after people in the world, an intoxicating mix of international players. God does indeed move in mysterious ways.

I was prepared to lose the house and everything in it. But the house was ultimately saved for me. That which I had surrendered was to be brought back.

CHAPTER 10

JOANNE KING

BY ANNE COOPER
Chronicle Staff

The daytime t e l e v i s i o n scene will be a little less bright and beautiful after this week, for Joanne King is departing her daily duties on Ch. 11's "News at Noon." Friday will be her last day.

When Joanne first went on the air nine years ago, she'd had no- television experience and, she says, she didn't quite know how to approach the job. "After my first show, I asked my mother how she liked it and she said, 'It was nice, but who was it?' So I decided then to just try to be myself.

"I said to myself, 'What on Earth can I give these people?' I'm not a comedienne, I'm not an actress.' But I'd worked at organizing social and charity functions and I was accustomed to talking to women, so I tried to present things in an interesting way. I just talk — I say exactly what I think every day, like a friend."

When she first went to work for Ch. 11, Joanne says, her bosses told her, "Our only concern is that you won't talk with the people."

"'Talk with the people,'" Joanne puzzled, "what does that mean? So just tried to do it.

"I talked about how I had braces when I was a child, my dyslexia, and my problems with my children — as long as they'd let me — and letters from all kinds of people (surprising enough, we have a large number of men and young people in our audience) told me how much it helped, how they appreciated hearing these things aired.

"A lot of people tell me they watch the show just to see what I'm wearing. And I do go through about 240 outfits a year — which makes for a very extensive and expensive wardrobe."

It can also get pretty boring, she says. She's been holding down the fort at the "News at Noon" practically since the moment Robin, her youngest son, was born. "After a while it got so that he'd see me dressed up and he'd say, "You not g o i n g out Mama? You just going to look in the mirror?'"

But, she emphasized, "I try to show people how they can use the wardrobe they have. I never talk about how to spend people's money, but how to save it. I'm very practical.

"I'm convinced things have to be practical. We researched everything and tried never to put anything on the air we didn't have an answer to. And I practiced everything on my family. It's amazing my skin isn't like leather." In nine years of broadcasting, the family went through numerous diet and beauty regimens.

Once, researching a diet, "I went on a fast for five days and ran a mile every day to see how the diet worked. I lost 10 pounds, but I got SO bored. After the fast, I went home and ate the whole weekend — night and day, day and night — and I gained every pound back."

It all sounds rather like the fare you might find in a beauty parlor library, but Joanne has also opened the forum to such topics as the China vote in the UN; a discussion of the VD problem in Houston; preventive dentistry; vasectomies; an examination of a diet for hypoglycemia; as well as beauty tips, recipes and family relations.

86

As for her interviews with the beautiful people of this world, Joanne admits she's been very lucky. "I know the people — or I know someone who knows them. When you meet someone under those circumstances, they're much more likely to sit down and talk.

"If I don't know my guest, I try to make friends before the show and I find then that the person really wants to give, to help. If I have a difficult or embarrassing question, something people want to know about, I always talk to my guest about it beforehand to find out if he's willing to discuss it.

"And I only had one bad experience—with an actress who had recently posed for nude photographs, for Playboy, I think. When I talked to her about it before the show, she was quite pleasant. But when I asked her on the air how she felt about posing in the nude, she became very rude.

"The director came over to me and said, 'You don't have to take that from anyone. Tell her to leave.'

"I've been the luckiest person. I couldn't ask for a better crew. A short show is so difficult. I have to program in my mind how I want the conversation to go and what the audience wants to know.

"Sometimes I'd creep into my chair just two minutes before we went on the air, but

King of the Airwaves

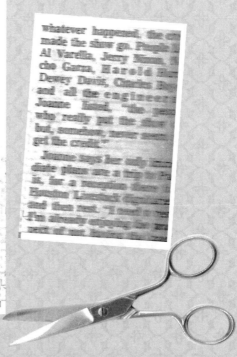

whatever happened, the crew made the show go. People like Al Varelli, Jerry Nelson, Pancho Garza, Harold Davey Davis, Charles and all the engineers Joanne lists, "the men who really put the show but, somehow, never get the credit."

Joanne says her only immediate plans are a trip to it, for a reception there Ernestine Lieschat and then rest. "I had an ready enjoying the next of my

KHOU•TV 11

A CBS Affiliate
RON STONE

A Corinthian Station
12-20-72

JOANNE

I got a most DISTURBING bit of News today. I CAN ONLy hope it is NOT TRUE.

IF, INDEED, You have DECIDED TO MOVE ON... MY LOVE FOR You, AND DECP RESPECT.. Compells me TO wish you All the Best.

IT HAS NOT AlwAys BEEN A smooth VOyAGc, AS A MATTER of Fact it has GOTTEN RAther Rough at TIMES. But, GOD, How you HAVE BEEN ONE of the few Lasting BRight SpOTS.

A CBS Affiliate
RON STONE

A Corinthian Station

I REMEMBER the FiRST DAY You CAME FOR AN iNTERVIEW. AL & I ASKED You And SOME other lADy, DUMB QuESTiONS, AND CAL JONES FliPpED. BUT I NEVER FIGuRED You WOULD LAST. 1/ou DiD..... AND BECAme the Biggest thing iN TV iN this TowN. I'll miss you — So Will A Couple of Million OtheR folks. good LuCk — AND IF you EVER NEED SOME ONE TO TALK TO —— CAll ME

Ron S

Houston now has two candidates for queen of noontime TV and one of them is already a King. The other, of course, is Joy Noufer.

Just why Joanne King decided to leave Channel 11 for Channel 2 after nearly a decade is a bit cloudy. Over lunch last month, she said it was a touchy subject and she didn't know exactly how to talk about it. Indeed, further discussion led nowhere, really, yet it did seem to lead to a conclusion: Apparently, Joanne wanted more flexibility than the station would or could allow.

She said she is grateful to Channel 11, but felt that after nine years, she had justified the station's investment in her and that the time was right for a change. "They were sellin' a great deal of t h e i r (studio) time for commercials and so some of my taping got difficult to get. Any show, you have to tape parts of (and it's) more interesting if you have several things in it and you can't, in one day, get a lot of those things or go out and make a film."

The station, she said, was nothing but good to her in every way and it was regrettable that things went awry after she gave notice of her departure. "I wanted to give them time to get another show on the air . . . so it would look normal for me to come back (from Paris) and go to another station."

Joanne got together with her new boss, Jack Harris, through old friend Chris Chandler, who felt she would like the new facilities at KPRC-TV. But word got out, she said with regret, but not from her and she tried to adjust, changing the subject when someone asked about post-Paris plans. Thus her departure was not as graceful as she had planned out of love and respect for Channel 11 and its staff.

Joanne happily admits to being a professional Texan, a term she feels connotes genuine warmth and hospitality. She was born in

The King who was queen

Joanne, that is, and she hasn't given up her noontime throne; she's just moved

By ED SWINNEY
Post Television Editor

Joanne the First

San Antonio, grew up here, did one year at Lamar High, then lived briefly in South America with her parents. Unhappy there, she surveyed relatives and their surroundings, chose an aunt in Bryan for three reasons: Allen Academy, Texas A&M, and the local high school.

Like a couple of UT contemporaries (Kathy Grant, Jayne Mansfield), Hollywood beckoned early. She was a sophomore, but her parents' condition to travel — a firm screen role — came through as she was having her wedding pictures made. She was Mrs. Robert King until last April.

"I was really married to the nicest man in the whole world," she reflected in an accent tinged with magnolia. She blames their age difference for the break up of a marriage from which came two sons — Beau, 16, and Robin, who is 10.

BTV (before TV) Joanne travelled abroad extensively and her activities as a socialite put her at ease before crowds and helped prepare her for TV. But, because her general background is well-known, some viewers seem have the impression that Joanne has always had it made, that life has been one ball after another. Not so, says she.

Until she was about 11, Joanne Johnson King considered her an ugly duckling. She also had dyslexia, which means you read backwards and she thought she was dumb. When she wrote her initials, JJ, they came out GG.

The Johnsons were down to earth Presbyterian folks, she said, but the love for antiques and music and the other arts was ever present. Without realizing it, she studied architecture most of her

life. At 5, her father was boring her with books on that and other subjects such as Chippendale. He was a builder but he told her ladies must know these things and later she learned to love them. Still later, she helped her husband design houses and draw the floor plan (copied from her great uncle's) of her present home, which she'll let go reluctantly for $600,000. Her husband, she said, was both successful and generous in allowing her to build an early French dream house.

Her first-born was considered a miracle. At 19, doctors told her she would either die on the operating table or be a cripple for life. Till then no one had survived removal of such a spinal tumor, much less walked or had children and went skiing. "I decided anything was possible with God," she recalled. "I got Beau by prayer. I'll just get another."

Her mentor, Cal Jones, sensed that she, like former Astro Judy Temple, had innate qualities that made them suitable for TV. Though it may sound corny, Joanne says that honestly, she has never considered herself a star or even a TV personality. On camera she feels as though she's talking to individuals.

"People I like, getting together at noon. When I first went on he 1960s and 1970s were a very liberal time. I was a conservative and my TV show reflected that. We conservatives believe a government is like a family. You do not spend what you do not have. The government is not a genie in a bottle, and it cannot grant wishes. The government we deal with daily is not the president. It is our neighbor, the guy at the post office or city hall. Conservatives want to keep control of our money, not turn it over to others, not see it wasted while we struggle. Government is not a magic wand but rather a wizard that restricts and takes away our freedoms, one bad spell at a time. Too many rules and agencies rob us because they are funded by our taxes without giving us an opportunity to determine how the money is spent. I said all that on my TV show.

At first, viewers screamed, "Get her off the air!" The liberal station manager would then call me in. "Why did you say that?" he'd ask.

"What did I say? Did I say that?"

"Don't do it again!" he'd admonish me.

I'd wait about a month and do it again. I offended liberal CBS, but what could they do? My ratings proved the people liked conservative thinking. (Years later, when I went off the air, the station got more calls than at any time in its history, saying "Thank goodness some-one told the truth!")

Bella Abzug and Gloria Steinem came to Houston with great fan-fare. These leaders from the Women's Movement who started the National Women's Political Caucus complained that the television stations in town had no women representatives.

"We have Joanne King," they were told.

"Oh, she doesn't count," they replied. "She's not like us."

They said that — until they met me. Then they did a complete turnaround. We actually became friends. I even introduce Gloria occasionally when she speaks at events. We discussed their objec-tives to "liberate" women and to see that females got the jobs they deserved. I want that too. We just have different methods.

They made demands. I made suggestions. I found I achieved

more with suggestions than with demands. Intelligent people recognize ability and know in their hearts what is right. Demands will never break the glass ceiling.

Men of that era were not ready to relinquish their positions or their territory to women. Even today, I still think it works best if they invite you in. If you force them, they can make the job so difficult that you do not achieve the success you're capable of because they put so many roadblocks in your path.

I think whatever it is you want to accomplish must always be the man's idea. The woman's job is to sell it. Let *men* fight your battles for you. They will do it.

On my TV show, I also referred often to God and thanked Him publicly. It shocked people, especially the liberals who had openly declared that He didn't exist. God was almost a dirty word in the sixties, when "god" was considered the individual.

My television career brought me many things that were fleetingly wonderful and flattering. For instance, Barbara Walters and I were added to the prestigious Who's Who organization in the same year. I ended up making more money than anyone else at the station. I had offers to go elsewhere, such as weekend host of the *Today* show in New York, but Houston paid to keep me. And I *wanted* them to keep me in Houston because of my family. "Don't you dare take those boys to live in New York," my mother would say.

I had a lot of amazing experiences because of being on television. But my TV career cost me a lot as well. My children used to give me dark glasses for Christmas so people wouldn't recognize me. We couldn't go anywhere without people wanting to talk to me. Some would say things like, "Oh, you don't look as good as you do on television." They seemed to feel that it was okay to say whatever they wanted to about and to me. I was a frog in a small puddle, but it was similar to what a lot of movie stars go through.

Julia Roberts told me that she had waited a long time to have her children. They are the real focus of her life. She said, "Now that I have them, I don't want to do anything after work but be a mother." She no longer liked to go to parties or do any of the things that she had done previously. She wanted to come home and be with her children. She changed diapers and did all of the things that people don't think movie stars do. She told me that motherhood was the most fun she had ever had.

I understood. I always felt very conflicted as a mother and a television personality. They used to joke that I would slide into the seat for the show seconds before it started. The station manager had told me as long as the ratings stayed up, they didn't care if I kept regular hours. One day I was so late, I completely missed the show. They had to run something else in its place. I guiltily said to the head newscaster, "I'll bet you have missed a show too." He said, "No, but I have had nightmares about it."

There were drawbacks to being recognized by the public, some of them serious. Once a woman called the station and said, "I'm going to kill Joanne King!"

"Why?" the operator asked.

"Because she's in bed with my husband!"

The receptionist said, "I know she's not because I just saw her. She's here at the station."

But the woman insisted she was going to murder me. The police had an officer follow me everywhere for three weeks, but I was terrified. I couldn't even open the door for fear this deranged woman might be standing there with a gun, ready to shoot me.

One night, I was walking through Neiman Marcus with the gun the police chief gave me for protection. Somehow it opened and the shells fell out. The other shoppers and salespeople didn't even look at me; they just politely walked around me, stepping over the shells, pretending everything was normal. Nothing ever came of the threat, but I was always uneasy.

I left CBS just before a big party they were giving celebrating my ten successful years. NBC had heard that I was unhappy at CBS because the station manager was having an affair with a woman who wanted my show. NBC offered me a big raise and anything I wanted.

The Joanne King Show was my new show in competition with my old one at CBS. I was in competition with myself. Soon my audience moved with me, I regained my ratings, and CBS fired the woman they had hired to replace me and canceled my old show.

It amazes me but thirty years later people still remember my daily show. The viewers felt like we were friends (except for the occasional crazy lady). I shared my problems and tried to solve theirs with the best problem solvers available. This was the first time in my life that I felt women really liked me, because, for the first time, they really knew me. Before, I think women only saw the "social butterfly" side of me. Until the television show, they didn't know about the part that cared deeply for them and tried to produce shows that would make their lives easier and more interesting.

Recently a beautiful woman came up to me and said, "My mother was sick with mono and was unable to have visitors due to contagion. She said, 'Don't worry about me. I won't be lonely. I have my best friend, Joanne King, with me every day.'"

I was touched beyond words.

Meanwhile, at home the real problem for me was that when we were low financially, I sacrificed everything to help Bob retrench. I closed the door on the world to do it, and I did it happily. Every thought and action was for him and the boys. When he began to revive financially, I wanted something for me. I wanted for him to see I needed a more open life. When he failed to see or care, the door began to close and love to disappear in a cloud of incompatibility and lack of similar life goals.

Did I love Bob when we married? Or did I love the life he offered and the fact that he loved *me* so much? I know that I *grew* to love him and still do in my heart for the fine human being he was. He was honorable, generous, and as handsome as a movie star. But did we have enough in common for a lifetime together? He liked working and exercise, period. I liked the high life, and I decided to find some. TV offered many opportunities. There was a world beyond Houston. I wanted to see it, and it wanted to see me. But this was not Bob's scene.

Chased, Chaste, and Conquering Spain

JOANNE HERRING

THE QUEEN OF TEX

When Houston's glamourous hostess sweeps down the red carpeted marble stairway of her 20-room villa, striking a commanding pose under a glistening chandelier that once belonged to Madame Pompadour, one is tempted to believe that the opulent stage has been set specially for such grand entrées.

Not quite, but there is indeed a dramatic aura about everything associated with the Queen of Te᾿᾿ ᾿nd that is most vividly manifested in her sp᾿᾿᾿d River Oaks domicile, where she regularly holds court to friends and admirers. The lavishly furnished dining room, with its French gilded and plush antiques, seats forty of the favoured few at her "small" soirées. After dinner, guests repair to the second floor "Arabian Nights" disco to dance on the zebra-skin patterned marble floor, flanked by life-size porcelain leopards and tigers.

But the aura is deceiving; there's more to the blond bombshell and whirlwind socialite than meets the eye. Joanne Herring is also a very shrewd businesswoman, with a seat on the board of a big bank, an oil company, and the Lindberg Foundation for the promotion of science. In her latter capacity, it's not unusual for Joanne to throw huge fund-raising parties for guests filling a hundred tables.

Not only that, for the past ten years or so, she has officiated as consul-general of Pakistan and Morocco, mobilizing US investments and development funds for the two needy countries.

The image, too, of a dynamic self-made woman is also deceptive. The daughter of a wealthy Texas engineer, Joanna acquired an early taste for good living, while still developing a spirit of independence and enterprise. She had her own popular television talkshow for twelve years.

It was her marriage to her late husband, Bob Herring, however, that projected Joanne into the rich and influential international circles in which her oil tycoon husband moved. Soon she was playing hostess to Saudi Arabian sheiks, English and French aristocracy, Swedish, Jordanian and Persian royalty, and the ubiquitous Henry Kissinger. And in these circles, Joanne Herring moves with regal ease, as befitting the uncrowned Queen of Texas.

Entering the River Oaks mansion o
Joanne Herring is a walk into Alice'
wonderland as well as a touch of the tenth muse. In a rare synthesis of style and espri
Joanne Herring has established herself and her home as the social Himalaya in th
Texan desert.

KING

some investment deals with her former in-laws, the **Cullen** clan . . .
Speaking of romance, socialite **Sue
(Mrs. Chad) Nelms** and her steady
fella, Dallasite **Gordon Guiberson**, are
just back from a trek to Manhattan.
Their pals won't be a bit surprised if
wedding bells are ringing soon . . .
Ch. 11's **Joanne King**, who really digs
royalty, has been hobnobbing with
the blue bloods a lot lately. You can
see her picture in the new Harper's
Bazaar. She's with **Prince Bernhard**
of the Netherlands and the picture
was snapped at a recent party at Palm Beach. Joanne is just
back from N.Y. and a visit with **Prince and Princess Paulo
Borghese.** Joanne returned only an hour before houseguests
from France arrived — **Henri-Francois Cruse** and wife **Gui-
aliaumette.** He's of the Cruse winrey clan and she's a former
Peugeot, of the auto fortune . . .

MAY 19, 1972

BY BEVERLY MAURICE
Fashion Editor

Mayor and Mrs. Louie Welch opened festivities officially with a delightful party in their Spanish style home Saturday night, honoring the guests who'll help make Foley's "Ole, Espana" festival a memorable two weeks.

The Marquis and Marquessa de Villaverde, high fashion designer Rodriguez and his wife and actress Nini Montiam arrived for a week's stay in our city. Daughter of Franco, Spain's ruler, the Marquessa is wed to Dr. Cristobal Bordiu, and they'll be honored with a party and tour in the Medical Center on Tuesday.

Rodriguez will be on hand at Foley's Crystal Room Monday at 11 a.m. to introduce his collection in a formal showing at the downtown store Then on Nov. 2, he'll be the guest star at the Houston Club luncheon fashion show.

Joanne (Mrs. Robert V.) King will also interview him during the week on her KHOU-TV show, as well as doing a thirty minute special on Spain Tuesday night.

Sir John Barbirolli and the Houston Symphony Orchestra will pay its tribute to Spain in Jones Hall on Monday night with a special selection. Store president Milton Berman and his wife will host the Spanish visitors for the concert and a candlelight supper.

Contemporary Arts Museum opens an exhibit of Spanish artists November 2.

In Foley's downtown store, a variety of Spanish pleasures are to be had.

Francisco Alarte of Barcelona, celebrated hair stylist, will be visiting in Foley's Beauty Salon during the entire two weeks.

Rick Sferra of the famous linens house of Sferra in Madrid will introduce a collection of fine table linens up to $7000 on the fifth floor.

Handbag designer Pedro Giner of Madrid will show his creations on the first floor.

Iron sculpture loaned by Essex of Madrid will be on display in the 9th floor Gallery.

And certainly not least—entertainment for the ch A puppet show of Ferdinand the Bull will be per

There'll Be Spanish Fun for Everyone

Winter white sparks romance in the Rodriguez collection. Pearl bead curtain earrings repeat the ball fringe motif at the hip of the white silk crepe fitted dress. White mink turban by Dior. There's a caramel wool coat to match the shoes.

I worked to save my marriage the best way I knew how. I thought by throwing myself into my TV career, it would fulfill the needs not met by my marriage. I tried always to remember what my mother had taught me — fairy tales don't come true if you step over the line — and I lived by that code when it came to men. But there were temptations. I was not always chaste by choice.

Yes, I was still married — technically, as they say. I was always careful about what transpired between my temptations and me. I offered nothing sexually. But I enjoyed the attentions of other men at this time, and they seemed to enjoy the chase as well.

Playboys never really interested me. It always surprised me that they were attracted to me at all. I enjoyed playing as much as they did, but for me, men of action and purpose were the aphrodisiacs.

Yet, we all like a little champagne occasionally, and that is just what playboys were to me…and I to them. Let's face it — it's fun to be chaste and chased. If you can pull it off…you have won the game. Everybody goes away laughing and free to play again another day.

I met one of my biggest temptations in Spain. When the Spanish government wanted to promote tourism, they hired me to make a film documentary. I was thrilled at the opportunity, and I needed the money. Although I was always sad to leave them, my boys stayed with my father and mother when I traveled, and they seemed fine. Bob was too busy with work to keep up with the children. Mother soon joined me in Spain to chaperone, but I knew the children were in loving hands with my father, and it was only for two weeks.

It was a great time to be in Spain. I loved meeting Manuel Benítez Pérez, known as El Cordobés. A Steve McQueen look-alike, this blond matador had the worldwide status of a movie star for his bravery, and his magnetism was beyond description. Even my mother chose going to his *finca* (country house) over having lunch with the Duchess of Alba. (We did have lunch with the duchess later in her palace and got to see her famous Goya paintings.)

El Cordobés was featured at the Feria of Seville (Seville Fair) in Spain with Jackie Kennedy and Princess Grace of Monaco. *Time* magazine described the fair as the essence of Spain, a six-day post-Lenten fiesta with bullfighting, flamenco dancing, and a marvelous ball. Wow, was it ever fun to be there. It was a big-time jet-set, and I got to play with them.

Both men and women ride beautiful horses in the traditional *traje corto*, stunning black suits with bolero jackets and tight, flaring pants that fit over boots. The hat is distinctive, with a low crown, a flat broad brim, and a chin strap. This is what Jackie, an excellent rider, chose to wear with such distinction. Princess Grace was not an equestrian. Too clever to challenge Jackie on a horse, Grace chose a carriage. She was strikingly lovely in her long, wide-skirted dress, big hat, and parasol.

There was fierce competition between Grace and Jackie. The American ambassador to Spain, Angier Biddle Duke, chose to inject me into the competition, on a small scale, of course. He said the other two women gave him a headache. El Cordobés dedicated one bull to Jackie and another to Grace, then found time to dedicate one to me.

Ambassador Duke was not a classically handsome man — but he had *something*. Whatever was interesting and different attracted him. Duke died at age seventy-nine, hit by a car while in-line skating, seeking excitement to the end.

Both Jackie and Grace were Americans and equally elegant and beautiful in my eyes, but according to the columnists, Jackie's *Life* cover won the contest. Some said she was more exciting than Grace, but both had no problem generating waves of interest. They played their parts well: Grace as the perfect princess; Jackie, the perfect wife of the president, whose family was American political royalty. It was exhilarating to be a part of it as the "queen of Texas" — a "title" the Spaniards often awarded me.

It didn't hurt that my name was King. Everyone wanted to associate me with the famous King Ranch. When asked, I made it clear that I was *not* a member of the King Ranch family. My answer was always, "I was born a Johnson, and I'm not related to Lyndon. I married a King, and he doesn't own an inch of the ranch."

El Cordobés was fascinating, but there was another that drove even the bullfighter from the ring of my attention: Cristóbal Martínez-Bordiú, tenth Marquis of Villaverde. At the *feria*, the royals and aristocrats had their tents set up, each decorated like a luxurious room. His was the grandest. When I arrived, the women ignored me. I could almost hear them thinking, "Who is this television person from Texas?" But the marquis came to me immediately. Sparks flew.

Cristóbal was one of the most fascinating men I ever met. A heart surgeon, he was the top playboy of Europe. His position in Spain was unequaled since he was married to Generalissimo Francisco Franco's beautiful daughter, Carmen. Yes, he was married. I was married. It was an impossibility. But, oh, my, the temptation.

Cristóbal loved Carmen, and he was a good father to their seven children — but he had another life, which she chose to ignore. Every woman he met seemed captivated. The first day I met him, I was transfixed... and, wonder of wonders, he was attracted to me. Cristóbal was to change my life in so many beautiful ways.

A few months later, I was surprised to learn that he and his wife, Carmen, were making a goodwill visit to Houston. I decided to give a ball. Even though we were having money problems, caterers, florists, and other party providers volunteered their services for a chance to showcase their talents. Participating in headline-grabbing events is a selling point for their businesses — and a great advantage to a hostess who is broke!

I asked the sheriff to send his mounted posse — dressed as Texas Rangers — to meet the guests of honor at the gate to Rivercrest, where we lived. One of my neighbors, Stewart Morris, had a collection of antique carriages. I requested that he drive the Villaverdes in his most beautiful open coach, surrounded by the Rangers on horseback. It was very colorful, very Texas, and very cold.

The guests of honor arrived, frozen but gorgeous in cowboy clothes. (The theme was Old West. Foreign guests always expected cowboys and Indians at parties in Texas.) A leading restaurateur had roasted an entire cow on a spit in our garden.

The evening was straight out of an MGM extravaganza. It played as well in Madrid as it did in Houston. When films of the party were shown to Franco and King Juan Carlos of Spain, they decided that Juan Carlos must come to Houston for his own visit, and that Cristóbal and Carmen should come too.

Cristóbal made two remarkable interviews possible for me. I eventually did King Juan Carlos's first interview. "Oh, I didn't know I sounded like that," he said. It was the first time he had ever heard a recording of himself. As for Franco, in his entire career, only two Americans were ever allowed to interview him — Walter Cronkite and me. I was also the only woman ever to interview Franco. For this interview, I won Spain's equivalent of a Grammy award, the Ondas.

After my party for Cristóbal and Carmen, the next night, Ricky di Portanova and his second wife (my friend Sandra was the third) hosted a party for the Spanish delegation. Ricky's wife decided to show me her power. I had thought I would be at Cristóbal's side, but I was wrong. Ricky's wife ruthlessly put me at a secondary table with the entourage of Spanish dignitaries accompanying the celebrated pair. Cristóbal was furious and I knew my seating placement was almost an insult.

Some guests change place cards or even walk out if they are displeased with their seat. I was not brought up that way. If you are a guest and have accepted the hospitality of the host, a real lady sits where she's asked to sit. So I sat.

Next to me was a wispy man. He was dressed well but was most unprepossessing in demeanor and appearance. "Oh, well," I thought. "I am here now and I cannot be anywhere else. Therefore, I am going to make this man have an absolutely wonderful evening."

At the end of the dinner he said, "My lady, you have given me the best evening of my life. Now I want to do something for you. I am the designer Rodriguez, who creates gowns for the crowned heads of Europe. I am going to make you the most beautiful dress in the world."

With that he bowed, kissed my hand, and walked out of my life. I never saw him again.

Within a year, I was at the wedding of Cristóbal's daughter, the granddaughter of Franco. She was marrying Prince Alfonso de Bourbon, first cousin of King Juan Carlos. I arrived at the ceremony in the most exquisite dress in the world — one that I could never afford but that had been delivered to me by a wispy man of his word.

During the wedding festivities, Cristóbal included me in the small parties reserved exclusively for visiting royalty. He would present me as "the queen of Texas." Because of who he was, people laughed and accepted me as just that!

I was accompanied to the wedding by an Austrian archduke, heir to the Austrian throne, who was exiled in Spain at the moment. He decided that ours could be a great romance. So on the day of the wedding, I glided into the cathedral, the archduke by my side. It was a very long way for a little girl from Houston to come. When I was twelve, I had dreamed of meeting an Austrian archduke. Any royal family that could stay on the throne seven hundred years impressed me!

There were a few problems with the archduke's fairy-tale romance, however. The duke was fat and asthmatic and had as many hands as an octopus has legs. No matter how thrilling his title, the rest was just too much.

It was heaven to be at the wedding with royals from all over the world, wearing the most beautiful dress in the world. But the next night, there was trouble in paradise. I learned, as it was March, that the ladies were going to wear floating, springtime floral dresses to the royal ball and dinner. The only really nice dress I had remaining was an elegant, fox-trimmed, high-necked, long-sleeved, very wintery dress. I would be totally out of season. In these lofty circles, what you wear is part of your credibility. I was already suspect as "the queen of Texas," with no real royal lineage. I didn't know what to do.

With a royal as an escort, you can wear an old blanket and be smiled upon. But by refusing to succumb to the archduke's charms, I was stuck with the repercussions of my out-of-season dress. I saw my new found social status evaporating. I was convinced my dress would confirm the worst stereotypes of American women.

God has a wonderful sense of humor: That night it snowed.

People were astonished. It *never* snowed in March in Madrid. It was so cold, the wind was like a saber. The snow swirled and leaves blew off the trees. I was the only woman at that ball who was appropriately dressed. The other ladies were shivering in their spring finery, while I came in looking elegant, appropriate, and warm. It was a moment of triumph in the most superficial way, but I had been reminded that any success I enjoyed in life wasn't because of me. God had given me a whimsical, loving gift. For some reason He wanted me in these royal settings, and in the process He had reminded me to honor everyone — including the wispy man, who in reality was one of the top designers in the world.

Dressed appropriately, I sallied forth with confidence as I strolled through palatial rooms filled with notable, interesting people. While the archduke frowned, royalty flocked to my side, even King Juan Carlos.

Mario D'Urso was lolling languidly on a chaise lounge beside Imelda Marcos, wife of the president of the Philippines. Mario was six foot four; thus, there was a lot of him to loll, all of it gorgeous. Some say men are not gorgeous, but he was and still is.

Of course, I was most pleased to meet the famous and beautiful Imelda of the five-hundred-pairs-of-shoes fame. Imelda never made a mistake as far as I know about anything pertaining to herself and her position. This was one smart cookie, with creamy white skin, big black eyes, and a lovely figure. She was very impressive, and she looked very much the queen with her courtier Mario. I was mesmerized by him, and when he said, "I am the prime minister of the Philippines," he said it with such imperious confidence, I almost believed him.

"Really! I am the queen of Albania," I replied with a smile.

"She is teasing you, Mario," said the Duchess de la Rochefoucauld. "She is the queen of Texas." "Oh, Lord," I thought when she mentioned that description, "here we go again." The TV show was trotted out into our conversation. I was praised as smart and talented. Beyond politeness, there was a reason for all this flattery. The duchess *had* to make me sound good. In environs like these, one must always have a very good reason to be standing next to the person one is with. On this night it was "Who *are* you?" and "*Who* do you *know?*" This was one-upmanship at its zenith, practiced to the point of art.

The air at the top was so rarified, I felt like I was standing on a steeple with little oxygen. Mario's sheer gorgeousness did not help me breathe any better.

Actually, he was an Italian count, a brilliant businessman who became a senator and deputy minister of trade for Italy in the coming European Union. As far as I was concerned, he could call himself anything he wanted. But he had been so disdainful, I was sure he would never deign to converse with me again. So I tried to amuse Imelda, hoping she might invite me to one of her famous parties in the Philippines — and she did!

I was happy to be mingling with the royal houses of Europe and beyond. I drifted away from Imelda, and to my amazement, the paragon of all things masculine drifted with me. From that moment, Mario never left my side.

Cristóbal was livid at my new attentive suitor, but he was very busy being the father of the bride.

Why was this wedding and its related parties important to me? My five days in the company of the most influential people in Europe helped me form international ties around the world, which would later give me incredible access to almost anyone. I could pick up the phone and get through to world leaders and people of royal influence, as easily as to my next-door neighbor. Normally one must be born into this kind of entrée. For me, God arranged it, because later, I was to use these contacts to pursue my goal of helping to defeat the threat of communism.

CHAPTER 12

Real Royalty, the Ritz,

Rolling out the red carpet
for royalty

and the French Connection

Rolling out the
red carpet for
royalty

By MARGE CRUMBAKER

IT NOW IS referred to as The Party.

And, in words of one syllable, it was:

In case you were on another planet that September week end, The Party is the one Robert and Joanne King and the H. H. Coffields gave for Their Serene Highnesses, Prince Rainier and Princess Grace of Monaco.

The Party was beautiful and things went so smoothly that observers were inclined to think that it was put together at that great big party-place-in-the-sky. Actually, it took a lot of hard work and a few near-panic situations to get it all stuck together.

The Party took place late on a Friday night. But at the King home, a miniature Versailles far out Westheimer, activity was in high gear early the day before.

On that Thursday, Joanne King rushed in her own front door to be greeted by dozens of people doing things for The Party. Over the roar of a vacuum cleaner, Joanne explained:

"I hope you understand about pictures not being allowed during the actual party but I guess They don't want to be constantly photographed like a pair of prized cows."

OUTSIDE, Robert King was engrossed in conversation with a gentleman who'd just rolled up in a green Mustang, hopped out and introduced himself as Rose of Abbey Rents.

"Now we could," Rose suggested, "set up a cloakroom right here on this spot." He indicated the very place where a big brown and white dog was sleeping under a pine tree.

"That would be fine," Robert King said agreeably.

"And then," Rose continued, "we could bank flowers all along here."

"Fine," Robert King said.

"Or," Rose persisted, "we could put flowers down the path and rope off the front."

"That sounds good," King agreed again. He kept glancing toward the door and when his wife emerged, they got into their big black Caddy and zoomed off to the airport and San Antonio and the first round of parties for Prince Rainier and Princess Grace.

And suddenly they were walking up the steps, making the red carpet seem completely justified

Regal applause for the serenade by the Pasadena Civic Chorus

The beautiful main ballroo

The long wait was worth it: Joanne King introduces Princess Grace and Prince Rainier to her guests

The receiving line turns into a giant circle of guests anxious to greet the royal pair and make them feel welcome

I've been given an opportunity to entertain Princess Grace and Prince Rainier of Monaco," I told my television station manager in 1968. He knew that entertaining this storybook couple was a coup, a high-ratings certainty, so I filmed everything, including the preparations for the ball I was giving them at my house.

Bob and I rallied as a couple, presenting a united front when the occasion warranted it. A party for royalty qualified.

I had met Their Highnesses through my friend Count Charles de Chambrun, the deputy minister of foreign affairs for France. Thus began my heady intoxication with all things French. It happened because of the world's fair — the HemisFair 1968 in San Antonio. The French consul general knew about my connection to George

Washington and that Charles was the nephew of the Marquis de Lafayette. We would make a good pair!

The day we met, Charles invited me to come to France. He wanted to lavish a great deal of money on the French Pavilion at the HemisFair by providing a superlative French restaurant. He thought my representing Texas among the French would help. Governor John Connally immediately made me the HemisFair ambassador to foreign countries.

I was ecstatic.

When Charles and I first discussed inviting Grace and Rainier to Houston, he said, "These people do not like to stay in hotels." Their entourage included French ministers, nobility, and jet-setters whose names were often featured in the press.

"Well, where do they want to stay?" I asked.

"They want to stay in private houses," he replied.

"Houses? Charles, there are forty people!"

He shrugged and said, "So get forty houses."

So I did. Imagine asking forty of your friends to put up world-famous celebrities they hadn't even met. I was young. I didn't know that I couldn't or shouldn't, so I just asked my friends to accommodate them, and they did.

I also asked them to provide limousines to transport these guests. If the friends I asked didn't own a limo, they rented one. Then I requested that they provide these awesome people with breakfast and that they press their clothes and, basically, give them royal accommodations and pampering. It's a wonder my friends didn't disown me.

Next, Charles said, "We also need airplanes."

"What?" I asked.

"They need to have private planes to fly them from the HemisFair in San Antonio to Houston for your ball."

Not many people had private planes big enough unless they were attached to companies, which would certainly not lend them for this purpose. The planes had to seat twenty people each. The prince and princess flew on separate planes (for the sake of their children, in case disaster struck) and divided their guests between the two of them. I found friends with the two planes with twenty seats. However, I gave no thought to the luggage. When the big day arrived, it was chaos. Once those two private planes were unloaded, nobody knew which luggage was to go in which limo. I had no way to help sort it out.

I remember everybody milling around the airport tarmac, disgruntled and hot under the Texas sun, asking these very elegant people which of the bags belonged to them. These people were not accustomed to being involved in anything so mundane. The limousines puffed away, while dukes and duchesses and ministers of this and that waded through piles of suitcases to claim their personal belongings.

I decided not to worry about it. I was going to take care of Grace and Rainier. So off I went, leaving everybody else to deal with the luggage fiasco. I wouldn't do that today, but being young, I thought, "They'll manage." And they did.

I had heard that the couple's favorite song was "True Love" from Princess Grace's film *High Society*. I thought, "I'll get the Houston Choir to sing it when they arrive." How romantic — a one-hundred-voice choir trilling in the soft night air. I asked the choir members to dress in black because I didn't want them to look like colorful lollipops.

I wore a beautiful white organza dress with bronze beads and an organza purple coat, another gift from Rodriguez. Local jewelers offered glittering accessories. I chose a magnificent sixty-carat sapphire surrounded by diamonds on a diamond chain. I had the finery but had only fifteen minutes to dress, with so many party details to check! I didn't have to ask people for favors; God provided. Something always appeared when I needed it. The ball was a success. Everyone had fun, and Grace and Rainier danced and talked to the guests as if they were old friends. They stayed until long after midnight, enchanting everyone. (They must have liked us because they invited Bob and me to accompany them on their trip to Mexico to see the ruins of Chichén Itzá. We accepted and had fun!)

When we aired the show about the prince and princess's royal visit to Texas in 1968, it was a ratings bonanza. I had come a long way from those early days in my TV career.

I had hoped my TV show would assuage my need to socialize, and it did for a time. But my marriage encountered other obstacles that proved insurmountable.

While the men in my social circle to this point had been tantalizing, a man was about to enter my life who seemed far more than a temptation. He made the prospect of leaving my old life a much more enticing notion.

Charles de Chambrun, the man I had met through the Hemis-Fair event, had invited me to France. I went, even though, with children and a daily TV show, it was not easy. As charming as Charles was, I felt I could not go alone. So I invited Camilla Blaffer to chaperone me. She spoke perfect French and was thrilled to be introduced into the circle of the oldest and best titles of France.

We arrived in Paris to find that Charles had been called away on state business. But he had arranged everything perfectly, asking the Duke and Duchess de la Rochefoucauld to become my guardian angels. She was the most celebrated hostess in Paris and he was the twenty-first duke. These French aristocrats invited me on boar shoots and for breakfast, lunch, and dinner at a glamorous palace every day. It was heady wine — and plenty of it flowed in the goblets of this gilded group.

Charles de Chambrun returned and said, "This is amazing. I come back to find you are everybody's best friend."

Charles had arranged for me to stay at the Ritz Hotel, where I met the exclusive and reclusive Charles Ritz, whose father had built both

Ritz hotels. Ritz had no children and took a fatherly fancy to me. He took great pride in my social success. I became known at the hotel as the "daughter" of the Ritz, where I never took the elevator but always ran the stairs to exercise. The staff loved to tell Mr. Ritz that I ran up and down five flights of stairs in high heels. I never paid a hotel bill at the Ritz, and I was even allowed to have parties, all a gift from the legendary Mr. Ritz. As if that wasn't enough, he had me to lunch with Coco Chanel and the Cartier family before I left.

Meanwhile, Charles de Chambrun introduced me to the heirs to the French throne, Princess Napoléon and the Countess of Paris, granddaughter of the last king. I learned to curtsy and to whom. With the Ritz as my palace and sponsors such as Charles and the duchess, I was enjoying the bubbles of my frothy new life. And romance in Paris, the most romantic of cities, did come.

By the end of the trip, the only Frenchman I considered marrying was Raymond Marcellin, French minister of the interior. This minister appoints the governors and the mayors and controls the French equivalents of the CIA and FBI. Everybody admired and feared Marcellin, as he had access to everybody's secrets.

I met him with Claude de Kemoularia, who became French ambassador to the UN. Claude's wife laughingly introduced me often as her husband's American girlfriend. (As there was no romance whatever, I thought it was funny. But my mother said, "She introduced you as what? That's not funny!") With Claude I met the Rothschilds and had lunch at Château Mouton Rothschild, the château that produces the famous wine.

Then he introduced me to Raymond Marcellin. "You will not be sorry," he said. I was not sorry.

Maxim's was then the grand restaurant of Paris, not because of the food, but because of its ambiance. It was the place to see and be seen. Marcellin came driving up in a ministerial car with flags flying on the fenders. Everyone was bowing and saying, "This way,

Monsieur le Ministre." The waiters stood at attention and the other guests were awed. I was impressed.

When I arrived back at the Ritz, there were flowers. After that, there were flowers every day, the car with the flags at my disposal, and dinners for whomever I chose at his palace on the Place Beauveau.

In France, the ministers reside in the palaces of former kings. Marie Antoinette's silver "resided" at Marcellin's palace. Fully uniformed grenadiers stood guard in the courtyard. The grandeur of another era unfolded before my eyes.

Raymond did not play the society role; thus, naturally, everyone wanted to know him. He took me on wonderful outings, including a helicopter ride over château country and dinners with celebrities such as actress Brigitte Bardot and with the most sought-after couple in the world, Liz Taylor and Richard Burton.

When I refused his expensive gifts (as a lady should), he bought me jewels, had them wrapped, and sent them anonymously to the hotel for my mother. I thought these were little remembrances from friends — until I got home and my mother unwrapped some magnificent pieces. (She really thought they were for her and wore them all.)

Marcellin had another marvelous asset as far as I was concerned. He was strongly anticommunist. At a time when the world was afraid of communists, placating them, and refusing to acknowledge that they wanted to conquer us all, Raymond stood firmly against them. Of course, being the head of the French domestic and international intelligence agencies, he had knowledge that few people in the world were privy to.

Charles de Chambrun felt differently. "The world just has to accept communism for a while," Charles told me. "It will probably only survive a hundred years."

Aghast, I protested, "You cannot mean that you will just lie down and accept their rule?"

"There is nothing we can do to stop them," he replied. "No country is strong enough. You think the United States is so strong. But your armed forces are in disarray. The communists have the bomb and they will use it. We must not destroy the world."

"Charles, what about you and your children? Don't you care that you will be a slave and your children even worse?" I asked.

"There is nothing we can do," he said again with a shrug. "It is inevitable."

I remained silent. I knew he would never listen to me. But in my head, I screamed, "I will never ever accept communism. I will die first." And I meant it.

Marcellin took me seriously. Together we had some intense evenings, planning and hoping that somehow, some way, the world would wake up in time, rally its forces, and fight. He shared my fear that communists were slowly taking over the world and its resources while America slept and played and talked about the awful Nazis. The Nazis were indeed awful, but they were gone, while the communists were planning a Cuban empire in South America, a new communist Africa via Angola, and a trap for the oil of the Middle East. Every day they were moving. They absorbed the governments of Tibet, North Korea, and the five countries around Afghanistan. They controlled Eastern Europe and were moving toward Vietnam and Cambodia.

I had no time for Brigitte Bardot. I wanted to save the world. The world, however, thought I was crazy. Even my mother wearily said to me one day, "Must we *always* discuss communism and how we must save the world? I don't want to save the world. Please save the world without me."

I was outraged. How could my mother care so little when the world was crumbling around us? She didn't care, and the world didn't either. But Marcellin did.

He told me, "You think like a man and look like a woman. I adore you. Marry me!"

I discussed it with one of my closest friends, Isabelle d'Ornano, born a Polish princess. Her uncle was married to Jackie Kennedy's sister, Lee. She had married the Conte d'Ornano, the owner of Orlane Cosmetics.

She said, "Joanne, you are entirely too American. If you become a French political wife, you will have to change. French politics are different from America's. The wife must submerge herself in her husband and stay in the background. Can you do that?"

I said nothing, but I had my doubts.

Another friend, the beautiful Sophia Bouboulis, who was to become the muse to artist Fernando Botero, said, "Marcellin fell in love with you as you are. He has had many mistresses. He can have any French woman he wants. He has given this a lot of thought. As a French politician, he is taking a big chance, marrying an American. He fell in love with you as you are. Do not change."

But there was a larger concern than whether or not *I* would have to change. I had two little boys who had always lived in the same big house on twelve acres with everything little boys want: a pool, a lake, horses, and dogs. They did not speak French. I spoke enough French to manage and even spoke enough to lunch with President Bourguiba of Tunisia, who spoke no English. How could I uproot them and move to a city where they knew no one, among people they did not understand in a tight culture of rules and regulations? They were accustomed to a free and easy life. To place them with a man who had never married and who did not have any interest in them? No, no, no.

And, of course, there was the same old problem that prevented me from accepting Marcellin's or any other proposals. I was still married.

Bob and I had basically been going our separate ways for quite some time, but as long as I was married, I was not going to tarnish my husband's or my name by stepping outside the prescribed rules.

And I didn't. But men such as Marcellin were being introduced into my life, and Bob was not alone at this time either.

Bob and I were mostly happy for sixteen years before our goals became too divergent to reconcile. I am forever grateful that we had two lovely children, the Kings of my heart, my sons, Beau and Robin. I will always love Bob for the fine man he was.

People

Big city beat
by Maxine

TRIPPING THE NIGHT FANTASTIC: Maria McRae hosted a seated dinner Sunday in her posh hacienda for **Ariana Stassinopoulos**, who was in town to tubthump the paperbak edition of her book, *Maria Callas*. She was here a year ago with the hard-cover version and made quite a few friends. Ariana, naturally, hails from Greece but lived in London for 13 years before moving to NYC a year ago. She's a grad of Cambridge with a degree in economics. Although *Maria Callas* first gave her national fame, Ariana had published two earlier books dealing with economics and politics. She's hard at work on her next tome, the life of **Pablo Picasso**, which will be published by Simon and Schuster. She's finished a book about Greek gods titled *The Gathering of the Gods*, which will be on the book stands in October. **Joanne Herring**, just back from NYC with **Baron** and **Baroness Ricky Di Portanova** attending attorney **Roy Cohn**'s big birthday bash, was on hand. Joanne and Ariana are friends. Joanne says her son, **Robin**, who wants to be a movie producer, is in China as part of a film crew working on a documentary with producer **Bill Fawcett**. Her other son, **Beau**, is just back from biz in Austria. Folks at the dinner included David Webb's **Elyse Robins, Bob** and **Gudrun Evans, Mari** and **Jimmy Papadakis, Warner Roberts, John Callas, He** Foster **and Gunter Richter**, an executive of the Remington hotel, currently under construction . . .

Houston Chronicle
Section 2 ★
Tuesday, Oct. 14, 1986

Prince Moulay Abdullah, third in line to the throne of Morocco, will be making a rare royal public appearance Friday night when he attends the performance of TUTS' *Desert Song*. **Robin King**, Houston's vice consul to Morocco, will escort Moulay, who, by the way, will have the former Miss Houston **Kim Greer** on his arm. Robin's date for the evening will be **Victoria DiMaria**, and after *Song*, he's hosting a small private party for Moulay . . .

Kings of Heart

My sons, Beau and Robin King, born seven years apart, seem more like only children to me than brothers. They do not resemble one another in looks or personality. What they have in common are character traits: both are Christians, and both are honorable, honest, and patriotic Americans.

Beau has a gift for conversation and a caring and understanding personality — when it really matters. When it is not crucial, you may not see much of him. We can talk, working out our problems through open communication, and Beau never holds grudges. If he gets mad, he gets over it. That is the mark of a real man.

He is always there to support and protect me too, often saying, "Mother, why do you work so hard? Don't worry about the future. I will take care of you." In fact, a few years ago he picked me up, took me to his home, and said, "Mother, this is your room. Anywhere I live, you will always have a home. You will never be alone and never have to worry about money because I will always take care of you."

Though he wants to take care of me, he knows my work is important to me, so when he realized that I needed to learn how to use a computer to accomplish my goals, he bought me one, and he also paid to set up my website (www.joanneherring.com). Without the computer, I would never have been able to write this book, and by spreading the word about my desire to help the people of Afghanistan, the website has helped my work immensely.

Beau is a practical man. Nothing interferes when he homes in on a target. He needed to know law and accounting, for example, so he studied them. He spoke Spanish, but not perfectly, so he went back to school, and now he speaks and reads fluent Spanish. No minute is wasted (no words either). He rises at five a.m. each day to work out, then takes his Rollerblades or bike to the office. I could not possibly keep his schedule or want to!

Maybe he was exchanged in the hospital nursery.

He is totally dependable, but he is not nurturing. (Neither am I. I so appreciate those people in my life who are! Like Desiree Howe, my best friend and the most nurturing person I know. She taught me how to express love and has a rare gift of relating to people. She has been an inspiration to me and to Beau. Hers is a true gift.)

My other son, Robin, is enchanting, an amusing conversationalist who is extremely knowledgeable about politics and history. He reads the *Encyclopaedia Britannica* for fun! (How did I *get* these egg-heads?) Robin doesn't talk about things, though; he just does them: he thinks deeply and analytically about a situation, then gets the job done. His talents have led him to work for the Reagan administration, as assistant to celebrity promoter Earl Blackwell, and for business tycoon Donald Trump.

His love of animals has led him not only to own racehorses but also to adopt dogs from the roadside — and he cares for their health and well-being more than he does his own.

His concern for others extends well beyond dogs and horses, of course. He also cares for my health and well-being, studying my needs and making me exercise and eat the right foods. When I am sick he is there, and he stays with me until I am well. He gave me a 4G smart phone so I can stay in touch wherever my work takes me, and he's teaching me to use it. He also brought me an iPod, which can read to me and does everything but dance, really. Robin also made me go to handgun school so that I could carry the derringer he gave me — a gun so small it fits in a purse. He made me learn kick-boxing too, so don't fool with me, buddy. I'm prepared!

When the boys were young, we lived in a gorgeous house, and at various times in their lives, we could have bought them whatever they desired. But we believed that things become meaningless when you can have everything. When I didn't have anything, I learned to yearn! Anticipation is half the joy of getting what you desire. So instead, each year, months before Christmas, we told Beau and Robin to choose two big gifts and three small presents for Santa Claus to bring them.

"Remember," we told them, "there have to be toys for everybody. Don't ask for too much." They anguished for months over their choices. Then, a week before Christmas, we cleaned out their toy boxes and gave everything away to needy children.

As a matter of fact, Beau didn't get a bicycle until he was eleven, *and* he had to work to pay for half of it by using it to deliver heavy newspapers. (Most of the other paper boys did their deliveries by car.) Sometimes we helped him if it rained, but sometimes he delivered the papers by himself in the rain. That was tough training, but it paid off: today he is a responsible, upstanding man.

My parents ("Dee" and "Granda" to the boys) lived just down the street when the boys were growing up. My father in particular helped raise Beau and Robin. He believed that all children need to feel they are the best at something — anything! His goal was always to teach the boys self-worth through accomplishment. He would spend hours launching clay pigeons for the boys to shoot, for example. They started shooting at age four and became such brilliant shots that we were told by some that they were Olympic material.

On one topic, however, my father and I disagreed. I said the boys could never have motorcycles. They were too dangerous, and that was final (which would be any mother's response). Often when I'd drive in our neighborhood, I'd notice kids on motorcycles and tsk-tsk at their risky riding. When the kids saw me, they would disappear into the woods like roaches scattering in the light. "Who are those kids?" I idly wondered.

You guessed it. They were *my* kids. My father had defied me and bought them motorcycles. I was livid. "How *dare* you do this!" I yelled. "You know I am terrified of those contraptions. They're dangerous!"

"But the boys spend most of their time fixing them!" he countered. He was teaching them about business, he told me. The boys were buying and selling used motorcycles.

Beau, fourteen at the time, had to write the ads, bargain with the customers, buy the used bikes, and learn to repair them until they were functional enough to sell. I think that early work is part of what makes Beau so successful today at buying and selling land. Today he has twenty companies in five states and has sold more than one hundred subdivisions.

Robin, only seven at the time, also had to have a motorcycle. Fixing motorcycles was second nature for Robin, who always had a knack for such tasks. Even before he could read the instructions, Robin could assemble the most complicated model airplanes by himself. He was a marvel. Putting those toys together foreshadowed his ability as an adult to understand complex machinery, including his boat, huge tractors, and the other ranch equipment that he needs to maintain the hundreds of acres at his country house.

Bob and I were different parents with each child. We were afraid that the wealth around Beau would spoil him (we were rich in those days), and we wanted to make sure he did not mistakenly believe money made him better than anyone else. If he learned early on the value of hard work, my husband and I thought that would ultimately make life easier for him.

But by the time Robin was born seven years later, we had reevaluated (not the part about the money but the part about how hard we made our sons work for the things they wanted). We felt that we had been too hard on Beau, and so we were easier with our second child.

I think, too, that because Robin was sick when he was little, we found it hard to discipline him. Robin had asthma when he was a little boy. He had matchstick legs and arms, but because he was on so much medicine, he was never still. He was upside down and backwards every waking minute of every day, but he was so frail, he looked like he was starving.

To me, asthma is the most terrifying illness that a parent and child can endure. When your child cannot breathe and you cannot help, the fear is beyond description. The years between birth and age six for Robin were a competition with death. He almost died four times before he turned three, but I vowed that my child would *not* die.

Once when Robin was hospitalized, the hospital staff rolled in a breathing machine to help him. When I saw his tiny body relieved of his struggle to take his next breath, I wanted that equipment available to him all of the time.

"I will mortgage my house, my virtue, and my life, but I want that machine," I declared.

The doctor looked thoughtful, then said, "Why not?" He knew of a smaller machine we could take home. "Keep it with you at all times," he advised. "The moment Robin coughs, start the machine. Perhaps you will be able to stop or even prevent the asthma attacks."

I would have done anything to minimize the attacks. It was horrifying to watch Robin's chest suck *in*, not out, with the sheer effort of breathing, hour after painful hour . . .

He was so brave, though. He never cried or complained. His stoicism hurt me more than anything else. "Mommy," he said, "please don't look so scared. I'll be fine." *But he wasn't fine!* I was so in tune with his body, I could hear his first cough from the opposite end of the house, the length of a football field. Then everything stopped, and the machine was turned on.

It seemed to me that my *darling* children disappeared at age thirteen. That's when my not-so-darling children went into a cave. They came out three times a day to eat and grunt "uh-huh" and "uh-uh." Around age seventeen, my darling children came back, but I never felt important around them.

I always felt that this was a sign of God's cleverness. Think about it: If our children remained as adorable as they were when they were young, we could never bear to let them go. But when they are teenagers, we become . . . rather willing.

Every working woman fears that her children may not have gotten the attention they deserved. I know I worried about that. When their father was no longer there, I tried to provide masculine experience for my sons, as well, including thrilling activities such as riding galloping horses on pencil-thin ledges (but *not* riding on motorcycle death machines).

I'm glad my sons made it to adulthood, not a sure thing given their daredevil sensibilities. I think it was just these risk-taking tendencies, though, that gave Robin and Beau the desire to push themselves more than most people.

Both of them got pilot licenses. Beau has an Airline Transport Pilot License for multiengine, complex, and float planes. He is instrument trained, meaning that he can fly under any conditions using instruments only. Continental Airlines begged Beau to come to work for them, and he considered the offer, but he decided he wanted his own business. He made a good choice, and he eventually bought his own plane — without the burden of passengers in the back.

In the water Beau was known as the miracle man. He could free dive to a depth of sixty feet, then find and shoot a fish with a challenging bow-and-arrow device called a Hawaiian sling, rising to the surface triumphantly with a big squirming fish as his prize. It takes huge discipline to get in that kind of shape. Even today being fit is a priority with Beau, who works hard at exercising and staying healthy. And it works: he looks like a picture on a magazine cover.

As a teenager, Robin was often written about in the paper, sometimes on the front page, for his daredevil activities. I would know nothing about his recreational pursuits until I read about them. He would get injured, not from a fall on the stairs or working as he would tell me, but from riding broncos in a rodeo, for example. He didn't want to worry me, he said. Robin got several types of pilot licenses and worked his way through college as an offshore helicopter pilot. He flew when and where others refused, for instance, landing on wet, sloping decks in the middle of a storm. Like me, he isn't afraid of *anything*. (It was the rattlesnake cure for me. I shudder to think what my daddy cooked up for Robin's "cure.")

The boys' daredevilry continued on other continents. Once, when we were on vacation in Africa, an elephant chased Beau while he was out taking photographs. To escape the charging elephant, Beau climbed up a tree — but he continued snapping photos the whole time. The pictures showed the elephant at different angles and then looking straight up at Beau as he perched on a limb. Thank God for the tree! The images were so remarkable, I showed them on my television program. Unfortunately, the production department never returned them, and Beau, of course, never forgave me.

Beau is a father. He has two boys, my beautiful twin grandsons, Beau and Beckett, who have big blue eyes and blond hair. Beau's beautiful Barbie doll wife, Stanisse, can do anything — and do it well. The chief financial officer of Beau's many companies and a very good mother to her boys, Stanisse has a special quality that draws everyone to her and makes them love her. She dresses her sons like pictures from a magazine, and everything around her is sheer perfection. That takes time and effort, and I don't know how she does it. I wish I had accomplished half of what she has.

Robin has girls coming and going like streetcars. I have liked those I knew, but as yet I have no daughter-in-law or grandchildren from my second son. Still, I have him, and that is enough.

Beau and Robin are the men they are. I accept their differences and glory in their strengths. If I could have any other sons in the world, I would never trade mine. Would you? Of course not!

CHAPTER 14

Suzy says

Joanne rounds up 'tout' Paris

JOANNE King (Mrs. Robert Herring) of Houston is in Paris producing a TV documentary for the Bicentennial. She's rounded up *tout* Paris for the film, practically all tiled.

No commoners need apply — unless papa or mama had noble blood, of course.

Joanne has herded the blue bloods out to Versailles, where they waddle around in enormous heavy costumes and wigs, patiently waiting to be called before the camera. The heat has been unbelievable, but that's show biz, *mes amis.* Either vanity or patriotism propels them through the nightmare. There is nothing worse than Paris when it sizzles, no matter how the song goes.

The documentary, entitled "A Thirst for Glory, A Taste of Freedom," will have its premiere at the Eisenhower Theater at Washington's Kennedy Center in October. John Warner, the Bicentennial biggie, will be the host for the film and the gala reception later. Everyone hopes for a mini-"Barry Lyndon." (They can dream.) At least, the same soft focus camera techniques will be used. and haunting 18th-century music will prevail.

Some of the noble swelterers who have been tripping around Versailles waiting for their moment on camera include Nathalie, daughter of the Duke de Noailles, the Duchess de la Rochefoucauld, the Vicomte and Vicomtessa de Rosiere, Prince Giovanni de Bourbon-Sicila, Princess Ghislaine de Poliganac, Princess Jeanne Marie de Broglie, Prince Bernard de la Tour d'Auvergne, the brilliant Paris architect, Prince Dimitri of Yugoslavia, the Com-

Houston Chronicle   Wednesday, July 28, 1976

Dilemmas: Divorce, Debt, Dates, and Bangladesh

vergne. the brilliant Paris architect, Prince Dimitri of Yugoslavia, the Comtesse de Chambrun and on and on into the Almanach de Gotha. The title of the documentary is from a quote from Lafayette to Washington. So now you know.

MARY Ballou Reynolds married Michael Ballentine Tuesday in Bethesda, Md., in the lovely garden of Mr. and Mrs. William Cafritz. A hundred or more were invited to a reception afterwards, and once that was out of the way, the bride and groom and the bride's four children left for a 6-week honeymoon in Scotland where they've taken two houses, one in Invernesshire in the Highlands and one in Ayrshire in the Lowlands. No sense in being cramped.

Mary Ballou was given away by her three sons, the twins. Joseph and Edward Stettinius grandsons of the late secretary of state and Richard Roland Reynolds son of the late lieutenant governor of Virginia. The twins are 13 and Roland is 5 Mary Stuart Stettinius, 9 years old and called Cricket, was

Ballentine of Maryland and Massachusetts, was his best man.

Halston made Mary Ballou's blue chiffon wedding dress, and with it she wore a hat made of fresh lilies of the valley. Cricket wore yellow. The groom's mother wore a gray and white polka dot Givenchy and a white panama hat.

Ed Carnevale of Harry Winston executed Michael's design for the wedding present that he gave his bride, diamond and platinum earrings in the shape of the famous Ballentine three rings. Her gold wedding band has been in the Ballentine family since 1856.

After the honeymoon (Cricket calls it the "familymoon" and the kid's right). they'll live together in Mary Ballou's house in Richmond. Michael is keeping his Washington apartment, where he works as a fund raiser. in the arts.

127

EYE ® VIEW

Filming another French connection

WASHINGTON, D.C. (FNS) — **Joanne Herring**, 10 suitcases, a dozen cardboard boxes, three sacks of wigs and a 14-man crew are crisscrossing France and the east coast in search of super-rich, well-connected people. Her objective: a 60-minute, Exxon-financed documentary on **Lafayette** and the American Revolution's French connection.

So far, she says, she's bagged the **Duchess D'Uzes**, the **Duchess de la Rochefoucauld**, **Princess Ghislaine de Polignac**, **Prince Dimitri of Yugoslavia** and **Candy van Alen**.

While Herring's latest foray into skittish Washington society is proving a slight bomb, with locals deciding to stay out of the project, the Kennedy Center has agreed to show the film — "A Thirst for Glory, a Taste of Freedom" — at a private premiere in October.

"It's tricky. Americans are afraid they may lose some of their stature by appearing in a movie. In France is was more or less the same thing. The biggest problem was getting them, but when you got one or two, when the Duchess

"It's a terribly sad thing about John Connally. Everyone talks about him as a wheeler-dealer. They forget he was a very wealthy man before he ever was governor of Texas . . .

---

de la Rochefoucauld came, others came," says Herring, who until her marriage, was in television in Houston for 12 years.

Following her second marriage, to Houston Natural Gas president **Robert Herring** in 1974, she quit her job hosting a daily TV talk show for NBC affiliate KPRC.

"They were so nice to me. They let me travel with my husband. Sometimes I was gone

their chateaux, even for the French film abo
the life of Lafayette. La Grange has never be
opened. Rochambeau has never been filmed i
We also filmed in Les Petits Apartments of Ve
sailles. The French are just a very priva
people," she explains.

"One of the things that helped us with t
owners of the chateaux was having **Rober**
Vega of Elizabeth Arden making them up. Y
see, he kept them very busy putting on wigs at
costumes. Then they had such a good time th
they ended up giving dinners and luncheons fo
us."

To make the film, some 30 French notables,
the midst of a heat wave, dressed up
heavy costumes on two consecutive Mondays
film at Versailles.

"Dealing with curators can be terrible. B
Versailles was very nice. They didn't want
open the windows because the fabric in th
rooms where they had reconstructed was $3,0(
a yard and they didn't want the sun, or wind

. . . To think that Connally
would sell the most valuable
thing he has, his name, for
$10,000 in that milk scandal is
ridiculous."

---

damage it or anybody touching it. And of cours
we were using candles for some of the scene
because 'Barry Lyndon' did it, and Versaill
was about to die. They had special firemen con
in and everything."

Slipping out of a bright green Valentin
skirt and blouse as she talks, Herring pee
down to her pantyhose and then slides, bra-less
into a black decollete Sant'Angelo jumpsuit
attend a cocktail party given by Treasure asse
tant secretary **Jerry Parsky.**

Herring says she convinced Air France
fly her and some of the crew to France for thr

Aug 30, 1972

SHE SNOOPS TO CONQUER: Joanne King, who g
from Europe last week, took off again today for Ger
a few days. She's jetting over to attend Prince and
Von Bismarck's big party at their castle near Ham
cidentally, Joanne, who divorced builder Bob King
back, has the Smart Set's tongues
wagging with her dating activity.
She's seriously seeing an Austrian
prince, a Spanish prince and a
French minister, and no one will be
surprised if she announces marriage
plans soon. FYI: I hear the most likely contender, though, is right here in
the USA. . . . Speaking of romance,
Baron Ricky DiPortanova has bought
a big sparkler for his gal, Houston's
Sandra Rivas, and pals say they

*A*fter sixteen years of marriage, Bob King and I divorced. I thought carefully and for a long time before I left my husband. He was such a fine man, but our life goals were too different, and the gap between us widened until it became too great to bridge. The divorce was hard on me, of course, but it was very hard on Beau and Robin — so hard that if I had known beforehand, I would not have done it. My life would have been different, I know, and some say history would have been too.

So in 1969, I found myself a single mom responsible for two boys and for my aging parents as well. Everything I had was mortgaged to the hilt except two hundred choice acres we were trying to sell (which were later worth millions). Bob owned a third, I owned a third, and the boys' trust fund owned a third, but 100 percent of the title was in Bob's name. If I could make the payment for the boys and me, I could save our shares.

My children's trust fund and the land were my family's future. There was nothing else for me and the boys. We had huge payments coming due, however, two-thirds of which I was accountable for, as I assumed responsibility for the trust fund. Bob told me he could barely make his own payment and could not help me. He said the boys' trust fund had to go. "Forget it," he said. "There is no money to make the payments."

I refused to give up on my boys' only financial hedge. I tried selling my jewelry, but my lawyer laughed. Its sale would make only a pinhole in the debt. I asked Mr. Coffield (my almost-father-in-law) to back my loan. He ran so fast you couldn't see his smoke. Prior to this, I had lots of men tell me, "Honey, if you ever need anything, you just come to me." But when I went to them about my house and land, they ran like rabbits.

One man was willing to help — but he attached strings. I was not raised that way, though, and it was essential to my sons and to me that I remain respectable. So word got around that there were limits to what I was willing to trade for financial security, and I became known in certain masculine circles as the "Unf — able Joanne."

It crushed me that I couldn't count on the people who had vowed to be my friends in good times and in bad. I wasn't asking for money. All I wanted was someone to sign a note at the bank so that I could get a loan to make the imminent payment. This would give us time to sell the land. The land itself would serve as collateral until I did. It was pure business. But since I had no title to the land, everyone said I had no real collateral, and so requests for business help became baseless. Any future calls I made would be purely to request charity for a destitute woman.

My only income at that time was the TV show salary, which fed us. Viewers thought I was still living a fairy tale. In reality, it was the lowest point in my life. When I had been sick to the point of dying, that was hard, but this was a different kind of despair. This was as close to hell as I ever want to come.

I never anticipated the difficulties I would encounter as a single mother, chief among them the financial burden and the burden of simply coping. This is perhaps the toughest job in the world.

I was taught to live by a code. No charity, no bankruptcy, no breaking your word, no stealing of husbands or money, no reneging on a business deal, no selling of virtue.

Now I had good land to sell, but no one would buy it.

My last hope was Vince Kickerillo, a hugely successful land developer who had built hundreds of houses. Born the twelfth child of an Italian sharecropper, he started with nothing and earned millions. He made so much money, he started his own bank. If Vince did not want to buy the land, I was licked.

When I drove from the house to my appointment with Vince, I felt despondent, desperate, and defeated. I couldn't consider my father's offer to sell everything he had, to save me. I had tried everything else I could think of, with no success, and I had not one cent beyond what I earned at the television station. But as I drove down the drive, at that instant, the Lord sent me a message: "Consider the lilies of the field, how they grow: they neither toil nor spin; and yet I say to you that even Solomon in all his glory was not arrayed like one of these." After that, He said into my consciousness, "The Lord knows you have need of these things" (from Matthew 6:27–29).

The Lord knew I had need of *everything*. All alone, I was faced with supporting, educating, and housing my children, helping my parents, keeping a demanding job — doing so much with so little. But these Bible verses changed everything. I suddenly knew in my heart that the Lord was walking beside me. I didn't know how or when, but I *knew* there would be an answer.

Going to Vince's bank that day, I dressed in my best, smiled, and held up my head as I had been taught (shades of Scarlett and her dress made out of draperies!). I was trying desperately to keep up appearances, even with my own children, whom I was trying to shield from our dire circumstances.

The longest walk in the world starts with one step. You just keep putting one foot in front of the other. So I got out of my car and walked to Vince's bank.

Houston is a business town, and businessmen make it *their* business to know everybody's business. An astute man, Vince *must* have known of my desperation.

He looked at the plot of the land, paused, then turned to me and said, "Joanne, you are asking more than I usually pay for the land I buy. I don't want to bargain with you." (So many others had offered half of what it was worth.) "I cannot buy your land."

"However," he added, "I am also a banker and I admire you. I will lend you a million dollars [a huge amount of money in 1969] on your name alone...No collateral or interest necessary."

I must have seemed terribly unappreciative because I simply thanked him briefly and left. When Vince said he was not going to buy the land, something in me folded in on itself, and I didn't hear another word. I just knew it was the end. The light around me disappeared, and I felt blackness envelope me.

"Joanne, do you realize what he said?" asked the friend who had accompanied me. I shook my head in despair. He took me by the shoulders and said, "He said he would lend you a million dollars on your name alone."

Realization struck me. I was paralyzed with surprise. It was one of the most amazing moments of my life. I had never had an experience like that. I was saved.

The money had to be repaid, of course, but there was time. The dreaded note that was due immediately could be paid. For at least a year, I could make the payments on my house, keeping it until I could sell it. Most importantly, I could take care of my boys and help my parents.

God had created a miracle, but the money wouldn't last forever. I had to get married. It was all I knew how to do. But the world had changed since my cloistered childhood and early womanhood. Most of the men I met didn't have marriage in mind. Their proposals were for "flings and things," and I wasn't a seasoned player in this market. I had flirted with playboys under the protective cloak of marriage, but now I was out there, fair game...and I didn't know how to play.

The funniest "candidate" was an Arab prince, a slim, attractive sheik whom I had never met before. He flew in from Marbella, Spain, where he lived, and earnestly explained in perfect English why I should marry him. He spent a week pressing his case. Then, rejected, he flew away in his private jet. I later saw pictures of him and his new wife (an Italian movie star) in *People* magazine.

And there was Raymond Marcellin, the French minister of the interior, waiting in the wings. He knew I was married when I met him. Now I was not. But was he suitable for my boys?

Although we didn't know it, for a time I dated the same man as Joan Collins, star of the television series *Dynasty*. Our mutual boyfriend had a house in a posh London neighborhood and the de rigueur château in Provence, France. He was young, good-looking, and hot stuff, he thought.

He suggested that he have a dinner in my honor, but he had invited Joan to the same dinner. Joan plopped herself down by his side and explained to all and sundry that she was there to stay the night — and I do mean *all* night.

I had no intention or desire to change her plans. I ate and ran. In fact, I ran (literally) every time I saw him. What was that idiot thinking by inviting us both to the same dinner?

Louis Dorfman, another big-time playboy, invited me to come for a week of skiing at his home in Aspen, Colorado. I suspected that I might not be the only ski bunny in his hutch, so I brought my children and an Italian princess with me to the mountains. Sure enough, as I deplaned from Houston, I saw him bidding good-bye to actress and Bond girl Jill St. John, who had just spent a warm and cozy week with him in his chalet. Now he was ready for the next adventure... me. But as he saw my entourage, I explained, "I was *sure* you wouldn't mind." I smiled, and you should have seen his face. He was a darling, and he entertained us all like the good sport he was. Louis and I became friends, and I love him to this day.

I had one more Louis Dorfman weekend, which was almost beyond belief. Louis and comedian Buddy Hackett were fast friends ("fast" being the operative word — they scooted around the world with the fastest hot ladies in Christendom on their arms). The only problem was that Buddy loved to drink, carouse, and curse. He could not utter three words without using the foulest language ever invented. Louis wanted me to meet him because Buddy was considered the funniest man in show business at that time.

"Buddy, you cannot do bad things," Louis told him, "no matter how funny you think you are. And you can't drink or curse the whole weekend. Joanne is a real lady, and you must behave like a gentleman."

"Okay," Buddy responded.

So when Louis and I walked into the suite for the weekend, Buddy met us with his head, face, and neck completely covered in shaving cream. "Louis says that I must be lily white around you, so I'm practicing," he said, smiling wickedly through the shaving cream. Louis looked worried.

At that time, there was a trendy psychological counseling movement popular with the glamour crowd that taught that it was healthy for you to sit in groups of people and — no matter what question was asked — to answer with the complete truth. Even if you were asked the worst and most embarrassing question — about your menstrual cycle or any other intimate thing; *nothing* was out of bounds — you had to tell the truth.

Buddy had just arrived from such a clinic outside of San Francisco and suggested that *we* all sit in a circle and re-create his experience. We were up for it.

But Buddy had decided in advance that I was a prude and that he wanted to punish Louis for making such "clean-living" demands of him. So Buddy planned the whole sequence to embarrass me and show me a thing or two. His scenario was diabolical.

As we sat down, Buddy introduced his date, who was very pretty and nice. As we went around the circle introducing ourselves, each of us explained exactly what we did with our lives. There were many interesting explanations, and then we came to Buddy's date.

"And what do you do?" Louis asked.

"I'm a whore. That is my full-time profession."

Buddy had hired the genuine thing just for the occasion. He sat covered in shaving cream, holding his sides with laughter. Louis almost fainted. It didn't bother me at all.

"How interesting," I replied. "Why did you choose that particular profession? I'm sure you had a good reason."

Buddy had warned her that I might insult her, slap him, and leave the room. "Be prepared for anything!" we found out later he had gleefully told her. "She's a real hoity-toity gal. A real turd!"

He was *not* prepared for my interest in her and what she did. He almost cried when we talked companionably. She told me that she could not make much money at anything else, but now she had enough to care for her daughter and to be a real stay-at-home mom, so she only worked nights most of the time. Buddy had paid her handsomely to work this "day job." Her task was to "expose" me to Buddy's best friend and let him know he was wasting his time with me, a heartless woman with a snobbish lifestyle.

Instead, Buddy and I became friends. He saw my heart go out to this sweet mother who was doing the best she could with her life to ensure that her little girl had a better one. We all felt the same way and had a fun-filled evening that none of us would ever forget. And there was no more talk of what anyone did for a living. I think Buddy's date felt accepted for the sweet person she was.

Some playboys of my acquaintance were strictly friends — lifelong ones at that. They weren't part of my quest for a husband but they were wonderful all the same.

Baron Enrico "Ricky" di Portanova was one of the men that I was urged to call before I approached Vince Kickerello. He was the grandson of Hugh Roy Cullen, one of the wealthiest men in the world. When cosmopolitan Ricky came to Houston to receive his part of the fortune, he was a sensation. He ultimately married one of my closet friends, the beautiful, intelligent, and delightful Sandra. Every item in their houses — a palace in Acapulco, the royal suite at Claridge's in London, and a home in Monte Carlo — was a museum piece. They had their own jet and more staff than most hotels. Ricky told me that before he met Sandra, he had wanted to marry me but was afraid of taking on two young boys.

Before Ricky met his wife and came into his fortune, he and my other dear playboy friend, British expat Charles Fawcett, were the two most popular bachelors in Rome. Charles was to play a critical role in my Afghan adventures. He was one of those bigger-than-life characters who pass through history from time to time. He had distinguished himself in the French Foreign Legion and the Royal Air Force during World War II, then had gone on to become a screen star and global adventurer. His unselfish, constant support fueled our friendship for thirty years. Without him, I never would have gone to Afghanistan. I would also never have produced and narrated the TV documentary *A Thirst for Glory, a Taste of Freedom*, about the American Revolution. Every revolution must have arms and money supplied by an ally to succeed. True in Afghanistan today.

Ricky and Charles would stroll down the Via Veneto, Rome's main street, home to the dolce vita (sweet life) and lined with outdoor cafés and blossoming umbrellas that resembled flowers. The pace was leisurely, the atmosphere festive. Soon the two would be surrounded by admiring women, random waiters, film stars, and adventurers — and even romantic, swashbuckler actor Errol Flynn when he was there shooting the film *The Sun Also Rises*.

I'm sure that if I had gone to bed with Charles or Ricky or any of the others who were to play defining roles in my life, I would never have enjoyed their long-term friendships. They would have left me, never giving me another thought, just as they did the other women who tumbled into their beds. I was convinced of that much, even with the changes in the world of dating. Still, it was an uncertain time in my life, especially when unanticipated situations arose.

Bill Powers, of my high school days, came back into my life, suggesting that we try again. It seemed unlikely to me after so many years that there could be anything meaningful between people who had not seen each other in such a long time. I did not think it could work.

When I told him so, he asked, "What are you going to do with your life?"

I said, "I have given it to God."

He looked at me disdainfully and said, "Joanne, do you mean to tell me that if the Lord told you to go to Bangladesh as a missionary, you would go?"

I was dumbfounded. I could not answer that question because I had never even considered being a missionary, and certainly not one in Bangladesh (previously part of Pakistan). (I have always wondered if that question was a predictor of things to come since I was to go to Pakistan and Afghanistan and work among the very poor in their villages.) But at that moment, I understood what Bill meant: *Do you mean that you could literally do it?*

I knew what I should answer, but I was horrified by what that would mean. Could I actually be a missionary in Bangladesh? You cannot lie to the Lord.

I went home and thought about it. I thought deeply. I really faced what it would mean to be a very poor missionary in a ravaged country. I actually pictured in my mind living barefoot on the banks of a muddy stream. I knew that I was promising God, and if I promised, I had to go.

Suddenly I felt a lightness of the spirit, a surety that I could do it and that I would be happy to do it because it would be His will if it were to happen. He had never failed me. I always found happiness when I walked with Him.

"All right, Lord," I said. "If You want me to go to Bangladesh and live like that, I can do it. I know I will be happy because it's Your will. I accept it. Yes, I can go to Bangladesh." Acknowledging that I really could go was simply a way of saying, "Not my will but Yours be done."

That decision changed everything. Now every time I face any

problem, I ask myself, "Could I go to Bangladesh?" meaning, "Do I really give this problem to the Lord?"

God smiled. He simply wanted my total acceptance of His will. When I did that, He gave it all back. Instead of the slums of Bangladesh, the Lord gave me one of the richest men in Houston — and all the joy my heart could hold.

HERRING

HAVE TONGUE, WILL TATTLE: The hottest buzz among the Smart Set is that Ch. 2's **Joanne King** and Houston Natural Gas Corp. prexy **Robert Herring** are planning a waltz to the altar next month. They've been telling close friends for the past couple weeks . . . Maestro **Henry King** has suffered

FRIDAY FLASHES: Ch. 2's **Joanne King** and fiance **Robert Herring**, the Houston Natural Gas bigwig, are telling pals they'll fly to N.Y. to be married next Friday. **Dr. Denton Cooley** and wife **Louise** will fly up with them and be their attendants at the ceremony. FYI: Joanne will be back in town in time to be on the tube Monday. She says she intends to continue her noon show for some time . . . **Warner Roberts** and **Jonni**

BIG CITY BEAT by Maxine

THE SUNDAY SNOOPER: Houston Natural Gas prexy **Bob Herring** and wife **Joanne** are home from Paris with the word they'll have some very interesting visitors from "over there" come November. They're **Count and Countess Patrice de Vogues**, who live in the famed chateau, Vaux de Visconte, after which Versaille was patterned. FYI: The Count wants to visit a real Texas ranch while here—not only that, he actually wants to work cattle for a week. Meanwhile, the Herrings still haven't decided where they want to settle permanently. They'd like to sell his mansion on Inwood and hers on Rivercrest and start all over . . . Talk

build a townhouse there . . . Houston Natural Gas prexy **Robert Herring** and bride **Joanne** got back from a week in Saudi Arabia in time to toss a poolside party Sunday for **Cristobal de Villa Verde**, who is here on a visit from sunny Spain. FYI: Joanne and her children have moved to Bob's River Oaks mansion, but the Herrings are still househunting for a larger one

MEMOS FROM MAX: Nancy and Jimmy Brennan's guests at their big aniversary party last week were unaware that Nancy was in a lot of pain from a scorpion bite on her foot. She's better now . . . Incidentally, Houston Natural Gas bossman **Robert Herring** and wife **Joanne** missed the party because they're honeymooning in Paris. They've traveled extensively since their recent marriage, but until now it had only been on Bob's business trips . . . Tidelands bossman **Dick Maegle** happily reports that the Tides and Tides II were

at College Inn. . . . **Count Alain de Taillach**, who has homes in Paris and Beirut, wound up his Houston biz visit and headed to N.Y. before joining his family in Paris for Christmas. He was royally entertained by the local gentry, including the **George DeMontronds**, the **Oscar Wyatts** and TV doll **Joanne King**. . . . Biz exec **Leonard Rauch** was busy getting congrats from his pals at Wednesday night's basketball game, because he was just appointed to the Board of Regents of UH. . . .

CHAPTER 15

Bob Herring: A Great Man Is Hard to Find

I don't remember meeting Bob Herring. I knew about him, just as everyone in Houston knew about him and admired him. My first memory of him is at a dinner party where he was my dinner companion. I remember coming home and thinking how clever I had been in my conversation. When I knew Bob better, I understood that he had a talent for making everybody feel clever.

I decided I needed to know him better, but I wasn't sure how to get closer to him. He was a widower who had absolutely closed his door on the world, determined to simply raise his children and to continue his successful career. Though he had started with nothing but his abilities, Bob was at the top of the ladder. He was president of the country club, chairman of the chamber of commerce, and so on — there was no honor that he had not had. He became the chairman of the board at Rice University even though he was a graduate of Texas A&M and Georgetown University.

Bob came from a modest, middle-class family. A successful family before the South was wiped out, the Herrings very much valued their family's history.

During World War II, when he was only twenty-three, Bob flew B-17s and was shot down four times. He was the youngest colonel in the Pacific War at the time of his promotion and served on General Douglas MacArthur's staff as chief intelligence officer for the war in the Pacific, an incredible feat for someone so young. Among his contributions, he helped develop the low-level bombing that hastened the end of the war.

MacArthur was scheduled to accept the surrender of the Japanese Army in Korea himself, but due to a storm, communication between MacArthur and U.S. troops in Korea was interrupted. Bob, who headed the advance team, did not know that the general and his entire staff had returned to base.

An entire army, tens of thousands of men standing at attention, swords carefully laid on the ground, awaited the general. Bob sat in his plane anticipating MacArthur's arrival too. After waiting all day with the Japanese army standing at attention in the hot sun, and unable to call headquarters about the situation, Bob decided to accept the surrender in General MacArthur's place. The paper the next morning said that a young colonel on MacArthur's staff had accepted the surrender of an entire country. MacArthur was not pleased.

Bob remembered spending the night at a local hotel. The next morning the hall was covered with gifts from grateful Koreans. He did not know how to return them because there were no cards. Two huge Satsuma gold vases from the imperial palace were among them. They depicted scenes from the proud Korean history with gold filigree surrounding each scene. The vases were so impressive, he could not leave them behind. He carried them home on his airplane and eventually gave them to me as a very special present. I still have them.

Bob had many medals and was twice recommended for the Medal of Honor. This was a soldier!

His climb in the business world was slow, however. He had no money and no position, yet he wanted to "play in the oil patch," as we say in Houston. It takes a big corporation, a consortium of businessmen, or a very innovative person to gain entry. Bob was innovative but he had no connections. By the time he entered the game, the big players were no longer roughnecks. They were generations into this very difficult field. Although they were referred to as "good old boys," they were far from that. They were educated and distinguished men. Everywhere Bob went, he met a closed door.

Business magnate Ray Fish had made millions, and Bob wanted desperately to join his organization. After sitting in Fish's office for what seemed like years, he was actually able to meet the man. Fish was impressed and sent him to Calgary, Canada. In Calgary Bob was his enormously successful and innovative self. This so impressed Fish that he made Bob president of a small company called Valley Oil.

Bob's success attracted the attention of the officers of Houston Natural Gas, the city's utility company, who offered him the presidency. Bob told them he would not accept their offer unless they bought his company. This was always Bob's way of doing business. If he made one company a success, and another company wanted to have him — which many did, including Conoco, Transco, and other big boys — he always insisted that the purchasing company buy his company along with him. Through his brilliance, his company stock was often worth more than the giant that wanted to acquire him. He transformed an aging utility and pushed it into the top echelon of the oil world.

This company was renamed Enron after he died. Alas, Bob died of lung cancer in 1981 at the age of sixty. The company that he built was later leveraged into extinction by people who came after him. Enron became a huge tragedy. Had Bob still been in charge, it would never have happened. During his scandal-free leadership, he would *never* have gambled with stockholders' money and people's pensions. He valued his stockholders and coworkers and talked about his responsibility to them constantly.

The company he built ended in disgrace and bankruptcy and tragedy for many. After filing for bankruptcy in 2001, Enron sold its last company in 2006. It also established a pattern that other businesses emulated, which led to their crashes in the late 1990s and early 2000s. Bob would have abhorred these practices and choices. He made credibility his winning strategy.

How did I get him? I really *had* to marry an important man. People expected it. There were very few like Bob running around loose. He was everything I admired in a man, and I felt extremely attracted to him. I also knew he was not unaware of me.

A mutual friend invited us both to a Christmas party. I called Bob's office and asked if he would like to go with me. He said he would. That was a very special evening. I wore the most alluring dress I could find in my closet. It was very high-necked and long-sleeved, but it was jersey and left little to the imagination. The night was a success. But Bob did not call me.

Of course, there was still my beau in France, Raymond Marcellin, the French minister of the interior. At that moment it was likely he would become prime minister under General Charles de Gaulle. It was a dazzling prospect. There were others, as well. But the bells had rung in Texas. I could not forget Bob Herring.

The glitter that would surround me in France was not as enticing as it had been prior to Bob. He was actually so much more appropriate for me. We had the same friends. We lived in the same city. I would not have to move my boys to a totally strange country with a man who had never had children. Bob had three, mostly grown, all outstanding, and all very nice.

I had a previously scheduled trip to France, but I called Bob's office and asked if he would like to accompany me to an awards ceremony after I returned, one at which both of us were on the program. He said he would, but I forgot the date and stayed in France, missing this opportunity. When I returned home, I called Bob and asked, "When is the awards benefit?"

"Last night," he said. He did not call back.

I later found out that he was dying of casserole poisoning. Every unmarried woman in Houston was bringing casseroles to his door. He finally stopped answering the door. He was a target, and he knew it. When I called, he never refused to take my call, but he never called me back. I always had to initiate the dates.

One night *he* finally asked *me* to act as his hostess for a party he was giving for the top business leaders of Houston. He was, at last, inviting me. But my competition was like a tsunami. His secretary had her eyes on him too. It got to the point where she would not pass my calls through to him. Not to be deterred, I pretended to be the English wife of the president of Shell Oil. Speaking with a very distinctive British accent, I called and said, "I am Mrs. Harry Bridges. I would like to speak to Mr. Herring, please." She fell for it, and the rest is history.

We had only five dates, but they were spread over three anxious months. When he finally proposed, what he actually said was, "Shall we live in my house or yours?" I remember thinking, "I hope he intends to marry me." He hadn't said a word about getting married; he'd just asked about our living arrangements. I should have known that Bob would never make such a remark unless he was serious.

That evening, I called my mother and said, "I *think* he proposed!"

"Thank God!" she said. And I did.

I think one of the reasons there was so much time in between our five dates was because he had to think very hard about it. He may have wanted me, but, being Bob, he must have carefully considered assuming my mountain of debt. He must have seriously thought about taking on two boys, then ages seventeen and ten, who would need everything, including college educations (though they both ended up paying for their own). He already had three children and a very busy and rewarding life. No matter how attracted he was to me, it was a lot for a man to consider. So many men had considered two kids too much, but Bob said yes to all of it.

The marriage was a gift from the Lord. Bob was the kindest, most unselfish, caring person I had ever met. He never waited for anyone to ask for assistance. He saw anguish and found a way to help, asking nothing but the joy he must have felt in doing it.

He paid all my debt off in full. He paid the enormous notes that I had dreaded so much and prayed so hard to be able to meet, making it possible for us to keep our land until it was sold to Shell Oil, leaving us all rich. He paid the taxes on other land I had had for years, so that one day this too would save me when I needed money. He paid the Vince Kickerillo note and joined me when I went to Vince's office to thank him for his amazing generosity. Vince told Bob, "I never worried a minute about that note. I knew she would pay me. But I'm happy she found someone to take care of her."

And Bob did take care of me. Without saying a word, he sent Bob King a loan of a million dollars, which removed any regrets or sadness I had about Bob King. Herring's trust was well founded. Bob King paid back every cent and rose from the ashes to become prosperous again. He worked hard to do it and deserved every penny, but he needed that loan to succeed. Bob Herring told me he did it because he saw that it made me desperately unhappy to see Bob King suffer.

"I never want you to be unhappy again," Bob Herring declared to me.

My former husband went on to have a new wife and two beautiful children. His happiness saved mine.

Bob Herring loved the "roar of the crowd" as I did. He was so confident in who and what he was. He never thought of me as a competitor but as a complement to anything he did, and I was delighted to be his copilot. I had tried flying alone and could manage, but I didn't like it. I love working with others. Who cares who gets the credit? It's the job that counts.

A man I worked with in television once said, "Joanne, you like the race. You do not care about the cup." That is true. I love the race and I like very much to win. But after the race, I like very much to find a new one to run.

In Bob I found the soul mate who understood me. He wanted to play on the big stage of world affairs. He was a genius and I enjoyed supporting him. He never made a business decision without discussing it with me. That was crucial for my development. It taught me about corporations. This was to be an essential tool in the toolbox of my future.

Bob had built his dream house. It was huge, with twenty-foot ceilings and beautiful walnut paneling in almost every downstairs room. It was very grand but not very me. When Bob asked me to marry him, he gave me a choice. "I will buy you any house in Houston, or we can live in yours," he said. "In fact, you can have anything you want in the entire world. The sky is the limit. You name it, I'll get it." He meant it. And, indeed, I am humbled by the sky he opened for me and how he let me fly. Bob Herring never said no to me in anything, and we never had a cross word.

I looked at all the homes available and decided that his house was the best choice at the time. It was close to his office. There was not much available in the "big house" market because in the early 1970s

Houston was booming, and building at that time would leave us too long in limbo.

A woman should never move into a house another woman has shared with her children. The Herring children welcomed me, but the minute I made any changes in their house, it upset them. It was also a difficult move for my boys because they had lived surrounded by twelve acres in a house they loved and thought was equally beautiful. Now they lived in a grand house that had everything, but very little property around it.

Moving in and sharing rooms when none of them had ever shared before was hard for everyone. We built an addition, but it took a year to finish. I was so relieved and happy to have our problems solved by my marriage that I did not realize how hard this was for my sons — and for Bob's children too. My children were made to feel like intruders in the Herring house. This was unconscious on the part of Bob's children, but it happened just the same.

Eventually, with my son Robin and my dad, we also took on the enormous task of buying, moving, renovating, and rescuing the Johnson family country house, which resembled Mount Vernon. It was on land so valuable it was sold by the square foot.

No one thought it could be moved; the general consensus was that it would need to be demolished. A movie producer saw it, though, and felt it should be saved. He thought it would make a fine chicken-fried steak restaurant. *My country home,* a chicken-fried steak restaurant! Over my crispy bottom.

When I looked at the house, I saw it as a beautiful woman with a black eye and her teeth knocked out. I couldn't stand it. I wanted it.

We decided to move it. Every electric line, every telephone line, and every computer had to be turned off as the house passed by. Eighteen police cars were required to block the highway as this three-story monolith rumbled by at three a.m. Saving the family home was just one of the many ways that Bob indulged me.

One of the most meaningful things that Beau ever said to me was this: "Mother, I know you feel bad about not staying married to Dad. I'm sad about that too. But, you know, I would have hated to miss knowing Bob Herring." I know he said that just to make me feel better (he does that often), but it worked.

On the other hand, Robin, who was very young and the target for most of the dissension, and often meanness, in the house, said to me, "I am so lonely for my house in the woods." Robin was devastated by it all, and it showed.

"Well, darling," I said, "please try to count your blessings."

"Mommy, *you* are my blessing," he told me. He had a remarkable sensitivity and sense of caring for someone so young. He was trying to help too, yet it was hard for us all.

I was very protective of my children. Bob Herring once said, "You are three against the world, and there is a wall around you that I cannot penetrate." He was right. I'm not sure that my children recognized it at the time, but I did have a wall around them. I would kill to protect them.

The boys and I never truly repaid Bob Herring for what he did for us. (At that time, of course, we had nothing to pay with.) His generosity fueled our futures. He did everything he could to ensure that the boys and I were safe. (Alas, he couldn't have predicted Houston's economic crash in the late 1980s and early 1990s, which left us in dire straits again.)

Can you imagine how this debt to him affected me? I, who felt the necessity to return money, kindness, or a debt of any kind? This weighed on me so heavily that I felt like Atlas carrying the world on my shoulders. How could I ever repay this man? What could I ever possibly do? I had taken a great deal from Bob Herring and I felt an urgency to repay him.

I decided to give him my life. It was all I had to give. I never told him; I simply decided to show him. Anything important to him took precedence over everything else. What he wanted, I would give. What he needed, I would do.

Bob traveled a great deal and wanted me to travel with him. I felt terribly guilty that I had to leave my children so often. Every time I left them it hurt me, so, I'm ashamed to say, sometimes I would leave without even saying good-bye (which was *terrible*). That was not the way to manage this difficult situation, and oftentimes, by the time I got on the plane, I'd be depressed. Though Beau and Robin were too young to understand that Bob had saved us from the direst of circumstances, I felt that he had done so much for all of us that I had to put him first.

As I lived with Bob Herring, I began to see the depth and breadth and heights of what a human being could be. When I think of him now, I feel so humbled to have had the privilege of even knowing him. That he should actually love me and share his magical life with me was a gift of gigantic proportions.

God does indeed listen.

Bob said he did not like the French or Paris, but we went to Paris on a fairy-tale honeymoon in 1973. When we arrived, our suite was filled with flowers from dukes, counts, and countless others of my acquaintance in Paris. Invitations were everywhere. Bob was overwhelmed. Fourteen black-tie dinners and fourteen very special luncheons were given for us in French homes. Who says the French never invite you into their homes? They do if they like you.

The French are a difficult tribe. Americans speak to everybody using first names, but unless they know you very well, the French would never intrude on your acquaintance, assuming that you might not want familiarity. We Americans think everyone is our friend, even if we never see them outside the office. To the French, a friend

The Quaid-i-azam award—the highest honor Pakistan gives to a civilian. It means "great leader." I never dreamed of being decorated for my services. Much less having two important ambassadors give me parties to celebrate! This moment was special to me because of the friends who cared and came. In this photo are four of the top figures of my life and the time (l–r): Ann Duncan, wife of Energy Secretary Charles Duncan; Alan Shepard in the back, the first American in space; Robin King, who made the Afghan documentary that got Washington interested, and Henry Kissinger. (Joanne Herring Personal Collection.)

Julia Roberts played me in *Charlie Wilson's War*, and for the Los Angeles premiere, I borrowed an emerald necklace. I was humbled by Julia Roberts's unassuming star power and blinded by the flashbulbs. (Robin King)

At the Los Angeles premiere of *Charlie Wilson's War*, December 10, 2007. I loved my borrowed "jools." Mmmm—green, the color of money. (David Gabber/ PR Photos)

My grandmother Ruth McGill holding my mother, Maelan McGill.

My father, William Dunlap Johnson, captain of the football team at Texas A&M University, was the first All-American from the Southwest Conference. The hero of my life.

The three-year-old future ambassador to Pakistan. From little girl to honorary man?

The River Oaks Elementary School class of 1938. I'm the ugly duckling in the first row, fifth from the left. I was the tallest, skinniest child in the class, male or female. (Houston Metropolitan Research Center, Houston Public Library)

In high school, things got better. The ugly duckling began to change.

Bridal portrait from my first marriage, to Bob King, in front of the fireplace of the family home. (GH Gittings Archive)

In my natural habitat—in front of the mahogany wood bar in our Rivercrest home. This photo, part of a photo shoot from the *Houston Chronicle*, won an international photography contest. (Jim Johnson)

"Pardon me, Princess! I'm the 'King' around here," Coke, our lab, seems to be saying as I mount the stairs of our Rivercrest home with Princess Grace and Prince Rainier. (Jim Cox)

That Was The Party That Was

A ROMAN ORGY CIRCA 1959

by Bill Roberts

Fifteen caesars ran around the marble halls, togas flying, chasing vestal virgins, drinking love potion and dancing a ballet of love.

Vestal virgins?

The virgins dreamily eyed the lusty caesars and applauded their feats of derring-do. Later, one virgin swooned as the caesars carried her outdoors to be burned at the stake. She had hoped for a fate worse than death.

It was the last Age of Innocence in America and one of the best private parties of the century. At least below the Mason-Dixon Line. It was the grandest private party ever held in Houston. It was a Farewell to the Fifties and none other than Joanne King Herring Davis (minus the Herring and Davis) reigned supreme.

Joanne knows how to throw a party. This most adored of Houston hostesses gives parties in London, Paris, Madrid, Washington and Houston attended by enough royalty to make anyone without a title seem an absolute misfit. Many real kings

(including the crowned heads of Sweden, Jordan, Morocco, and the Shah of Iran), five princes and princesses, twenty-four ambassadors, and God knows how many prime ministers and other heads of state—Sadat!—have come when Joanne has said, "Let's party!" Once, she entertained Princess Grace and Prince Rainier at her home.

She is the honorary consul general of Pakistan and Morocco, the first and only woman ever chosen by the King of Morocco to be his ambassador. She is one of the great beauties of the Western world. She is very, very rich. She does things. Properly.

This gorgeous woman was queen of Houston television during the sixties and early seventies. She has done a few TV specials since those days, one a year or so ago on General Maurice Hirsch, a "Texas Hero." She chairs a gala ball or two each year.

But her most famous role will always be as hostess of the legendary 1959 Roman Bacchanal at her marble mansion on Rivercrest Drive in Houston. Some called it a Roman Orgy.

Deep in "debauchery" at the orgy. From the Roman holiday party I gave in 1959, before I started giving parties with a purpose. Covered in *Life* magazine, Bob King and I are dining on a roman couch.

"The King who was queen." That's what the press called me when I started my TV career. This is my publicity photo for Channel 11.

The icon, Barbara Walters, and me. She was, and is, wonderful.

I'm dressed as Marie Antoinette, making my own French connection.

Mardi Gras photo of me on the set of the movie *The Thief Who Came to Dinner*, filmed in Houston. They cut my scene, but I still get $1.68 every time it plays!

Houston Chronicle photo of Majia, my horse, and me in the Rain in Spain outfit I wore at the Feria of Seville with Princess Grace and Jackie O. (Roger Powers)

Dancing into the future, as I began the Bob Herring years. Here I'm in front of the stairway of our River Oaks home, looking over my shoulder, but never looking back. (Peter Moody Meyer)

The King (Bob Herring) and I with King Hussein of Jordan. He had an entourage of fifty men so I invited fifty beautiful women, who came from all over the world. My invitations to Jordan were fervent.

His Majesty Hassan II of Morocco, wearing the white hat.

Prince Saud, the foreign minister of Saudi Arabia, is one of the handsomest and most brilliant men I have ever met. (Copyright 1976/ Jimolivephotography.com)

General Zia, president of Pakistan, was one of the greatest minds and kindest hearts I ever encountered. He was a great friend of the United States and a champion of free enterprise for his people.

Somewhere, among the mujahideen. My eight-foot-tall bodyguard complete with captured Kalashnikov. (Robin King)

Joanne Herring
With our very best wishes,

Ronald Reagan
Nancy Reagan

At the White House with the Reagans. It was the first night they introduced the controversial new china. I felt the controversy was ridiculous because their friends paid for it.

With my parents and my sons, Beau and Robin, the night Bob and I were named Cultural Leaders of the Year. Sadly, Bob was too ill to attend. It was an empty evening without him. I used the opportunity to speak on free enterprise, to the delight of the audience, who felt the talk was well-timed and needed as the Soviets were moving. (Betty Jukes)

Queen of Denmark

Ambassador John Loeb

My broken leg, broken heart, and broken dreams begin to mend at a party in Denmark with Ambassador John Loeb and Her Majesty, the Queen of Denmark. (Ambassador John Loeb)

Laughing again with Charlie Wilson (l) and Senator John Tower (r) at the Paris Air Show. (John W. Craddock Jr.)

Nancy Reagan checks my dress (because it resembles hers). Ronald Reagan shakes hands with Charlie Wilson.

My favorite president, George H.W. Bush.

To/ Joanne — Greetings from Air Force II
1983   G Bush

On Air Force Two with Vice President George H.W. Bush.

With President George H.W. Bush, President George W. Bush, and Governor
Jeb Bush at the Bush Ranch in Crawford, Texas. (Joanne Amos / Reflections
Photography / Washington, D.C.)

Front row, third from the right, among these amazing women—Barbara
Walters; Liz Smith; Beverly Sills; Nancy Kissinger; Carolina Herrera; Marva
Collins; Ann Fowler Arledge; Comtesse Michel d'Ornano, mayor of Deauville;
Duchess of Bedford; Hillie Merritt Mahoney; Me; Helen Boehm; and Shirley
Lord Rosenthal. (Birmingham Southern College)

Prince Bandar, Saudi Ambassador to U.S.

H.R.H. Prince Bandar of Saudi Arabia was the star of a banquet given for me by the marine commandant and Mrs. P.X. Kelly. I gave my best Washington party for the prince and his wife, Princess Haifa. Please read the articles about the party in chapter 22. You'll laugh, I promise.

In the arms of my last husband, Lloyd Davis, on our around-the-world honeymoon—in a yurt in Mongolia, with all the yak butter we could eat.

Calendar photo of me and a couple of salukis from the movie *Charlie Wilson's War*, in which two greyhounds escort Julia Roberts and Tom Hanks (playing me and Charlie Wilson) upstairs. (Brett Chisholm)

Walking into the surprise dinner dance my "brother" Larry Brookshire gave for me to celebrate the Texas premiere of the movie *Charlie Wilson's War*. (Jillhunterphotography.com)

Saying good-bye at Charlie's grave in Arlington National Cemetery, February 23, 2010. My final farewell. Everyone from the whole of *Charlie Wilson's War* stayed back with us and waited patiently. When the Wilson family left the gravesite, all of us stood on the pathway reminiscing as, one by one, each major player went up to Charlie's casket to say good-bye alone. I was touched by everyone's love on that cold, gray day. (Paul Erikson)

HRH Prince Jean de France at Houston luncheon where the money was raised to fund the model village. Penny Lloyd, HRH, Joanne Herring, Susan Krohn, and Margaret Alkek Williams. Houston raised the money! (Michelle Watson/CatchLight Group)

Beau King as a young adult on the ski slopes. My daredevil son! (Stanisse King)

Portrait of my precious family—Beau, Stanisse, and my grandsons, Beau and Beckett. (Stanisse King)

Robin with the mujahideen in Afghanistan, making the film that engaged Charlie Wilson in the Afghan war. (Joanne King Herring)

Charlie Fawcett and my son Robin King at the movie premiere of *Courage Is Our Weapon*. It was that film by my son Robin that opened wide the eyes of the world to the reality of the Soviet atrocities in Afghanistan.

Robin King, who made the film that changed the world, in front of the family home—the Mount Vernon replica that he purchased from the family trust when he was twenty-nine years old. (Betty Tichich)

is someone you see often, someone with whom you share your life. We Americans pick up people like cornflakes and toss them when they grow stale. Once the Frenchman gives his friendship, he gives it forever.

Bob decided he liked Paris very much — and Paris liked him! My friends lost their hearts to this elegant, lovely man, as I already had.

The Mating Dance

Another Texan at the Golden Door was **Joanne Herring** of Houston, who hobbled around on crutches most of the time but, in spite of a bad leg, still managed to do water exercises in the pool, arrive at lunch in black leotards and generally look like a Southern belle the rest of the time with flowers in her hair and — was that a ribbon around her neck?

Joanne Herring

Eugenia Sheppard Around the Town

Lee Thaw mixes guests the way a good chef mixes a salad. Last night at her dinner for the Duke and **Duchess d'Uzes** and **Mr.** and **Mrs. Robert Herring** (who flew in from Texas for the evening) she put together such international favorites as **Carolina** and **Reinaldo Herrera** from Venezula, the **Marquis Raymundo de Larrain, Mrs. Pierre Schlumberger** and her traveling companion Egyptian **Prince Nageeb,** Argentinian **Ambassador** and **Mrs. Carlos Ortiz de Rosas** with such New Yorkers as **Mary Lasker, Jeanne Murray Vanderbilt, Estee** and **Joe Lauder, Dr.** and **Mrs. William Cahn, Serge Obolensky** and **Tatiana** and **Alex Liberman.**

The Duchess d'Uzes was wearing one of Balmain's barer black numbers. **Joanne Herring,** in blond lace from Cardin, is in the process of producing a film that will be shot in some of the great homes of France, to reflect the French interest and enthusiasm for America at the time of the American Revolution. Sponsored by Exxon, it will be shown some time during the Bicentennial year.

Between visits to France and stops in New York, the Herrings will stay at home in Houston long enough to host a big dinner May 20 that will draw guests from all over the country.

*　　*　　*

of the Whooping Crane

84 or No, Rose Kennedy Cuts A Mean Dance Beat

FOR SHEER glamor the party the night before Barbra Streisand's TV special almost equalled the show at the Kennedy Center.

Rose Kennedy, small and frail in a rosy red dress that blended with the rosy pink tables and gorgeous pink, red and white flower centerpieces, danced with son Teddy to Howard Devron's hot beat, causing others to comment: "I hope I can still dance when I'm 84." "I'll settle for breathing," reported Treasury Secretary Bill Simon.

Simon, who was deep in conversation with Barbara Walters when not dancing, turned round to gaze at voluptuous Joanne King Herring doing a terrific wiggle in her low-cut, skin-tight gown. "Your bifocals are steaming up, Bill," cracked a friend at his table.

Betty Beale's Washington

Benefit Premiere

WASHINGTON, D.C. — For sheer glamor the party the night before Barbra Streisand's TV special last Sunday almost equalled the show at the Kennedy Center. President Ford wasn't at Iranian Ambassador Zahedi's wingding for 240 and Streisand, who was there, didn't sing, but it was a glittering smash notwithstanding.

Bill Simon, who was deep in conversation with Barbara Walters when not dancing, turned around to gaze at voluptuous Joanne King Herring doing a terrific wiggle in her low-cut, skin-tight gown. "Your bifocals are steaming up, Bill," cracked a friend at his table.

BILL SIMON
QOU+O

153

The Washington Star

Founded in 1852

MURRAY J. GART, *Editor*

SIDNEY EPSTEIN, *Executive Editor* WILLIAM F. McILWAIN, *Deputy Editor* EDWIN M. YODER JR., *Editorial Page Editor*

SUNDAY, NOVEMBER 18, 1979

Joanne Herring's gracious gesture

I read with great interest Joy Billington's Nov. 11 article on Joanne Herring ("Is she a Texas cliche or royalty with impeccable connections?"). There always seems to be a tendency for Washington newspapers to look on Joanne Herring from a strictly political or social point of view. In doing so, I think there is the danger of overlooking the fact that she is a very considerate, humane human being.

This spring, when I was in Houston, I attended a party given by Mrs. Herring for the West Point Glee Club. Since she is a hostess who thinks of every comfort for her guests, she had invited a bevy of young ladies to fill the void, so to speak, of young men without young women at a gathering which could have had all the overtones of a stag party. But the young ladies were there and the West Pointers were obviously delighted with the thoughtfulness of their hostess.

But, alas, even though Mrs. Herring had thought of everything, she suddenly was confronted with something she had not had an inkling could ever take place. Out of the mass of white faces appeared that of one lone black man, a member of the West Point Glee Club.

Everything stopped in its tracks.

Houston has come a long way racewise, but a lone black face in the middle of a sea of white faces, some of them belonging to young women, caused heads to turn.

Mrs. Herring realized in a flash what the black Glee Club member must have been feeling, and realizing that there were no young black

JOANNE HERRING

ladies in the crowd, she stepped forward, greeted the cadet and without so much as a pause she asked him to dance.

What she did was natural, gracious and so thoughtful that many who might have criticized her did not even glance in their direction.

While it is certainly possible that Mrs. Herring may produce expensive parties for the Arabs and Pakistanis, it is also possible that basically she deplores humiliation, either political or social, even when she has nothing to gain but the rewards of the gesture itself.

Richard Lebherz
Frederick, Md.

King Hussein of Jordan

Would-be hosts scrap for honor

Rumor has it that they're all out there tossing and scratching like the gingham dog and the calico cat to have the honor of hosting King Hussein of Jordan when he comes to Houston.

The U.S. State Department, the Jordanian government, the honorary Jordanian consul in Houston all wish to sponsor events when the Arab ruler and his entourage are here for five days on a "semi-business" basis.

The afternoon of May 1, the king is planning to attend a barbecue at the Douglas B. Marshalls' Gleannloch Farms ranch.

May 2, he will attend a very small private party at the Robert Herrings, the only such event the shy, retiring king will permit.

Then he is scheduled to check into the hospital for a medical check-up.
— JUDY LUNN

WOMEN'S WEAR DAILY. THURSDAY. DECEMBER 9, 1982

THE SAGE CONTINUES: First, there was the big Metropolitan Museum party in New York Monday night where **Nan Kempner** and **Nancy Kissinger** showed up in the same black and white **Yves Saint Laurent** dress. The next night, YSL struck again — this time at the White House. **Joanne Herring** and **Annette Reed** walked into the state dinner for Pakistan president **Mohammed Zia ul-Hag** wearing the same slinky black velvet Saint Laurent — except for one thing: "Hers is cut much lower," said Reed. **Nancy Reagan,** also in black velvet, didn't know who designed her dress. "It's either **Bill Blass** or **Adolfo.** I can't check the label now." It was a Blass.

The senator was attending a dinner party for Henry Kissinger at La Cirque in the Big Apple. Does that mean that Javits is going to give Kissinger his blessing in seeking his Senate seat? Or was Jack just keeping a nervous eye on his biggest threat? Maybe neither. But it is known that Henry has asked a senator or two about the life of an elected official.

It was the Bob Herrings' dinner at the super swish New York restaurant and it was a delayeed party for Kissinger's book. The list numbered 50 and what a list it was.

The Isaac Sterns were there, and Happy Rockefeller, John J. McCloy, maestro Zubin Mehta, and his wife, the Lane Kirklands, Marietta Tree, Pauline Trigere, the Oscar de la Rentas, the Bob Wagners, the Peter Duchins, Bess Myerson, Alan Greenspan, Dick and Cynthia Helms, the Irving Kristols, the Herb Schlossers, Irene Selznick, Earl Blackwell and Eugenia Sheppard, Lee Thaw, Kitty Carlisle, Shirley Lord Anderson and David, Jeremy Wren, Baron and Baroness Ricky di Portonova from Houston, and from Washington the Tom Clagetts, Sen. Larry Pressler, and Texas Rep. Charlie Wilson.

There were some serious remarks by Henry about the perilous situation in the Middle East, then a private super concert took place. Mehta conducted, Stern played the violin backed up by the strolling violinists, who provided dinner music, and Duchin played the piano. When it was over, Houston hostess Joanne Herring knew she'd given a smash.

Joanne Herring's list of honors

CHRONICLE COLUMNIST Betty Beale wrote: "There is one person who could become the No. 1 hostess in Washington, but Joanne Herring is not interested."

Husband Robert Herring said of his business interests: "We were not getting the representation in Washington that I wanted from our lobbying organizations. Joanne turned all that around with her first dinner party. She gets people to talk, to relax, to enjoy themselves. One of the statesmen turned to me after he met her and said 'Bob, what do you mean, bringing a secret weapon like Joanne to Washington!'"

Her party formula — the same whether it's a private dinner or a large public fund-raiser — has become famous since the early days of her Roman Evening, complete with fireworks in the Piney Point forest, or the first major civic venture, the Consular Ball.

"Get everybody involved," says Joanne. "Give them a job, a chance to show their talents." For example, she assigned a host couple to each country at the Consular Ball, set a limit on the number of tables so it would be hard to get an invitation, and then introduced everyone with fanfare in a gala Grand March, complete with flying flags.

Showmanship has been her forte, since early days in drama and music studies at UT, and her parties often feature a celebrity guest from one field or another. And, since guests are asked to move from table to table during dinner, all the guests get to chat with each other. In case they don't know what to say, Joanne usually provides table arrangements or whimsical place cards that offer conversation starters, such as a short horoscope of the guest.

Toasts are usually given during dinner, an opportunity for Joanne and Bob to mention guests' accomplishments. But basically, it's a warm, outgoing personality that makes all this so successful. Her list of honors:

•First woman in 50 years to be honorary chairman of TB Association Drive
•Board Member, Museum of Fine Arts
•Board member, Houston Ballet Foundation
•Board of Regents, Meridian House, Washington, D.C.
•Board member, Theatre Under the Stars Guild
•Board of Regents, Texas Southern University
•Board member, Charles A. Lindbergh Memorial Fund
•Chairman of the Opera Ball, the Consular Ball, the March of Dimes Rose Gala, the Houston Symphony Society Evening with Danny Kaye, the Muscular Dystrophy drive, the Multiple Sclerosis drive, the Easter Seal drive, the National Diabetes Foundation's Jack Benny Memorial Tennis Tournament, and the Just-One- Break, Feather Ball in New York.
•Hemisfair's international ambassador, appointed by the governor in 1968, and official hostess of Houston in 1965. Since then, she's entertained at least some 15 major heads of state from foreign countries.
•Appointment as Consul by two foreign governments: Morocco and Pakistan. Also, being knighted by King Boudouin of Belgium for arranging an exhibition of fine firearms (antique and modern) at the Museum of Natural History as well as entertaining the Prime Minister on his visit here. Also, presented the Star of Quadeszam by

NEW YORK POST,
MONDAY, JANUARY 21, 1985

AROUND the TOWN

JOANNE HERRING

WHEN Joanne Herring gives a party, you can be sure that there will be something unique about it that guests will remember.

The other night Joanne, who hails from Houston, and her close friend **Dodie Kazanjian**, who divides her time between Washington and New-port, hosted a black tie dinner at the Hay Adams Hotel in Washington in honor of Commandant of the Marine Corps, Gen. P.X. Kelley and his wife Barbara.

Instead of place cards, each guest had a balloon tied to their wrist with the guest's name on one side and table number on the other. Eva Gabor arrived with Merv Griffin, and the hostesses, who definitely aim to please, sat Eva at an all-male table. You can be sure that Eva just loved every minute of it!

THE BEST LITTLE HOSTESSE IN TEXAS

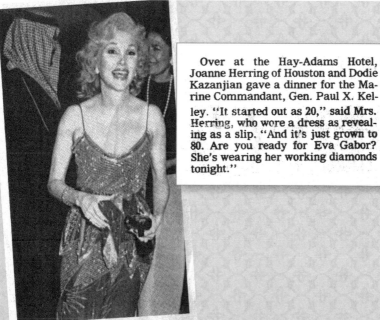

Joanne Herring Davis at a Saudi reception in Washington

Over at the Hay-Adams Hotel, Joanne Herring of Houston and Dodie Kazanjian gave a dinner for the Marine Commandant, Gen. Paul X. Kelley. "It started out as 20," said Mrs. Herring, who wore a dress as revealing as a slip. "And it's just grown to 80. Are you ready for Eva Gabor? She's wearing her working diamonds tonight."

At Joanne Herring and Dodie Kazanjian's dinner, from left, Eva Gabor, Gen. Paul X. Kelley, Barbara Kelley and Mrs. Herring.

TRENDS . . . IN GOURMET MUSICAL CHAIRS

Parties where the guests change with the courses

NEW YORK POST, THURSDAY, JULY 12, 1984

THE peripatetic dinner is here. In our fast moving, fast talking society, being sandwiched between the same two partners all night might seem as endless as waiting in line to get a passport.

To add pace to their parties, some lively hostesses are asking their guests to change paatners after each course. While the young guard seems to like the idea, the old guard looks down on this social musical chairs.

Joanne Herring, the vivacious Texas hostess, can be credited for turning the middle-class progressive dinner into a high society event when she asked top Washingtonians, international dignitaries,

By FRANCE-MICHELE ADLER

four-star generals and elegant socialites to pick up their napkins, grab their wine glasses and hunt up their next partners.

"It adds adrenaline to the party. I like the gaiety, the lack of protocol," says this free spirit.

Her first peripatetic dinner was given for **Prince Saud ibn Faisal** in the late '60s.

"At that time, not everybody knew someone from Saudi Arabia," explains Joanne, who was eager to introduce the "good looking and charming prince" to her friends and have him

meet the outstanding women and men she knows.

Not caring a hoot for convention, she even gave two male partners to the prince for one course so he could chat with astronaut Alan Shepard and heart surgeon Denton Cooley.

Since then, Joanne has duplicated this unorthodox social dinner all over the world and on a grand scale.

"The logistics are terrible," she admits. Although she provides cards indicating one's next partner for each course, she must remember the sitting plan for the entire evening because guests get confused.

"I've never had it backfire but I work at it all night long," advises Joanne.

Mix 'n' match no merry-go-round

Herring

66 When you look over an open fan, it means you're flirting . . . I use fans a lot for luncheon parties. And if I'm tired and don't want to be stimulating, I take a fan to a party to be amusing and let the fan do the work." — Joanne Herring, the Houston socialite.

Joan Schnitzer and Luciana Avedon

WOMEN'S WEAR DAILY, MONDAY, MAY 9, 1977

THE KING AND I: "We did a lot of research and found some of the most beautiful girls in the country to have here for **King Hussein**," said **Joan Herring**, at the party she and her husband **Robert** gave for Jordan's king in Houston.

"Since the King is traveling with all males, we didn't want this to look like a boys' fraternity party. And he does like to be around pretty women," she said.

The King, who stayed with Washington Star publisher, **Joe Albritton**, while in Houston, said during the party in his honor, "We are fast approaching a crucial point and something must be done," as he referred to the tension in the Mideast. Hussein also said that he favors **President Carter's** energy program and that he believes America should conserve energy.

King Hussein left Houston after his annual physical checkup, in the Texas Heart Institute.

*I*n the 1970s, Washington boasted black-tie events every night. The indisputable king of all this glitter was Ardeshir Zahedi, the Iranian ambassador. He was rugged, masculine, tall, slim, well tailored, and known to be a fascinating, polished man of the world. Calling on his enormous wealth, Ardeshir possessed a flair for the dramatic, driving a Rolls-Royce, throwing soirees at his gorgeous embassy residence, and causing a stir with lavish gestures such as sending kilos of caviar to a favored hostess. He was a playboy who loved women, and women loved him. Elizabeth Taylor had a crush on him. The *world* had a crush on him.

I despaired of ever meeting this intriguing ambassador. Then I read that he planned a trip to Houston for a medical checkup.

"Bob," I said that evening, "what do you think about my inviting the ambassador to dinner?"

"That would be great," he said. "Do you know him?"

"No," I said, "but I intend to." I explained my plan for an unannounced hospital visit. He laughed indulgently.

Earlier, I might have felt trepidation. But years in front of the television camera as well as thousands of hours perfecting conversational exchanges gave me hope. I was pretty good at getting through barriers.

Knowing the importance of dressing appropriately, I scrutinized my closet. Today, details were critical. Today, I hoped to leave a "scent" enticing enough to be followed by a person whose life already boasted rooms full of flowers and invitations to the most influential parties in the world.

At best, I had five minutes to make or break my plan. Everything I did, said, and wore would be analyzed with the speed of a computer. I faced no amateur, but rather a professional who could spot a phony, a climber, a bore at twenty paces. He would analyze me with the swiftness of a gunslinger at the O.K. Corral. I hoped our meeting would not end disappointingly, with me departing (at least metaphorically) in the proverbial pine box.

"So," I wondered, "what should I wear?"

Nothing from Paris, I thought, brushing aside French designer labels. Too obvious. To seem anxious would be deadly.

Nothing too chichi or sexy. That translates as untutored.

Nothing too dull. Uniform twinsets and pearls, while nice, spell "ho hum."

Hmm...I chose a boxy white jacket, piped in brown, with a

brown, cotton, high-necked, fitted, long-sleeved shirt that revealed a lot only when the jacket opened, while otherwise leaving lots to the imagination. The skirt was long, not tight, but slit to the knee. High-heeled shoes completed my outfit.

I debated, then chose one more accessory — an object I rarely use at night, much less in the daytime — my twenty-carat diamond ring. It is, as Zsa Zsa Gabor once said of hers, a working diamond, silent but speaking wonders, an indisputable sign that indicates wealth and position. An expert with a practiced eye can spot a fake ten yards away.

Bob Herring, always an enormously generous man, gave me the knuckle-to-knuckle diamond, which was almost as wide as it was long. The gift did not mark a special occasion, only an opportune moment when it became available. Our friend, jeweler Mike Kazanjian, let Bob know that he had an unusual piece he thought I'd like. The exquisite ring featured a square bottom and a marquis top, a combination cut I'd never seen before.

Sometimes people think, "Oh, what a frivolous thing to have." Actually, impressive jewels are good public relations and help tremendously in business settings. If you want to be accepted and remembered in a room full of Fortune 500 executives, wear a twenty-carat diamond. They immediately welcome you with open arms. It's obvious you're not a con artist, out to get their money. You clearly have your own. Such jewels grant you instant credibility and status.

(Alas, these days I wear only fakes. The real stuff lives in the bank. It was no longer fun to wear my jewelry after I learned of a friend's horrible experience. She was staying at a posh hotel. Two men stepped into an elevator with her and cut off her finger to get her ring. That did it for me. No more real jewels unless they belong to a jeweler and come with a guard!)

On this occasion, I considered the working diamond a fitting accessory for the event for which I was preparing.

Finally, I felt ready. I looked appropriate, hopefully attractive but not overdone, for a casual meeting on a hot summer day.

What was the cause of this intense concentration on my appearance?

Shortly after our Parisian honeymoon, Bob said, "I want us to do our own lobbying in Washington."

Many laws limiting the freedom of the oil business were at stake. He felt that this was bad not only for his company but also for the economy. I was intent on helping Bob in whatever capacity I could. He was hugely successful in Houston. In Washington, however, he was just another Fortune 500 medium-sized company competing with the giants. Enron wasn't Enron yet.

What could I possibly do?

I had noticed that most business dealings occurred not in legislative offices or staid conference rooms, but at fun-filled parties where people relaxed and conversed as equals. In an office, one person sits behind a desk and the other person is the supplicant. At a party, however, everyone talks on an even level. No person presides at a desk or takes precedence over another.

Parties were especially significant in Washington because they provided opportunities for people with differing ideas to hear another side. In a friendly, engaging atmosphere, you had a chance to explain why a particular idea or action would succeed or work for a constituency or help the country. People were more open to listening in a social setting, and, very often, they understood and agreed with what you were saying. It worked well also because, at a party, no one was being asked to make a commitment, but merely to consider an idea.

"I'm Mrs. Robert Herring and I would like to see the ambassador," I requested with all the charm I could muster to the nurse stalking the lobby desk at the hospital. I was directed to the ambassador's aide, a young, exceedingly handsome fellow, groomed to a fault. At a glance, I took in his hand-tailored suit, his John Lobb shoes, and his princely manner. He made a similar lightning-quick assessment of me.

The gracious man greeted me with a look of curiosity easily interpreted: why was I here? Something else played across his face as well: attraction.

My father once said, "Joanne doesn't have one good feature, but you put them all together and they look pretty good."

At the time, looks were a woman's only platform for advancement. You *had* to use your looks to be noticed. My mother said, "Why are you wearing those little 'slippy' dresses? You should be wearing gray flannel that looks businesslike." "Mother," I said, "I would never get in the door!" Once you get in, you must know your subject, have it be relevant to his objectives, and be brief. Then you will always be welcome. But first you must get in.

In Washington, if there were going to be a hundred people at a party, and I wanted to meet a certain person, what did I do? I tried to make that person want to meet me. Toward that end, I often wore what the press called "slinky" dresses.

My next move was to say, "Let me introduce you to my husband. He supports your programs," or "He would like to hear more about your programs. May I introduce you?"

If you were smart, you developed other facets, such as understanding the problems the person faced. I liked parties and the la-di-da part of socializing, but I had discovered that the machinations of business and world affairs interested me more.

But for a woman to play on the big field, she must learn to play "the game." It's complicated and nuanced in ways that distinguish skill levels. It is not flirtation. It is more subtle, a careful application of talents, with definite limits. What I refer to has little to do with sex — which is common and available on every street corner.

I laughingly refer to the game sometimes as "the mating dance of the whooping crane." Just as whooping cranes have a dance in which the male and female advance, then retreat; advance, then retreat; so, too, do men and women as they relate to one another — even if the sole goal is friendship. This game has many rules.

As I stood before the charming aide of the Iranian ambassador, I played the game to win.

"I have heard of the ambassador and what an interesting and

fascinating man he is," I said sincerely, holding myself rather aloof and impersonally. The aide quickly proved to be an advanced player. He took my hand, bowed over it, and responded, "Ah, but not nearly as fascinating as you, madam."

I knew this was my cue to retreat. When physical contact is made, the woman must become more reserved. I gently withdrew my hand, smiled, and said, "My husband helped found this hospital with Dr. Denton Cooley. I think the ambassador would find Bob interesting." Mentioning my husband at this juncture was deliberate and crucial. (The game is much more complicated, alas, for women who have no husband to invoke at the appropriate moment.) "I think they would enjoy knowing one another," I continued. Then I added, "I'd very much like to give a party for the ambassador while he's in Houston."

Walking to the window and changing the subject, I asked, "Have you seen much of our city?" The aide joined me and lamented that his only view of Houston had been from a hospital window. We laughed.

"Oh, that's a shame because we have a very green city," I said. "It's more like the Old South than the Old West. In fact, in the *Guinness Book of Records*, we are listed as having more trees than any other city in the world."

"That's interesting," he replied. "We always think of the West as being a desert with tumbleweeds and cowboys."

"We have those too. Most people don't realize how big Texas is," I said. "It's larger than France. It would be a *shame* to leave without knowing us."

"I will ask the ambassador," the gentleman responded, "but having met you, madam, I certainly agree it would, indeed, be a shame. May I call you?" I handed him my card, which I had had carefully engraved at Amorial in Paris. The French company's work was immediately apparent to those interested in such things, and I saw recognition in the eyes of the ambassador's aide.

I thought again about how details mattered in playing this game:

from the power of dressing appropriately down to the wearing of the diamond that spoke volumes. Now this attractive card would represent not only a final, telling detail for the aide's benefit, but also a first impression for the ambassador when it was presented to him on my behalf.

We said our good-byes and I practically waltzed away. Two hours later, the ambassador phoned to accept.

Even now, I have a sense of joy as I remember that initial encounter. Ardeshir became a dear friend and a strong part of our lives. We were always his houseguests (which gave us enormous cachet) when we visited Washington.

While it's true that I saw him as a door to that glittering city and its people, I always made sure that he understood how much I valued him as a person. When someone does something for me, I always want to reciprocate in a way they value. It's a point of honor.

Fortunately, if you play the game correctly, every player can help the other and wins a friend in the process.

I may have been the "queen of Houston," as the papers called me, but that was *no* help in Washington. Bob and I needed to establish ourselves in Washington society. But how?

Ardeshir's job was promoting friendship between Iran and the United States, which was strong at the time. He had to keep those ties firm. But he was a kind and generous friend. He made it possible for us to enter the Washington hierarchy from the top. Because of him, everyone we met greeted us with open arms.

For example, one night I was at a very large reception. Right in front of me was Barbara Walters. The embassy secretary, who was an elegant, lovely lady, tried to introduce us. "This is Mrs. Herring," she said.

Ms. Walters gave me a bored glance.

"She and her husband are the houseguests of the ambassador," the secretary continued.

"Ooh," said Barbara, turning completely around, not at all bored now. "How wonderful to meet you. I just adore Ardeshir."

"Everyone does," I replied, smiling.

Barbara became a person I saw often and who usually came when I invited her, even from New York. I discovered a Barbara Walters who was not caustic and inquiring but sweet and caring. She actually tried to help me in whatever way she could. Under the veneer that careers demand, we often find wonderful hearts.

Parties in the 1970s were elegant and opulent: black ties every night, limos, caviar, champagne...oh, it was grand. The problem was that everyone wanted the same top people. The "important" people received as many as twenty-five invitations a night. The ambassadors, cabinet secretaries, and members of Congress were the ruling stars of the party circuit. Bigger corporations than Bob's were competing for their time.

Bob had a few acquaintances among the senators and he had his sterling reputation as being one of the cleverer innovators in the oil sector.

And we had Ardeshir. To maintain this relationship we had to reciprocate. What did he want and need? He wanted and needed people to enjoy his parties enough to secure his goals for the shah. Our "job" was therefore to help entertain. During the day, the problems of the world rested on the shoulders of this group. Thus at night they liked to laugh and have fun. Many of these men were good dancers and loved to show off their talents. They did not have the slightest interest in me except as an amusing companion. We laughed, drank a little champagne, and went home with our mates. It was "Scarlett at the picnic," a game I knew so well. Bob was equally successful with the women. He made them feel important in his inimitable way, and, in so doing, we became known and made real friends.

But all of this was under Ardeshir's umbrella. What if we stepped out and invited these people to our own parties? Would they want us without Ardeshir?

All of my life was a challenge, and now I faced a big one. We could not match the splendor with which Ardeshir entertained. Our parties had to be different, fun, a real diversion. We were now one of those twenty-five invitations arriving every night, and I worried that no one would accept — but they all did.

I did everything but backflips to ensure that our guests had fun. I invented diversions such as having the guests change seats after every course. As we always had five courses, including coffee, each guest got to have five different dining partners, a new one with each course. This was in fact extremely difficult to orchestrate because I needed to give careful thought to ensure that every new dinner partner was interesting to the other. The guests were all interesting, of course, but not all were compatible. I agonized over each move, even though I invited the most beautiful women and the most fascinating men, and naturally the young and delicious girls that flocked to Washington, as well. I was never afraid to have these young, fresh beauties around. I liked them and they liked me, and they appreciated the attention because many hostesses overlooked them unless they were heiresses.

I looked for the lonely and shy, as well. The new ambassador to Washington from the Emirates, Saaid Ghobash, was one such. Twenty-eight years old, from a rich, distinguished family of sheiks, he moved with ease within his world of men and sequestered women. Washington was another world entirely. I could tell he felt alone and disassociated (just as I had felt in Saudi Arabia) when he first arrived. His friendship, though, was such fun. I teased him unmercifully about the girls. He would blush and smile and, I think, feel comforted to have a friend that did not ask him for favors but liked him only for himself. A brilliant man, in years to come he became a great bridge between our two cultures. The support of the oil-rich Emirate states was essential to our security and to our oil supply.

I tried to make everything I did different from other parties. I gave after-dinner speeches, for example, that I tried to make funny yet comfortably complimentary. Betty Beale, a top Washington columnist, said my remarks were a "tour de force." I'm glad to say, I made our guests laugh. They went home happy and lighthearted, a real change from the daily grind of their days, during which millions of dollars and millions of lives were at stake. They needed this respite and I gave it to them. Bob was always there as ballast, quietly using his amazing abilities to make people feel comfortable, to do the business he was there to accomplish.

This is how we worked together. On the way to Washington, he would coach me in the nuances of what he needed to enhance his business and the fortunes and jobs of his employees and stockholders. I listened, using the skills of memory retention I had perfected to conquer dyslexia.

I could explain Bob's needs succinctly (due to my experience in TV) as I sat next to the congressmen and senators whose votes could make the difference. They enjoyed hearing the requests and recommendations from me rather than from somebody in their office. They listened and nodded. The next day Bob went to their offices and often closed the deal by getting their vote or support. I set the deal up, then went on to play, ending the evening in fun and games. Bob followed through with the details. It was a strategy that seemed to work very well.

Bob's business soared. He bought every pipeline in sight, every form of energy known, and helped every person who had an idea to develop alternative energies if he thought it had any merit. He saw far into the future, recognizing the problems that face us today long before they became realities.

Talking to anyone at all was second nature for me by now; no one frightened me. I used every ability I had spent years acquiring. I had the foundation of the European grandees to make me feel comfortable anywhere and often knew crucial people from almost any country. All that I had learned, every day of my work on TV, topped with the educational base my father had provided, prepared me for this new stage of my life, the most difficult of any I had been asked to face. This was business. Every word I said could be used for or against Bob and his company. It was a heavy responsibility.

Hosting parties *was* business. It was fun, sure, but ultimately it was business.

Washington wasn't the only place we threw parties, either. We entertained everywhere, mixing business and pleasure in such popular spots as Acapulco. Many times we had dinner in New York, breakfast in Paris, and dinner in Riyadh.

The years my mother made me be nice to the chaperones at parties, the years of trying to live up to what I thought was honorable and right: these early lessons paid huge dividends at these times. When the press made caustic remarks my powerful older friends (Princess von Bismarck, Duchess de la Rochefoucauld, Lady Barbara Colyton, and Helen Coolidge, to name a few) stood staunchly in my defense, so I never experienced lasting damage. These older bastions of society were my best defense; they stayed loyal to me when Bob died and I was vulnerable.

Of course these remarks hurt. I would be crazy to say they didn't. Sometimes I would anguish over them, but then I would say to myself that it was ridiculous to dwell on it. When someone told me that so-and-so didn't like me, I replied, "I don't blame them. I don't like myself all the time either," which invariably made people laugh. In the end, no matter how much they shot at me, I was just fine. My life went on exactly the same. Sally Quinn of the *Washington Post* wrote a half-scathing, half-flattering article, her special talent. It saddened me, but Henry Kissinger cheered me when he said, "Joanne, nobody since John Kennedy's funeral has had five full pages in the *Washington Post*. Be flattered that they think you're important!"

CHAPTER 17

Exotic Adventure in the Middle East

To find the Pakistani and Moroccan consulates in Houston, visit the twenty-three-room mansion of Robert Herring, chairman of Houston Natural Gas, and his wife, Joanne. She is the consul, but he is so actively involved that calls himself the "assistant honorary cons Mrs. Herring's southern charms help sell th Pakistani and Moroccan products on the sta

Perhaps the most intriguing, and certainly the most glamorous, honorary consulship in the country involves Robert and Joanne Herring of Houston. He is chairman of Houston Natural Gas, a $1.8-billion company that does substantial business in the Arab oil-producing countries. In 1974 the Pakistani ambassador in Washington tried to persuade him to serve as honorary consul in Houston. Herring declined. So the ambassador launched an end run and tried to get Joanne. Well aware that the Arab oil nations look kindly on those who help out their poorer Muslim brethren, Bob Herring had no objections and Joanne accepted. Then, three years ago,

the Herrings had an audience with the Ki of Morocco. The King soon sent word t he also wanted Joanne as his consul Houston. She accepted that one, too.

To date, neither country appears to gret choosing the Herrings. Joanne, a f mer TV talk-show host, is a renown party giver and has not hesitated to use connections in her consular work. S roped her dress-designer friends, inclu ing Oscar de la Renta and Geoffrey Bee into running up creations for a fashi show to publicize Pakistani fabrics a leathers. Then she dragooned friends at department stores to send their buyers

© 1980 BOB GOMEL

$\mathcal{B}$ob told me over and over how much it meant to have me travel with him. Running a major company is hard work, and with many lives depending on his decisions, he said being with me gave him something to look forward to after a very hard day. I was despondent about leaving my children, but they were not alone: my parents moved into the house with them while we were gone, and there was always our dear Leonora Gaudin (a beautiful woman from Honduras), who, more than anyone else, gave them continuity. Later, Reverend Stevens, the man who had worked for Bob King and me previously as a nanny and a driver, had financial problems, so he moved in too. Somehow, though, knowing all these loved ones were there didn't help at all. *I wanted to be there!*

But it helped to know how much my presence meant to Bob, who was carrying a major burden not only for our family but for his thousands of employees as well. If he felt he needed me, I had to be with him. I was a sounding board for him, he said; he had never before had anyone like me on his travels. "You have changed my life," he told me.

Bob's business took us to the Middle East for oil, Saudi Arabia in particular. Saudi Arabia was a challenge in 1973. Today it is a brilliant world of skyscrapers and every modern convenience. The government of Saudi Arabia has shared the wealth and created a new world in the desert that would rival the dreams of any city planner. When Bob and I first visited, however, this incredible change had not yet occurred. Riyadh was a city of unpaved streets and buildings made of mud. (Mud made an effective barrier against the desert heat.)

We stayed at the Sahara Palace Hotel, which was similar to a Motel 6 in a ghetto. There was little air-conditioning, and what there was rattled like a screen door in a tornado. There was no room service and there were no restaurants. Arab families did not go out; dinner was eaten at home.

We knew nobody except our lawyer, who had been hired to introduce Bob to the ministers Bob needed to see. The attorney, who was
kind enough to invite us to his home to eat our meals, also had a big
party in our honor. As it turns out, people are the same everywhere,
and parties work! You can meet several people at a time at a good
shindig.

Parties in Saudi Arabia started at seven p.m. and went on until
one or two a.m., and for good reason — the heat! The people lived at
night to escape it, but we were not accustomed to this schedule. Our
body clocks were on U.S. time, and so were our workdays and
playtimes.

Our first night there, I thought I would die of hunger. Numerous
cups of rose-flavored tea were served in crystal glasses resting neatly
inside beautiful filigree holders. I did not enjoy rose-flavored tea.
Plus it was served hot and I had never sipped from a crystal glass cup
before; it burned my lips. (Think how hard it is for foreigners to
adjust to U.S. food and customs.)

The men sat alone and talked business. I was left with the ladies,
who had never met an American; coincidentally, I had never met a
Saudi. The women, all wives of critical cabinet ministers — very crucial to Bob's business — sat silently, unaccustomed to mixed parties.
(Most of the time, Saudi men and women entertained separately.)
Even though in this instance the men and women were seated separately, we were all in the same vicinity. It was a great honor for me
that the ministers' wives all appeared together to make me feel at
home. They had prepared several delicacies themselves to honor me,
brought on beautiful silver trays. I was touched by their kindness, but
I starved until we finally ate at around one o'clock in the morning.

I thought, "How do I interest these lovely women who have been
so kind and are probably as nervous as I am?" Actually, these ladies
were much more sophisticated than I realized at first. Under the
veils, they wore Yves St. Laurent dresses cut above the knee and the
last word in snappy shoes. They were very knowledgeable about what

was in, but none of this was evident as I sat down with them that evening, my knees knocking.

Their lives had been so different from mine. I thought, "Nothing has prepared me for this." But I was wrong. People are the same everywhere. "Just do what you did in Colombia at age fifteen," I told myself. "You *have* been a foreigner before."

They were so kind, and they spoke English perfectly. I was ashamed that I didn't speak Arabic. I wanted to be careful of every word so as to not damage Bob by my ignorance. "Oh, Lord, help me," I thought.

Bob was doing just fine, as usual, sitting comfortably among the men, talking animatedly. I took a deep breath, said a prayer, and jumped in like a kid at the swimming hole. I was supposed to make friends and talk. So I talked.

"How did you meet your husband?" I asked of one. "He is a famous man. You must be very proud that he chose you." This was before I knew anything about the Middle East and the acknowledged tradition of arranged marriages. Most brides in this era never even *saw* their husbands before the wedding night.

The woman replied that her husband had seen her at her school. He fell madly in love and went immediately to her father to ask for her hand. He was years older than she, and I wondered about their compatibility because she was interested only in conversation about movie stars, fashion magazines, and girlish chatter. She was a plump little dumpling but delightful, as dumplings always are.

The next minister's wife was very different. A sharifa, she was descended directly from Muhammad and had black hair and startling blue eyes. She was studying to become a doctor. When she told me of her daily responsibilities, I was stunned and asked, "How do you do it? When do you study?"

"After midnight when the family is asleep," she said.

I was lost in admiration. I thought *my* life was complicated, but I had much to learn. I was on the first of what would be eighteen trips in seven years to Saudi Arabia. My misadventures were just beginning...

On another trip, I was sitting in a beauty salon and had almost dozed off — the relative comfort of this salon was much better than the one I had tried during my first visit. There, the attendant washed my hair in a toilet used as a shampoo bowl. The wire curlers were full of previous customers' hair and pressed indentions in my head. The ladies of Saudi Arabia, I learned, have their own private beauticians, while ladies on the street — and American visitors — are forced to use a toilet bowl. But since hair *must* be curled and coiffed wherever you are, I sat, waiting... drowsily.

Suddenly, a woman in a veil and flowing robes grabbed my hand. This got my attention because it was my *left* hand, which not coincidentally had my twenty-carat diamond ring on it.

I was tempted to squeal, "Who in the devil are you, and why are you attaching yourself to my ring?" It wasn't that I didn't appreciate the attention. In fact, when you wear a twenty-carat diamond, it's hard to pretend to be surprised when people notice. This was my working diamond, remember, and it worked well, helping me to fit in among the higher echelon of this society.

This Saudi lady had a killer grip. She twisted and turned my hand to reflect the light. Perhaps, I thought, it was time to start a conversation.

"I'm Joanne Herring from Houston," I began. "I'm here as a guest of the king."

I'm pretty sure that the people in the salon didn't understand a word I said, until I mentioned the word "king."

Of course, I was technically lying, but I thought I might intimidate the lady into releasing my diamond and the aching hand attached to it.

Her eyes were wide, and I figured she was impressed to know someone who would merit such an invitation, so I prepared to excuse her so I could get back to my high calling of a toilet-bowl rinse.

But I could tell by the looks on the faces around me that I'd done something wrong.

She slowly lowered my hand and looked at me suspiciously, as everyone in the salon stared at me. The woman admiring my jewelry was none other than King Faisal bin Abdul-Aziz Al Saud's daughter, a royal princess of Saudi Arabia.

My mind raced. I'd already told her my name — and my hometown — and there just weren't many more clues needed to trace me back to my husband's company, with negative consequences. This society didn't seem like the most forgiving place, and it was unlikely they'd have much patience with the Westerner who'd lied to a royal princess. It was very difficult to know the proper protocol, let alone follow it. This meant the possibility for miscommunication was high.

I decided to just tell the truth.

"Honestly," I began, "my husband is here to form an oil partnership with His Majesty's government."

The princess, I noted, didn't seem to be particularly concerned about my honesty and any violations of king-knowing protocol. She continued to hold my hand, evaluating my ring with the precision of a Swiss diamond cutter. She didn't even need a loupe. Her people had been nomads who carried their wealth with them. She must have known the real thing since infancy — just like the generations of successful traders who came before her.

To my shock, she invited me to come back to her splendid palace for tea. How did I know? Well, realizing that Arabic in Houston was as scarce as a bikini in Riyadh, the delighted onlookers translated for me. What a story this would make around the toilet rinse — for the next week.

Had I stopped a moment to consider the situation, I might not have been so eager to jump onto this magic carpet ride. For one thing, the possibility of my offending her was great and Bob's embryonic operation could be shut down as a result. I had no idea of her true identity. Had she been a very beautiful, elegant thief, I easily could have been robbed. I had heard stories of unwary travelers who had fallen into the wrong company, been held up, and left in the desert to die. People have certainly been killed for less than twenty carats.

Yet, presented with an opportunity to see inside the sequestered world of the Saudi Arabian princesses, I didn't let the sand shift beneath my feet. I knew only that their world was like Ali Baba's cave — full of jewels and wonder. So I canceled my appointment, gently took my bruised hand back from the princess, packed up my things, and joined her.

We drove on an unpaved road that shot dust up onto the car's windows to an expansive building that seemed to be made of dirt. Even through the car's dusty windows, the two princesses standing at the gate saw my blond hair and started giggling. I was a novelty — a real, live American — and when I got out of the car, I was immediately examined with as much fervor as my ring had garnered previously. In retrospect, I see that the ring was my key into this palace. (That ring worked hard.) The princesses were curious about Americans but had never seen one who seemed close to their own social caste.

Sadly, they did not speak Texan, however, and I did not speak Arabic. Our interaction was like a mime show played by kindergartners at an ethnic retreat. There were the ever-present smiles, the exaggerated gestures, and the unnecessarily loud talk...as if the speakers were trying to overcome the sound barrier instead of the language barrier. Thankfully, it was a circus that excluded spectators, although at the time we were totally unconcerned with how we appeared. The easy warmth and respectful curiosity carried us to places that words could not have.

I gasped when my foot entered the opulent palace, a stark contrast to the dull exterior. Soft light played on the gorgeous rugs, like jewels scattered on velvet. The walls were hung with tapestries of shimmering silk, afloat with color. The depth of the colors on the walls and floors made me feel as if I was in a giant kaleidoscope, with each twist of the day providing richer and more glorious scenes. Because the Hadith (a book of the words and deeds of the Prophet Muhammad) prohibits the use of human features, animals, and flowers in the home, color and intricate designs provide the decorations.

Although I couldn't easily understand her, the princess was trying to tell me something. I later realized that she was indicating that the décor was so richly colored to make up for the fact that the rooms contained no real flowers. Only when she took me by the hand and led me into a lovely courtyard did I understand.

With the other princesses following her like little ducklings, we stepped into a green world. Cool water bubbled in a marble fountain. Birds flew from tree to tree and occasionally landed on the rich grass. A servant appeared, dressed in white and holding a brass tray about the size of a small table. It was full of dates, tarts, a curious paste, and a variety of breads. I partook of them all on a golden plate, closing my eyes and tasting almond, rose, and sesame seed. The rose tea was served in lavishly cut crystal nestled in silver- and gold-filigree holders.

Three maids appeared carrying a new curiosity, a three-foot-high silver stove that was smoking, emitting a terrible stench. While they set it on the priceless rug, I tried to restrain a gasp.

"Aah," the princesses trilled. Inexplicably, the main princess grabbed my skirt and pulled it above my thighs, guiding me toward the stove.

"Aah," said the other princesses in unison.

"Ooh," I replied. In all of the minilessons I was getting, no one had mentioned how to conduct myself when a princess hikes up your dress over a steaming silver stove.

The stove smelled of the luscious scents of a Neiman Marcus perfume counter, mixed with the unmistakable fragrance of an entire rugby team's mildewed athletic socks.

But the smell didn't seem to put a damper on the princess. She lifted her own skirt and placed it over the stove, and the other princesses did likewise. Their skirts billowed out with the warm air; then they danced around the room. It seemed that I was expected to dance too. So...I danced.

As I watched them dance and laugh, I knew I'd never be able to sit and have conversations with the lead princess about her life and ideas. It made me sad, so I simply enjoyed the moment in time, watching this young woman swirl and twirl around the lavish room, oblivious to the constraints of the world around her.

Suddenly, a clear voice rang out. It was prayer time — a deeply sacred moment. A servant appeared with carpets of silk so exquisite, I gasped when I saw them. Then a nervous dread washed over me as she placed the rugs on the floor and I realized what was about to happen.

One, two, three, four, *five* . . .

They expected me to pray too. The princess grabbed me and pulled me down with so much force (probably hoping to ensure my proper place in Paradise) that I hit my nose.

"Oh, Lord," I prayed, "please don't let my nose bleed on this carpet. That's probably worse than adultery, and they stone you for that."

I attended a Presbyterian church in Houston and we preferred a more . . . well, vertical form of prayer.

But I made it through, and the afternoon came to an end, like a brightly colored dream. Hours later I stumbled into my hotel suite to find Bob sitting on the couch. My skirt was crumpled, my makeup smeared from the steaming oven, my hair uncoiffed, and my nose red and feeling slightly askew.

"How was the beauty shop?" Bob asked, looking me over with a bemused smile. "You look lovely." Really, Bob was too much. I looked shot. Well, I sort of had been.

That night, I drifted to sleep with visions of princesses, palaces, and jewels dancing in my head. Even the memory of the silver stove's unusual smell couldn't ruin the fairy-tale world I'd seen. I awakened with a start the next morning when I heard a knock on our hotel suite door, my day at the Sahara Palace now a memory.

Bob opened it to find a servant attired in trailing robes and a snow-white turban.

"From Her Royal Highness," he said, holding out a heavy, intricately carved box.

"I assume this is for you, Joanne," Bob said, taking the big box from the messenger and setting it on the floor.

"What on earth?" I gasped.

"For remembrance," the servant said, waiting for me to open the gift. "Her Highness will live in purdah in total seclusion. She will never again receive an American," he added in broken English.

I carefully opened the heavy lid, tears stinging my eyes.

"For remembrance," the servant repeated.

There, in the box, was a crimson silk gown, embroidered with gold and precious stones.

"A Saudi wedding dress," the servant murmured.

Was it hers? Why had she given it to me? Although I didn't comprehend what had happened, I knew that some mysterious and wonderful union of hearts and minds had happened between me and a Saudi princess as foreign to me as this American was to her.

I felt a deep sadness that we would never meet again, but I would never forget her. That she should want me to have this gift touched a chord that would resonate through my whole life. She gave me a bejeweled wedding dress, but most of all, she'd given me something far more precious — an unspoken piece of her heart.

I sank to the floor, cradled the dress, and wept.

Postscript: The princess had darker days in her future — her father would soon be assassinated. On the 1,405th birthday of the Prophet Muhammad, the king would celebrate with a reception for a visiting Kuwaiti delegation inside his opulent palace. He'd recognize a family member — a cousin whose brother had been killed by the king's police when he launched an attack on a Saudi television station.

The king would lean forward to allow the cousin to fulfill the custom of kissing the tip of the king's nose. Instead, the cousin would reach under his white robe, pull out a gun, and shoot the princess's father three times in the face. As the king was dying, the cousin would shout, "Now my brother is avenged!"

Moroccan royalty to sit in

The Houston Post/Wed., October 15, 1986

SUPER PEOPLE — Moroccan Prince **Moulay Abdullah** is heading a dazzling lineup of dignitaries who'll sit in the dress circle Friday night when Theatre Under The Stars kicks off *The Desert Song*. His royal highness will be seated next to **Joanne Herring Davis**, the Kingdom of Morocco's honorary consul general to Houston. They'll be joined by Joanne's son **Robin King** (vice consul) and possibly by **Maati Jorio**, Moroccan ambassador to the United States. Moulay, a handsome 24-year-old student at UT-Austin, is third in line for the throne.

Other outstanding guests are New York City Opera general manager **Beverly Sills** and Los Angeles Music Center president **Frank Dale**. They'll view *Desert Song* with an eye toward adding it to their own rosters.

Tickets are selling like crazy because the word is out that its stars — NYCO baritone **Richard White** and Broadway's **Linda Michele** — are simply sensational as the Red Shadow and Margot. The musical is set in Morocco in 1925 amid the Riff uprising against the injustices of the occupying French Foreign Legion.

Above: Newlyweds Joanne and Lloyd Davis were hosted at a seated dinner in Tony's last week by Lynette Proler.

DAVIS:
Prince at her side

Following the opening, dress circle members will join the stars and the cast at 2016 Main for a Moroccan-style buffet stirred up by caterer **Kirk Schlein**. Both the sixth-floor poolside party room an 26th-floor penthouse (dramatically filmed movie *Urban Cowboy*) will be decorated sheik's oasis, even to a tented entrance. The is bound to enjoy the evening.

★ Antiques and art objects from the River Oaks home of **Joanne Herring Davis** were given a private preview at Hart Galleries, where formally clad guests paid $25 each for a peek. As a result, more than $5,000 was raised for the Children's Center for Developmental Therapy. Joanne and husband **Lloyd Davis** — who were recently married — eventually plan to live in a high-rise, so some of the possessions simply *haave* to go. Gallery bosses **Wynonne** and **Jerry Hart** have Joanne's beautiful collection of things earmarked for auction tonight and Friday, and on Sunday afternoon. Biggies in the dress-up preview crowd included **Eleanor** and **Mac McCollum**, socialite **Sandra Lawson**, **Ford** and **Patti Hubbard**, Wrapture Boutique's **Craig Kanyuck** and husband **Ed**, **Manny Mones** and wife **Yolanda**, and on and on.

CHAPTER 18

They Called Me "Sir"

To me, it's simple. Socialism and communism promise every-thing, but they're actually slavery. They *sound* good. They represent what I call the Robin Hood dream, where you take from the rich and give to the poor — it just never works. The rich stop giving and the poor stop working. The rich grow weary of giving handouts and the poor stop because they expect support. There *is* no taking from the rich to give to the deserving poor in any country that has tried communism. In fact, all communist countries have walls to keep people in, not out.

People usually run from communism, not to it. Why doesn't it work? Government cannot successfully make its people equal. Only markets can do that. It's been tried for years under many countries and leaders, and it always fails. We must be free to set our own des-tiny. Our enemies plan to change our thinking by using problems such as racism, poverty, homelessness, and illegal immigrants to make us feel guilty about the imperfections of capitalism. Then they promise they will cure the problem by empowering government. The only government solution to any problem is to make laws that restrict our freedoms. The government believes less human freedom, fewer human mistakes. I disagree. The communist way is an impenetrable bureaucracy that only the dictators can control. Where has that ever succeeded? Russia? China? Vietnam? East Germany? North Korea? Cuba? Chile tried it, and by a U.S.-funded revolution, the people freed themselves from the tyrants. Our press hindered their freedom at every step. Ask any Chilean about life under communism — I think they'd agree.

One look at the two Koreas shows the difference. The North Korean people are starving slaves in a dictatorship that threatens the world. South Korea, under capitalism, is rich and free and a threat to no one. And never forget the German wall, which kept the slaves in, while just across the street in West Germany, the same people became a world economic power.

Sahabzada Yaqub Ali Khan was the Pakistan ambassador to the United States (and eventually foreign minister) and a great friend of ours. It was through him that Bob Herring was offered the position of Pakistan's honorary consul in 1973. Bob would have been the only Pakistani consul in the United States at that time, so the offer was not to be taken lightly. Although consuls are not ambassadors and don't represent heads of state, honorary consuls provide assistance to citizens of their own country and the country they represent. They promote friendship and trade between the two countries.

This would be a distinguished position, a full-time job, with a lot of power to promote goodwill and establish trade. Bob would be called upon to work on many different levels. He was astonished that they would ask him. "I have companies in twenty-six countries, and that is really all that I can manage," he carefully replied. "I'm very grateful and appreciative and honored." Then he suggested, "Why don't you take Joanne?"

"Joanne!" They gasped. Their eyes widened and their jaws dropped. "Joanne!" There was nothing in the world they wanted *less* than Joanne. What in the world would they do with a *woman*? They had no women in government anywhere — and certainly *not* a blond American Christian who wore short skirts and kept her head uncovered. I was anathema to their every government and faith tradition. The *last* thing they wanted was me.

I think the only reason they decided to accept me was that they didn't want to offend Bob. They hoped that he would drill for oil in Pakistan. At that time, Pakistan was completely dependent on imported oil. Energy independence was essential to the Pakistani economy, and the Pakistanis saw Bob as their liberator.

Officially, I was first appointed honorary consul, in 1974, by President Zulfikar Ali Bhutto, Benazir's father. But then came this: "On April 4, 1979, the former Prime Minister [Bhutto] was hanged, after the Supreme Court upheld the death sentence passed by the Lahore High Court," according to *Story of Pakistan: A Multimedia Journey,* a best-selling CD-ROM and website that focuses on the political history of Pakistan. "The High Court had given him the death sentence on charges of murder of the father of a dissident PPP [Pakistan Peoples Party] politician."

President Mohammad Zia ul-Haq came into power, and the world said that Zia ordered the execution of President Bhutto. This was totally untrue. Bhutto had a political opponent that he thought might win the (very rigged) election...so Bhutto had him killed. He then was tried by his own judges and convicted of murder.

The Koran serves as the unofficial constitution of Pakistan. It exacts an eye for an eye and a tooth for a tooth. If you murder, you must die. The only thing that Zia did was to not commute Bhutto's sentence. In a country whose constitution demanded capital punishment for murder, Zia could not violate the law.

The communist press used Bhutto's death as disinformation in an attempt to destroy Zia, who was an encumbrance to the Russians. Zia, who had studied in the United States and was very Western and capitalistic, stood staunchly against the Russians and their form of government. The rest of the world didn't really know him or where he stood, and it didn't care. After all, Pakistan was unimportant to the United States in the 1970s and early 1980s. Thus, as always, the Americans did not take the time to understand Pakistan's law.

Why don't we ever ask if there is a good reason countries react as they do? We just judge them by our own standards and believe the destructive things that are said by those who profit from misunderstandings.

When Zia came into power, he kept me on as honorary consul. A miracle.

Zia invited Bob and me to Pakistan on the equivalent of a state visit. The fanfare and hoopla that accompanied such visits was trotted out, and Zia treated us like royalty.

During our first dinner, something clicked between Zia and me. From then on, we worked together often, though I never saw him alone. His aide was always with him, or if no aide was available, his wife was in attendance.

Zia respected my opinions and I respected his. If he had been the type of man many said he was, he would never have allowed a woman appointed by Bhutto to continue to serve as honorary consul.

If you watched *Charlie Wilson's War*, you saw how I stood up at the party I gave for President Zia in Houston and explained this publicly. Nobody could believe it. People of substance had come from England, Saudi Arabia, New York, and Washington to attend. I told them the story as I told it to you. I had thought about it a lot, and I realized I was risking everything I had . . . as I do quite often. But I was sick of the misunderstanding and wanted to tell the true story.

From the movie:

Charlie: "Want me to look it over?"

Joanne: "It's an introduction, Charlie. I'll be fine."

Joanne at the podium: "Today we honor President Zia ul-Haq of Pakistan. Before we go any further, I would like you all to know this: President Zia did not kill Bhutto."

Less than a decade later, Zia was killed by a bomb planted aboard his plane. Without him we could never have achieved victory against the Soviets in Afghanistan. He allowed the United States to send arms through Pakistan and held the line against the Soviet invasion. Far from being a despot, he was our greatest ally, and he desperately wanted to bring capitalism to Pakistan.

It's important to understand how disinformation works. A made-up story is sent to some columnist, usually at a small paper in a small town. The columnist prints it, thinking he has a scoop. He doesn't check it in any way. Once the story is printed, it is sent to a wire service. Sometimes the service sends it out, especially if it is startling and salacious. Remember, the press thrives on sensation. "If it bleeds, it leads" is the television journalist's motto. When the story gets on the wires, it goes everywhere (and that's not even taking into account the modern impact of the Internet in spreading these stories). No matter how untrue, if it's disseminated, it becomes accepted fact (something Mark Twain knew a century ago). As unimportant as I am, I have felt the bite of disinformation. Imagine how it works on an international scale for the president of a small country who was opposing a great war machine like the Soviet Union in the 1980s.

When Zia kept me on, nobody, including me, envisioned that together we would play a part in dislodging this danger to the free world. In my newfound position I simply tried to analyze what I could do for this country. I didn't want to merely get drunk sailors out of jail and give national-day parties, which is what the job often entails. Rather, I thought the best way for me to fight the communist encroachment on Pakistan's border was to show how capitalism works for the poor.

I wanted to work with the very poor, and eventually change their lives, by showing them how free enterprise works for people as individuals and for countries as a whole. It could lift their country from poverty to a better life.

America did not start rich. It took us more than one hundred years to achieve significant national wealth, and we're still working at it more than two hundred years later. With communism on their doorstep, I wanted the Pakistanis to see the difference between capitalism and communism. Instead of working in villages communally, Pakistanis could work in their own homes better, faster, and cheaper, capitalist style. By their own industry, they could make more money — and keep it.

Learning how to take good ideas and turn them into successful businesses takes experience. I didn't finish college, but I learned by working, first on Bob King's construction projects and later with Bob Herring, who showed me how corporations coordinate to achieve a specific goal. I also understood fashion design and had friends in the designer world.

"What does this country need?" I asked myself. "It needs money. How can I show people who are hungry that by embracing capitalism, they can make their lives better?"

I looked at what Pakistan had to offer. It had a wondrous display of artistic craftsmanship, but the designs were too exotic for Western décor. The pieces, such as an embroidered pillow or an interesting Oriental copper coffeepot, could be used as beautiful accents for the home. You might buy one, but you would not buy another. These were accent pieces, not items that would sell again and again. The Pakistanis needed to sell things to the West that would generate repeat sales.

How could I take these brilliant artists and utilize their talents to sell on the world market? I needed to think of mass-produced items that people would continue to buy — embroidered sheets, towels, handkerchiefs, and clothing. We would need to transform all of the designs into a more Western look.

Both Frette and Porthault made luxurious linens and sold them for thousands. The only thing that differentiated their products from the Pakistanis' fine sheets of equal thread count was the embroidery. Pakistan cotton was famous for its quality. I bought designer sheets as an example, sent them to Pakistan, and had them copied in new designs for a fraction of the cost.

Hand-blocked prints on fabric were a specialty of Pakistan craftsmen and women. These, too, were much prized in Western markets. In fact, *anything* handcrafted was a specialty skill the Pakistanis possessed.

However, the Pakistani Export Promotion Bureau was to become my enemy. Bureaucracies often are. They refused to rock the boat or their nice little niche that allowed them to pocket some of the bureau's money. I referred to them as "a sick ol' elephant." You can imagine the effect that had when the newspapers printed it. This endeared me to nobody.

I asked the designers I knew — Pierre Cardin, Yves St. Laurent, Givenchy, Oscar de la Renta, Bill Blass, and other big names in France, Italy, and the United States — to use the Pakistani hand-beaded sari fabrics in ensembles for runway shows. These generous geniuses graciously did it even though they were overwhelmed with the business of their own design houses. At that time, they were just beginning to expand the use of their names to cover everything from towels to tennis shoes.

The fashion shows with the Pakistani fabric ensembles attracted such notables as Nelson Rockefeller, movie stars, and the society people. Even Pierre Cardin himself came to help launch them. We did shows in Houston, New York, Atlanta, Washington, Tokyo, and London. The show in Japan was so successful, they demanded that we repeat it twice. Companies wanted to buy thousands of the out-fits. It would have revolutionized the life of the poor Pakistani women, who were confined to their houses by custom, tradition, and law, and who often had as many as sixteen or seventeen children. By making these clothes and using their embroidery on the wonderful silk and polyester fabrics already in production, they could actually feed their children. Through this initiative, I hoped that we could ultimately bring millions into the pockets of the poor.

But I learned that in a battle between economic development

and a country's cultural traditions, tradition wins. So while international designers clambered for Pakistani fabrics, the Export Promotion Bureau decided that it could not be responsible for producing the items on a timely basis. New demand would upset the stream of income the bureaucrats had constructed.

Still, while I was working with the villagers on the designer project, I became well-known in Pakistan, and the people liked and approved of me. Zia sent me by plane or by car to the villages and with great fanfare I would be introduced: "Mrs. Herring is here!" People lined up by the hundreds to see me. I was doing a man's job in a man's world, so... I had to become a man. And that's what they made me. Pakistani officials just started calling me "sir." I began to attend meetings with maybe one hundred businessmen and no women in attendance. Everybody addressed me as "sir," and I was given a seat of honor. When they called me on the phone, they would say, "Yes, sir," and "No, sir."

By now, I had become the consul of Morocco too. How did I become the consul of *two* Arab countries? It must have been the finger of fate... or was God again in need of a laugh?

Bob and I had been invited to Morocco for a New Year's celebration by the king's sister, Princess Fatima Zohra, and her husband. Her younger brother, Prince Moulay Abdullah (a well-known international playboy), was having a grand party in his specially built playhouse, which was fashioned after a Texas saloon. The Moroccans thought it novel in the extreme, but I felt at home. Black tie in a saloon was fun, especially as the prince chose me as his dinner partner.

The next night was the essence of Morocco. Musicians played and belly dancers swayed as course after course was placed before us. Moroccan food is fabled, a combination of French and Arabic, known to be one of the great cuisines of the world. It was served traditional style on huge, gleaming brass trays. Guests sat on tooled cushions surrounding the trays, on priceless Oriental carpets in silk-draped tented rooms … it was pure *One Thousand and One Nights,* come true.

Charles Fawcett was the darling of the whole Moroccan royal family and a special friend of King Hassan II. He had decided that I should meet the king to discuss the communist threat. I had no idea that with this simple invitation, Charles would set in motion a series of momentous events. I had several intimate dinners with Charles and various princes and ministers, who were looking me over to see if I was worthy of His Majesty's time. Women were not on the A-list in any way, shape, or form, in terms of seeing His Majesty. As a direct descendant of Muhammad, Hassan II was considered almost holy. Of course, I was moved from one event to another without knowing I was being judged. Behind the scenes, Charles was pushing every minute, and I had Bob's stellar reputation to support me.

One morning Charles Fawcett proudly announced that Bob and I had been vetted sufficiently to have a few minutes with His Majesty. For anyone to gain entrée to the king was considered equivalent to climbing Mount Everest. But for a woman to be included? Well, that was a peak beyond. Suffice it say, His Majesty gave few audiences.

We went to the palace, where King Hassan personally greeted us across acres of green marble bordered by sculptured fountains and arches. He led us to a beautiful, very minimalist salon. The décor was severely elegant, what one would see in a slick avant garde magazine. There was not an Arab element anywhere except in the tradition of serving tea. The silver service was a work of modern art, pure Mies van der Rohe. This was no ordinary king steeped in tradition, but a very modern monarch who played a crucial part in world history. He constantly acted as a balancing force among the Arab countries and the West. He understood both, and his brilliance and diplomacy are legend.

He was also extremely fit and handsome. He and his brother caused many a heart to flutter until he assumed the throne. At the time Bob and I met him, when he was king, he did not attend many parties and never included women when entertaining. When His Majesty gave a party, men and women were separated, and the ladies were not received.

I was intimidated by this honor, but I was sure that it was Bob that he wanted to see and thought that, by a miracle, I was allowed to tag along. The fifteen-minute audience stretched into two hours, during which His Majesty talked mainly to me. I was staggered.

When we returned to the hotel, standing in front of our suite was the chief of protocol of Morocco. He bowed to me, not Bob, and said, "His Majesty would like you to become the consul general of Morocco in America. You are the only government official his majesty has ever appointed personally. He usually leaves that honor in the hands of his ministers. You will be the only U.S. consul." He smiled, expecting me to swoon. That I didn't was a miracle.

At that moment I could have chucked Pakistan with its terrible problems and poverty into the cool Mediterranean! Oh, how I wanted to say yes. Instead I took a deep breath and said, "I am honored beyond anything in my life, but I am the consul general of Pakistan and thus am obligated to them. I am desperately sorry, but I must decline."

The minister staggered as if he had been shot. "*You must . . .* His Majesty said . . ." He could not continue. No one said no to His Majesty!

"Perhaps I could serve both countries," I said. "But you must ask His Majesty to request this, because I could not." The minister shook his head and went away. That night His Majesty had a dinner given for us which I was told I *must* attend. We explained that we had a flight at seven p.m. and thus must send our regrets.

"Impossible," said the minister. "This invitation is from His Majesty. The plane will wait!"

And it did. A commercial flight with two hundred very angry passengers waited until eleven o'clock that night so that we could savor a leisurely dinner. As we boarded the plane, the outraged, weary passengers indicated that impaling us on the nearest fence should have been obligatory. Fortunately we boarded first and exited ahead of the impromptu Moroccan lynch mob.

Two weeks later, some very displeased Pakistani diplomats reported that I was to serve both countries as consul general. At the time I thought back to a friend who had married into a multimillion-dollar business family from another country. I asked her, "Are you going to wear the saris and the national costume?" "No," she said, "I'm an American and I don't know how to wear them. I'm just going to wear what I've always worn." I related to her experience: I had been given many caftans, and walking in them was very difficult for me. The Moroccan ladies looked enchanting in them. They knew how to hold their caftans, while I just stumbled along trying to imitate them, but I looked like a bundle of laundry. I soon realized that you had to grow up knowing how to wear a caftan. In Pakistan I tried saris and they fell in my soup. Thus I decided, rather unwisely, to always dress as an American and to wear exactly what I wore at home — which was not always considered correct in either Pakistan or Morocco. The Moroccans were more liberal, though, and didn't seem to care.

The Pakistanis seemed to understand that my motives were pure and that I had never taken a dime in all the years of work and mountains of time that I had invested in their country. Still, some tried to bribe me. I don't know who was behind it — perhaps those who wanted to discredit me. Or perhaps it was those who wanted to control me. I'll never know. I should have told the president, but I just ignored it, as I did most insults.

This is what happened: I had an appointment with an army general whom I had never before met. He looked me straight in the eye and asked, "How would you like to have a little Swiss bank account?"

I said, "I would like that very much!"

"I think that can be arranged. Would you be open to that sort of thing?" he cajoled.

I had no intention whatsoever of accepting his bribe. I had made a promise to myself and to Pakistan that I would never take a penny for my services until I could see that my efforts were actually helping to raise the people out of poverty. So I said, "I cannot take anything but a thank-you." The look on his face was the most astonished I've seen before or since. He simply could not believe that I would turn down his offer.

In another unfortunate incident, two Pakistani ladies that I worked with took my designs and products to Saudi Arabia and sold them for thousands. They made a mint, while I never made a penny. In their defense, they tried to get me to join them. I said, "Remember, this is for the poor. They must make money before we do. I expect that to take five years. I keep my promises." But they did not, and they didn't give a penny to the poor villagers who should have received the money. They pocketed it. It was like a kick in the stomach to me, but it was a great lesson: I should have had contracts for these people. I lost that round but continued hoping for success, which I knew would come slowly, if at all.

The people I was working to help were so poor and isolated that their villages had no roads in or out. No one even had a bicycle. They had no electricity, so they certainly had no radio or television (so virtually no contact whatsoever with the outside world) or anything we consider necessities.

That's why their interpretation of my careful instructions on how to copy and embroider a handkerchief did not strike me as unusual. They knew how to do the work, but they didn't understand why it had to look exactly like the original I gave them to mimic. When some of the handkerchiefs turned up in odd shapes, often with three corners, I gently pointed out that the handkerchiefs must have four corners. They looked at me and said, "Why? You can still blow your nose on it." There was no arguing that!

I have never forgotten the handkerchief story. It taught me how far we had to go in this closed world and how little we understood each other. Our lives were so vastly different. (The American poor would be considered Pakistan's rich.)

In what became another unsuccessful attempt to foster capitalism in Pakistan, I also tried to help the country's small businessmen. I told them, "You aren't making enough money because you don't have the means to advertise your products. The boxes you are using are not attractive. Presentation is everything when you're selling.

"You don't have any money to export because you have to pay an agent in whatever country you're exporting to. You don't have any money for anybody to solicit business for you abroad.

"Why not form consortiums of five men in different types of businesses and pool your money to advertise and share transportation costs and the cost of an agent in another country to market your products? All of that is necessary to participate in world trade. This is needed or your business will not expand."

I started a box company whose sole purpose was to provide boxes to small businesses. By mass-producing the same box, but in different sizes, we made the process more efficient, cheaper, and faster. I envisioned the boxes being covered in shiny paper resembling black patent leather to make them look professional and attractive. The merchants could buy them to hold their products and customize them by adding their business name on top, along with a seal of gold, silver, or bronze. I hoped the idea would give the businessmen an incentive to get a gold seal on the box, which would mean, "top-of-the-line, quality products."

All of my work was in vain. At first the men thought my ideas were great. Then they looked at each other and said, "Why should I help him?" They had never tried collaboration and it was so foreign to them that they rejected it. Unfortunately, I faced this sentiment regardless of whom I talked to. The people were just not ready for Western ideas.

Predictably the box company ran up against the Export Promotion Bureau. The bureau did business with a box company in Switzerland and insisted that we use the same company. The Swiss are famous for everything from chocolate to finance, but in this case, design was not one of their strengths. The box venture, too, ended in defeat (and the Pakistani/Swiss boxes were awful!).

The market mentality of these countries is "Nothing is done for nothing. If you want something, pay me first." You might give alms to a beggar, but you don't give him a job unless he can benefit you in some way. The bureau personnel were not offered a percentage, so they blocked the orders.

My dream was shattered by what I call the "crust" of any developing nation. History has taught us that the crust is made up of the political potentates and the very rich families who often profit from selling goods at competitive prices on the open market, while gaining a sizable profit by paying workers a low wage. Under such a system, the middle class is often not allowed to develop — to break through the "crust" to a higher standard of living. Without a middle class, no country can ever be really self-sufficient and successful.

As you know, in the United States, the middle class is a true force and the true source of our strength. Our wealth is derived largely from the industry and integrity of our middle class. One of the great tragedies of today is that so many countries in Africa, the Middle East, and South America, as well as China, communist North Korea, and Vietnam, suffer from the lack of a middle class. The poor are kept on low wages so that the rich and bureaucrats can make big profits. They do not allow the poor to break through the crust.

It was this barrier that Pakistan could not break through, a barrier supported by people who would not profit personally from these plans to help the poor raise their standards of living by earning what they should.

I truly wish there were more leaders like Zia to help with our mission today. He knew how to break through the crust. Zia was a revelation. He was a truly caring leader who wanted his country to rise, and it did while he was alive. I saw it, and you could feel hope in the air. Bhutto had entranced me with his charm but certainly was no hero. He became rich on the backs of his people. Zia, a humanitarian, was his complete antithesis and yet the world considered him a monster. Every single person that I sent to Pakistan to meet Zia came back with the same impression I had of him. I was determined to do everything I could to dispel Zia's ill-founded "monstrous" reputation created by the Soviets.

Walter Cronkite, David Brinkley, and a host of other journalists begged me to get them into Afghanistan but didn't want anything to do with the Pakistan president. I didn't agree with everything Walter said, but, like all of us, I had a great affection for him. I said, "Okay, Walter, I will get you to Afghanistan, but you have to interview Zia."

"I don't want to interview Zia," he said. "He's a monster!"

"No, Walter, he's not, and that's the only way I'll get you into Afghanistan," I replied. I had to get him in through Zia anyway.

"All right, I'll do it," he said.

When Walter came back I sat next to him at a dinner party.

"What did you think of Zia?" I asked.

"I loved him," Walter said. "But he lied to me about having the nuclear bomb."

"Walter, he is the president of Pakistan. He doesn't owe you any explanations," I said. "His only responsibility is to the people of Pakistan, not to you and your television network."

Zia told me that it was ridiculous to think he would ever even think of using nuclear weapons, except for protection. He laughed when he said, "India has a bomb, Russia has a bomb, and China has a bomb. All of them are twenty times bigger than I am. It would be ridiculous for me to even think of invading them. I just don't want them to invade me, and they would like to very much!"

As a last rejoinder, Walter said, "Well, you know, the *Ladies' Home Journal* did a poll, and they decided that I had more integrity than God." He looked like a little boy, telling me some marvelous thing someone had said about him.

"Oh, Walter, you *are* wonderful," I said. And he was. But the *Ladies' Home Journal's* belief in his integrity didn't mean anything compared to the issues swirling around Pakistan and Afghanistan on the eve of the Soviet invasion of Afghanistan. Even the wise Walter Cronkite failed to grasp how important my friend President Zia was going to be in breaking the Soviet bloc.

With the compliments of

The Embassy of United Arab Emirates

Washington, D. C.

CHAPTER 19

Cross-Dressing in Afghanistan

*I*t all began one summer night in 1980, when I was sitting with Pakistani president Zia ul-Haq in the living room of his little bungalow in Islamabad. I had been described as the queen of Texas (*People*), a Marilyn Monroe or Zsa Zsa Gabor look-alike (the *New York Post*), and the Texan who acts like a duchess (*Paris Match*).

I was doing a man's job in a man's world, yet I could never escape these descriptions. The only time my intellect was ever mentioned was in *Fortune* magazine, and once by the BBC.

So here's one more description in those terms: I was blond and Presbyterian — a very unlikely confidante of the Islamic president of Pakistan. Zia was just about the most vilified man in the world at that time. The Soviets wanted him *dead*! He had revitalized Pakistan, and people were beginning to see changes. Pakistan was moving away from previous governments, where corruption reigned and hope had been squelched. I know because I saw it. Now, just as Pakistan began to rise, the Soviet Union invaded Afghanistan. Russian troops were poised on the borders of Pakistan, a heartbeat away from invasion.

It seemed like Zia and I were just about the most unlikely pair in history to stand against the juggernaut of the Soviet Union, but we wanted the same world — one where people could be rewarded for their efforts and where prosperity had a chance. There were many comments about our relationship, but nobody understood it.

George Crile wrote in his book, *Charlie Wilson's War*: "[President Zia] was so spellbound by Herring, and took her so seriously, that to the utter dismay of his entire foreign office, he made her Pakistan's roving ambassador to the world and even awarded her his country's highest civilian honor, the title of *Quaid-e-Azam*, or 'Great Leader.' Charlie Wilson says that Zia would leave cabinet meetings just to take Joanne's calls. 'There was no affair with Zia,' Wilson recalls, 'but it's impossible to deal with Joanne and not deal with her on a sexual basis. No matter who you are, you take those phone calls.'"

Actually, our relationship was a meeting of the minds and a similarity of objectives — nothing more. Still, because I admired his courage so much, I had a deep affection for Zia and what he stood for.

For example, Zia told me that President Jimmy Carter had offered him five million dollars in aid. Zia shocked the world when he responded, "Mr. President, that's *peanuts!*"

"Why didn't you take it?" I asked. "Any money is better than no money."

"If I took it," said Zia, "it would not be enough to save my country, but it *is* enough to trigger a Soviet invasion. They would call me an American puppet and take my country in five days." He bowed his head. "I cannot retaliate because they would accuse me of invading them. Their excuse for expansion has always been that they are protecting their borders and are frightened of U.S. incursions."

"Oh," I said, "really, 'protecting their borders'...Angola, Cuba, Nicaragua, El Salvador — those are pretty far-flung borders."

"Exactly," he said. "It's obvious that they are starting empires in every corner of the world. I ache with despair for my people. I have three million Afghan refugees in Peshawar. We have opened our borders to them and we have been giving them the best we can. My people are hungry. But they are sharing with the Afghans, who have nothing."

Pakistan was not in favor in Washington at the time. President Carter was calling the Soviet invasion of Afghanistan a "tribal war," as if the locals were peevishly killing each other and asking the friendly communists to come settle their village spat.

"We cannot hold out against the Russians when they come — and they will," Zia said.

"You have a great army," I said.

"But no arms," he replied. "Your president Carter refuses to believe that the Soviets have any intentions of capturing Afghanistan or Pakistan. He actually thinks he can talk to them and they will pull out. Right now their planes are overflying my borders, bombing my villages, and killing my people. I cannot retaliate because that will give them an excuse to invade us, saying *we* attacked first and that they had to defend themselves. That is always their answer and excuse."

In fact, the Soviets were unloading cargo planes full of tanks and Hind helicopters and weaponry every forty-eight minutes.

Russian Hind helicopters hovered over helpless Afghan villagers, shooting anything that moved: men, women, children, babies in their mothers' arms, sheep and goats. Soviet planes dropped small, shiny butterfly bombs that looked like toys…and when children would run to pick them up, the explosives would blow off their hands, condemning them to an agonizing death by infection and gangrene. By killing children slowly and painfully, they hoped to break the will of the Afghan people as the Communists had in Vietnam.

This was no tribal war. It was the domination of a proud people by a cold, voracious empire that would stop at nothing in its quest for global domination and a warm-water port in the Arabian Sea.

Earlier, I had asked myself why any country would take the trouble to invade Afghanistan. There was nothing there. No oil, no industry, few raw materials. Just stubborn, ragged tribesmen who wanted to be left alone. And why Pakistan? They had nothing either.

I looked at the map, and there was the answer: the Strait of

Hormuz, the enormously strategic, improbably constricted waterway between the Gulf of Oman and the Persian Gulf.

The strait is thirty-five miles wide at its narrowest point. It is bordered by Iran, the United Arab Emirates, and Oman. The only passage to the open ocean for large parts of the Persian Gulf, it is the world's most critical choke point for the millions and millions of barrels of crude oil that pass through it on their way to fuel the world — every day.

If the Strait of Hormuz was controlled by the Russians, they could cut off U.S. tankers. It wouldn't be our cars and our air conditioners that would be threatened. It would be our factories, our chemical plants, our building industry — the lifestyle and jobs of every American. The Soviets could take down the entire economy of the United States.

I read later that President Richard Nixon said in a conversation with the president of Somalia, "The Soviet aim is to gain control of the two great treasure houses on which the West depends — the energy treasure of the Persian Gulf and the mineral treasure house of central and southern Africa."

I had been spouting anticommunism for years. But when I went to Washington with this little message about the potential for the economic destruction of the United States at the hands of the Soviets and repeated it to any member of Congress who would listen, I saw some interesting changes in how powerful people reacted. The glazed expression on their faces that always appeared when Afghanistan was mentioned suddenly changed. A new understanding dawned. A new urgency emerged. Afghanistan mattered after all.

And now I was sitting with the president of Pakistan on a summer night with waves of geostrategic conflict washing over our thoughts. I felt the horrors of the human tragedy unfolding on his border. I knew the political importance of this moment in history.

But what could I do? I was of no importance on the world scene. But I remembered that in a toolbox even small tools can be useful.

"Mr. President," I said, "I have a thought. I don't have much to offer, but I do have one thing. A widow's mite, so to speak."

I wasn't sure if Muslim presidents of Muslim nations knew much about Jesus's remarks in the New Testament about the widow's mite, but I pressed on.

"I had a television show for fifteen years. I know how to interview people. My son Robin seems to think if we make a film showing exactly what the Russians are doing, the people of the West might listen. What if we showed what is going on in the refugee camps and the atrocities that the Soviets are committing against women and children? A picture really is worth a thousand words. People can argue politics and policies all day long...but if they see suffering with their own eyes, they can't deny it."

"How do you propose to do it?" he asked thoughtfully. "And how will you get it shown?"

"You have a television station," I said. "Can't we get what we need from your people?"

"I can send you to the refugee camps in Pakistan with my men," he said. "I can get you that far to film what is happening with the refugees. But I cannot be involved in Afghanistan.

"If you go into Afghanistan," he continued, "I will not know it. I will not know where you go, who you go with, or what happens to you. I cannot rescue you or help you in any way if you encounter trouble...which you will.

"If you do not return, I will not know that you ever went or what happened to you, because if I did the Soviets can accuse me of sending American filmmakers into Afghanistan. I will again be compromised as an American puppet. The least little thing I do will be exactly what they are looking for as a reason to invade Pakistan. I cannot risk my country in any way. You will be entirely on your own."

Fortunately, I was never on my own. Robin and Charles Fawcett were there. And God was certainly with all of us, or we would never have made it. We believed that He wanted us to help the Afghan people and also help our own country, which seemed oblivious to the gathering Soviet storm.

"Do you have any access to Afghan leaders or anyone else who can help you there?" President Zia asked.

"Strangely enough, I do," I said. "He's an American, but he's been living among the Afghans. He's one of the most remarkable men in the world. His name is Charles Fawcett." Galvanized by the Soviet atrocities in Afghanistan, my friend Charles had lived with the muja-hideen (Afghan freedom fighters) already, fighting beside them. Their leaders trusted and loved him.

Zia was as good as his word. I returned to Houston and laid my plans. Charles was excited about making our movie, and since no Pakistani cameraman could accompany us, my son Robin King volunteered. Robin was only seventeen, but he had an adventurous streak, and he already had experience beyond his years and multiple film credits under his belt, having been around the world four times working for different film companies. He was making progress on his career, but as he did many times, he gave it all up to serve his country.

Robin and I traveled to Pakistan, where we met up with Charles, and the three of us set off for Afghanistan — alone, unarmed, and with very little money — in December of 1979, the dead of winter.

The wind cut like a knife, but we arrived safely at the refugee camp at the Pakistani-Afghan border. I slept under about eighteen blankets and my sable coat. It was like lying under a dead hippo, yet I was still so cold, I could not sleep. Meanwhile, the refugees, some three million of them, stretching as far as you could see, were sleeping on the ground with no blankets, no tents, no shoes, in layers of thin, ragged clothing. At night, I could hear the children coughing. They sounded like little foxes.

The hard, brown soil was carved in grooves from wind erosion. There were no trees. The refugees had uprooted the small, dry bushes that had been there to serve as fuel for their small cooking fires. There was little water, and what water there was, was so polluted that it sickened and killed many. For people who must wash five times a day to prepare for their prayers, this situation was painful and dangerous.

Little canals were cut through the surface of this parched earth, so dry that it was as hard as iron. People washed their utensils in it, bathed in it, and drank from it. In warmer climates, cholera would probably have been rampant. Due to the extreme cold, there was none in the camp at the time, but many other preventable illnesses were rampant. There was no medicine.

The Afghan children were so thin, they looked as if they had matchsticks for limbs. Most were sick, their bellies inflated from starvation. Patient and listless, they had no energy to move. Some of the children tried to play with little stones.

I interviewed a widow who had had five children. Her three living children were all maimed, with stumps for limbs and empty sockets where their eyes should have been. Like many other little ones, they had excitedly run to pick up the brightly colored Soviet "toys." Their mother had shouted for them to stop, stop — there was death in the toys. Like kids everywhere, they had scampered ahead anyway and picked them up, only to fall, screaming, in an explosion of blood and bone.

In spite of their suffering, they were beautiful people, with skin the color of coffee with lots of cream, aquiline features, and green eyes. They weren't pitiful or defeated. They did not weep in public for their dead. They asked for nothing.

When we told them how we were going to use this film to get them medicine and food, they would shake their fists and say, "Don't send us food. Don't send us medicine. We can live without food and medicine. But we cannot live without *freedom*. Send us guns!"

They needed them — big ones. Their stories told us why. The Soviet Hind helicopters, flying just thirty feet above the helpless people, were shooting and shredding everything that moved. It had become a game for the pilots.

The Hinds, heavily armored gunships with titanium rotors, were fifty-five feet long and twenty feet high, with thirty-millimeter cannons, rockets, machine guns, and antitank missiles. The Hind was impregnable against anything the mujahideen could throw at it. The Russians called it the Crocodile. The Afghans called it Shaitan-Arba: Satan's Chariot.

On the ground, the Russians were using terror tactics and KGB-perfected torture, impaling the Afghan people and cutting off their arms and legs. They assaulted pregnant women with cattle prods until milk poured from the women's breasts. Gangs of soldiers raped women until their bladders burst.

They would take the children from a village, hold them in front of their parents and slowly, slowly cut their throats. They would pile dissenters on the ground like firewood. Then they would drive their sixty-ton tanks over them or set them on fire. I could not conceive of such cruelty. I felt helpless and sick, so inadequate in the face of such need.

We packed up our gear. It was time to leave the camp and go to the tribal area buffer zone on our way into Afghanistan.

This buffer zone had been created by the British in 1893 as a bulwark between Afghanistan and Pakistan while the latter was still part of India. The British had tried to conquer Afghanistan and met with decisive, violent failure…and this tribal area was still one of the most dangerous places on earth. There was no law. It was populated by various tribal groups, thieves, and bands of outlaws. They fought over turf and stole from travelers to support themselves. Drug dealers, outlaws, and fugitives were everywhere. There was no border control. The area belonged to no one and no government.

This would later be rumored to be the impenetrable hiding place of Osama bin Laden, but at that time it was simply a place where no one in their right mind would go. And there we were — Charles Fawcett, Robin, and I.

Charles led us to a small village from which a bus crossed into Afghanistan. He gave me some ragged Afghan clothes: a coat that came to my knees, baggy trousers, and a pie-plate hat covered in lambs' wool that almost covered my eyes. I pushed my hair up into my hat and wrapped a scarf around my face and neck. Robin and Charles wore similar clothes.

I had no idea where we were going or where we went. We simply followed Charles who said we were heading to a mujahideen outpost in Afghanistan, but he said he deliberately kept us in the dark about our location because if word leaked out about our visit, the Soviets would wipe out the camp.

We trudged. We rode in the backs of trucks and oxcarts. At dangerous checkpoints my comrades actually stuffed me into a big oil barrel and nailed down the lid. A woman — a white Western woman — was more dangerous contraband than heroin or weapons.

Tiny snowflakes swirled around us like lacy ash. The cold wind penetrated to our bones. But I was beyond caring.

At last, our truck arrived at the warriors' desolate outpost. I was suddenly more frightened than I had ever been in my life. I thought, "I have broken all their rules." Here I was, a woman, face uncovered, dressed as a man, walking among men. I began to understand what I had done. What had seemed a great adventure was suddenly a death trap. I had never experienced real war or suffering. I had led my son into this morass of danger where death was as close as a shadow.

I knew how the mujahideen treated infidels. Whenever they caught a Russian soldier, they'd give him over to their women to skin him alive. The women would skin him slowly, starting at the testicles, moving toward the eyeballs…and then they would take the body to a road, to send a clear, grisly message to the Soviets. Retaliation was their only defense against the Russian atrocities. They had to at least frighten the Russians, as they had no way to kill them. This was war, a brutal one-sided war, and the victims were striking back in the only ways they could.

At one time Afghanistan was the fruit basket of the Middle East, poor but viable. Women were not forced to wear burkas and were encouraged to go to school. The horrors of war had forced them to depend on their religion to unite the many tribes to fight together. They fought under the banner of Islam, and now they regarded anyone who violated it as worse than animals.

These fighters would think nothing of killing me — and Charles and Robin for good measure — and leaving our bleeding bodies in the snow. I had never felt such cold, heart-stopping fear for myself, my friend, and especially my son.

When we arrived at the outpost, Charles and Robin got out of the truck with their camera equipment, and I emerged from my barrel. Thousands and thousands of mujahideen sat on the cold ground before us, fanned out on the hills of a natural amphitheater, as far as I could see. We stood there like a sacrifice.

The men began to stir. I braced myself. They leapt to their feet, and all I could see were what seemed to be thousands upon thousands of ragged fighters, their faces streaked with dirt, raising their World War I rifles in the air, shouting and screaming.

"They're going to kill me," I thought.

They were not going to kill me. They were welcoming us. Cheering with gratitude, overwhelmed that someone had actually come to help them.

They had felt that no one in the whole world cared…and now our little trio represented hope.

From that point on, I never questioned why I was there with war-hardened Muslim men who waved captured Russian testicles at their enemies.

They had so little, but they had killed their only sheep, used all their flour, and made us a meal I will never forget. They found a table and provided wooden chairs. Where they got them I had no idea. There were even forks and knives for the three of us. As we prepared to eat, my Afghan guide whispered in my ear, "Do not eat it."

"I must!" I whispered back to him. "They've given us everything they have!"

"You cannot eat it," he said. "Push it around your plate. Eat a bit of bread. But don't eat anything else. It will make you sick." He was sure our Western constitutions would not be able to handle the nearly raw wartime food-preparation techniques of these warriors.

I swallowed my tears and did as he said, my heart aching over it. Hungry men crowded three deep around the table, watching us eat, so proud to offer us this glorious feast. It was an expression of gratitude, and it affected me almost more than any experience in my life.

It was decided that I needed a bodyguard. Our hosts chose a seven-foot Pashtun with a long handlebar mustache and a turban that made him seem even taller. He was straight out of central casting. His only weapon was a scimitar stuck in his belt. It was thought that he was strong enough to defend himself without a gun. Guns were scarce. We heard stories of how the Afghan men checked them out like library books and went out in groups with their treasured firearms. They survived on leaves, berries, and bits of dry bread. They fought as long as they could, and then returned to camp, and the next group went out. The guns were 1914 Enfield rifles, state-of-the-art during the First World War...more than sixty years before. That was all they had.

For a photograph taken at this lunch, my bodyguard was handed a Kalashnikov (an AK-47 captured from the Russians), but he had to give it right back to his superior, who needed it more than he did.

My bodyguard was to save my life and my son's too.

The next day, I visited the women's quarters. The women lived separately from the men in a camp made of ragged tents and shelters thrown together with packing cases or whatever large pieces of board they could find. Most had only thin rectangles of cloth that blew in the cutting wind.

The women were as thin as shadows. The oldest, around thirty, had no teeth. The harsh life and meager food, combined with yearly childbearing, took its toll. Every one of them had lost a child to disease or malnutrition. Every one of them had seen friends and children mowed down by the Hind helicopters. And every one of them stood straight and proud, as determined as their men to fight to the last drop of blood.

We wanted to film the terrain as part of the film, so we drove away from the camp, but the weather warmed up during the day and the sun felt so good that we traveled farther than we'd planned. We were standing on the side of a mountain when suddenly we looked up and saw a tiny speck. It was drawing closer quickly, and my brain just registered, "Oh, a helicopter."

Then I knew.

This Russian Hind, with its armored belly and its cannons and machine guns, was coming to kill. It somehow knew where we were, or where to look for us.

I thought, "I have brought my *son* to this, and now he might not live through it!" Besides the initial scare when we first arrived and the bitter cold conditions, up until that moment I had felt like I was on a great adventure, but not in a war. Being killed in a helicopter raid had never crossed my mind. Now we were facing it. I saw with clarity the gravity of my actions. What if my irresponsibility killed my son?

My giant bodyguard grabbed me by the belt. I folded like a kitten in its mother's mouth, and he stuffed me into something in the ground. Whether it was a hole or a rock crevice I am not sure. All I knew was that it was dark.

I was too terrified to remember to pray. There was shouting and noise, the whirring thump of the rotor blades, and a sensation of horror and guilt. I didn't know where my son was or if he was alive. I later learned he had been thrown behind some rocks and quickly covered with leaves.

The helicopter did not stay long. It sprayed shots and moved on. We were too small a target. Most likely its orders were to decimate a village, and we happened to be in its path. It had not been hunting us.

When they pulled me out of the hole, I shook uncontrollably for two hours. It was all so fast, unexpected, and horrible. That night I fell to my knees in gratitude.

In the end, the documentary film we made had no red-carpet premieres. It was not entertaining — but it showed the truth. It caught the faces and the stories of the people whose lives had been destroyed by the Soviets.

Robin was only a teenager when he filmed the Afghanistan warriors. Without my knowledge, he also lived alone with the communist guerrillas in El Salvador three times, bringing back footage and interviews to prove that the conflict in El Salvador was not a civil war but a communist revolution supported by Cuba and Vietnam. Robin is one of the few people who can say they've been shot at by both Soviet and American helicopters. He and Charles had led the first *60 Minutes* film crew to the Afghanistan border.

Charles Fawcett later showed the movie to large audiences in London, Paris, New York, Atlanta, Tokyo, Houston, and Rome. I would show it to Bill Casey, head of the CIA, Senator John Tower of the U.S. Senate Armed Services Committee, countless members of Congress — Republican and Democrat alike — and all those in a position to help, including Charlie Wilson...which eventually brought about some pretty big changes in the world as we knew it. It was this film that Robin, Charles, and I made that would pique Charlie Wilson's interest. Charlie would listen avidly as Robin suggested the Stinger missiles as a weapon to help the Afghans fight the Russians. He asked Robin many questions about the Afghans' ability to fight the Soviets and prevail.

But at this point all of that was in the future, and we were just concerned about getting our precious film safely out of Afghanistan. We jolted and bounced and staggered back to Islamabad.

Upon our arrival, just to keep things interesting, President Zia decided to host a state dinner for us.

I had no clothes to wear, and Robin and Charles didn't either. Robin still considers that dinner the most embarrassing experience of his life. Our Western clothes had all disappeared. Our Afghan attire was hardly appropriate, and besides, it smelled bad and was infested with fleas.

A Pakistani friend, Miriam, wife of General Habibullah, loaned me a beautiful salwar kameez (a long tunic over pants). I went out to buy some panty hose, but the locals had never heard of panty hose. The only thing available was stockings, but I had no garters or any way to hold them up. I tried to twist and knot them, but they eventually drooped and sagged around my ankles. The only purse I had was a Louis Vuitton satchel that I had dragged all over Pakistan and Afghanistan. By now, my satchel looked as weathered as a World War II French Resistance carrier bag. I placed it on the coffee table as I sat with President Zia before dinner.

"What is that?" the president asked, recoiling in horror. He motioned for a servant to sweep it away.

"Oh, Mr. President!" I bleated. "Please excuse me! That's my purse!"

Zia looked at me like I'd been toting my personal items around in a sheep's bladder, but he was as gracious as ever. "Ah," he breathed to an aide. "Please take Mrs. Herring's . . . uh, *purse* . . . to a safe place."

That evening Charles, Robin, and I were the shabbiest group that had ever passed the threshold of the president's house. No one raised an eyebrow or allowed a look of shock to cross their faces. Had I been in a tiara and resplendent clothes from head to foot, I could not have been treated more elegantly than I was, wearing a borrowed outfit with my nylons puddling around my ankles.

At dinner I was seated at the center of a long table as the guest of honor. The first course, an elegant soup, was served by white-gloved waiters with tall, snowy turbans with pleated fastenings that looked like beautiful fans. The military leaders' uniforms looked like something out of an exotic movie, every crease knife sharp, every gold button gleaming.

After the soup was served, I waited for Mrs. Zia, as hostess, to signal the dinner's commencement by raising her spoon, but she did not. No one moved. We sat and sat and sat in lovely silence as the soup cooled.

After several "centuries" of polite waiting, with the guests in their finest regalia staring blankly ahead, it crossed my mind that maybe in this country, the guest of honor was supposed to start the dinner. If I was wrong, it would be a great embarrassment in a country where manners had been passed down from maharajas and British viceroys.

"Oh, Lord!" I prayed silently. "Please let this be right!" I trusted that God knew about manners in all cultures. Timorously, I lifted my spoon.

For a moment nothing happened, and I prepared to die for the second time that week. Then, without changing expression, the guests reached for their spoons and began to eat.

Another bullet dodged.

Once we were back in the States, movie people and Universal Studios tried to buy Robin's film. They called almost daily, as did news organizations all over the world who wanted to get footage of battle scenes and a genuine helicopter attack. He wrestled with allowing them to use it, but as we had so little contact with these film reps and the first script was rough, Robin was concerned that it might be edited and used in ways that would be detrimental to the Afghan cause and the upheavals fomenting in Pakistan.

Betty Beale

What One Hears at White House Parties

WASHINGTON, D.C. — Ronald Reagan, who just celebrated his 71st birthday, is thanking God these days for the darnedest favor. At the luncheon the Reagans gave for the Roosevelt family, Mrs. James Roosevelt, who was seated on the president's right, told him her bright red hair was natural. "I don't have dyed hair," she told him, although many people who see her flaming locks apparently think so.

'Nor do I," said the president. Then, turning to Mrs. Elliott Roosevelt on his left, he said, "Look, Patty, I am getting some gray hairs. Thank God, because everyone thinks I dye my hair."

At his dinner for Egyptian President Hosni Mubarak, the president gave another reason for being cheered. Although he admitted he faces a battle getting government entitlement programs switched to the states, when it was suggested the governors will probably fight it, he said, "On the contrary. It's what they've wanted right along. I had a group of governors and mayors here and they are as pleased as they can be. And that includes some of the Democratic governors," he added, mentioning Arizona's Bruce Babbitt and Georgia's George Busbee.

Mingling in the Blue Room before the divine concert by violinist Itzhak Per-

-lman were Japan's number-one designer, Hanae Mori, and husband Ken, Hanae wearing one of her own rich creations, embroidered purple satin, and a most unusual hairdo. Did you ever see a Japanese woman with kinky hair? Well, the famed Hanae had her black, shoulder-length tresses permanented so tight the result was what black beauty salons call the "bush style." It's just another example of always wanting what you don't have.

David Mahoney and his beautiful wife Hildegarde were chatting with Secretary of State and Mrs. Al Haig. From Houston came the white-thatched corporation president Harris Masterson and wife Carroll, he wearing his long gold-and-malachite link necklace and little round diamond buttons on the vest of his dinner suit.

Also winging in from Houston for the night was curvaceous, blonde Joanne Herring, who, following the recent death of her husband Bob, is selling their Houston house and is uncertain where she will light. Now honorary consul for Pakistan, she may do something more for that country in the line of promoting their fabrics, arts and crafts, as she has done at fashion shows in this country. She said she may accept an offer President Zia made her a

WHITE HOUSE GUEST Joanne Herring of Houston spied a friend at the Reagans' dinner for Egyptian President and Mrs. Mubarak.

CHAPTER 20

When Dreams Die

Under the patronage of
The President of the United States
and Mrs. Reagan
The Committee
requests the pleasure of your company
at
The National Symphony Ball
on Friday, the second of December
at eight o'clock
Sheraton Washington Hotel
Washington, District of Columbia

White Tie

*T*he two most momentous events in my life struck within a week of each other in December 1979. One would rip at my heart, the other give purpose for my last days. The Soviet invasion of Afghanistan that month led to what has become a lifelong war to win peace in Afghanistan. The attack on my heart began on Christmas.

Bob and I had the best Christmas morning of our lives in 1979. It was warm and wonderful, everything Christmas should be.

Christmas afternoon, Bob suddenly said, "Call Denton. I don't feel well." He felt nauseated. I called our best friend and the best man at our wedding, the famous heart surgeon Denton Cooley, who lived just behind us.

Denton raced over. "He's my best friend, he's sick, and I don't even have a stethoscope," he said, apologizing with tears in his eyes. As a surgeon, he didn't carry one like a general practitioner would.

Refusing help, Bob retreated to the bathroom, and then we heard a crash. He had fallen. Denton immediately called an ambulance and rode to the hospital with him.

After virtually every consequential doctor in Houston had examined him, they said, "We have good news and bad news. You do not have heart trouble. The bad news is you have lung cancer. But there is a treatment that's been effective."

We had older friends who had been diagnosed with lung cancer and lived for twenty-five years after surgery. We did not realize for almost a year, though, that Bob's was the most virulent of all lung cancers and that it was also inoperable.

During the first year of Bob's diagnosis, we were convinced that he was treatable. He worked, I traveled, and we soldiered on. But near the first anniversary of his diagnosis, the monster roared, and I became a full-time caregiver. Bob began a special treatment program in which he was completely isolated in a germ-free atmosphere. I stayed outside on the other side of the window from morning until night. Again, I abandoned everything, even my children, to stay by his side. Just as he appreciated my traveling with him when he was well, he now told me how much it meant to have me there with him when he was sick.

We tried every new method of treatment known to man. I even took him to Mexico, where there were claims that they had cured lung cancer. I brought him home on a hospital gurney. Ricky and Sandra di Portanova found a doctor in Switzerland who was experimenting with interferon. Mary Lasker was one of the country's best-known advocates for medical research and its funding. Her institute had cornered the market on interferon to use for research. This great lady said Bob could have as much of the interferon as he needed.

The doctor from Switzerland had a delicate form of interferon that had to be handled by a doctor in-flight. It was against the law to prescribe it in the United States because it had not been approved by the Food and Drug Administration. I got on the phone with every significant medical man in Houston, but not one would let me use this new formula. I screamed and wept for hours with the doctors, until finally they couldn't take it anymore. They figured Bob was dying anyway. The drug was administered, and it *did* change the number of cancer cells in his blood, but it was too late.

I know Bob must have been in horrible pain, but he never once complained. He never said he hurt; he never said anything, except "I love you" every time I walked in the room.

I truly felt at the time that Bob was more worthy than I to live. I actually prayed that the Lord take me instead of Bob, and I meant it. One afternoon I got down on my knees beside my bed and said, "Lord, I have believed — against all unbelief, against every diagnosis, against every doctor — that if I believed enough you would save Bob. But now I cannot go on. I need to know . . . are you going to take Bob?"

As I had several times before in my life, I felt a flowing across my consciousness: "I am going to take Bob, but you will be all right." Those words were not comforting to me. I was very willing to give my life for Bob's. I did not see how I could go on without him. It would have been easier for me to die than to continue living without him. But from that moment, I knew that the Lord was going to take him.

My dreams were haunted by visions of what my life would be. How could I carry on? How could I manage? What would happen to me and my children? I had no preparations whatsoever for "carrying on." No one in my life had ever prepared me for actually running my own affairs — not my father, not Bob King, and not Bob Herring. I had never bought a car on my own. I had rarely even paid bills. These thoughts hovered over me like a black cloud. My whole future and my children's would depend on whether I could learn.

Bob went into remission, came home from the hospital, and never left the house again.

Bob left me the eleventh day of October in 1981. When he died, the pain was so terrible that I went into shock. His children handled the funeral, and I am happy that they could and that they did exactly as they wanted. This has always given me comfort.

I did not even go to the viewing. His family had this time for themselves. The funeral is a blur, though I know that Bill Bright, founder of Campus Crusade for Christ, did the service.

Several important media businesspersons came to the funeral, including John Kluge, a television entrepreneur, and *Vogue* editor Shirley Lord, who was married to the editor of the *New York Times*. Even my friends from France came.

That day, my dear friend the gorgeous Margaret Williams, the queen of Houston society and the head of a huge foundation, wanted to help. "What can I do?" she asked.

"Well," I said, "some important people flew down from everywhere just for Bob's funeral. Could you possibly have them for dinner at your house?" Naturally, I didn't want to be seen anywhere, but I had to do something for these gracious visitors. Margaret was not prepared to host such a gathering, so she took us to Houston's top restaurant.

I couldn't ask Margaret to host my guests without being present myself, so I went, hoping no one would see me. Of course, everybody saw me. Can you imagine what the newspapers said about that? "On the day of Bob Herring's funeral, Joanne Herring, John Kluge, and the wife of the *New York Times* editor went to dinner at Tony's" ... or words to that effect.

On top of that, Marvin Zindler, who did TV exposés, was there to cover the funeral. He wanted to honor Bob because, like everyone, he admired Bob so much. I recognized the gift, so I thanked him personally.

During the next few weeks, flowers from Bob's admirers covered the house, even the stairs. More than a thousand letters and cards of condolence arrived, many handwritten by heads of state and titans of industry. But my grief was so strong, I believed that if I read those kind letters, I would die. I stuffed them into designer pillowcases and threw them all away, unopened.

People thought that was a horrible thing to do. Even my friends couldn't understand why I did it. They were surprised that I had not appreciated their outpouring enough to respond. Of course I loved them for caring, but there was nothing to respond with. I was like an empty shell — functioning, but feeling only pain and inadequacy. I regret throwing the notes away now. Now I could read them and appreciate and cherish them. But at the time, I did what I felt I had to do to survive.

The first two people who came the morning after Bob died were businessman and politican Robert Mosbacher and Houston socialite Joan Schnitzer. Denton and Louise Cooley sent me meals for three days after Bob's death, when I couldn't even think about feeding my family.

I was horrified that *one week* after my husband died, men started coming to see me with marriage proposals. I could not believe they thought that I would be interested in somebody else at that point — or ever. One man even tried to kiss me. I looked at him — he was a dear friend who just was not thinking — and said, "I just lost my husband. Do you think I could possibly be interested in anything like that?" I even had an Arab prince visit, a stranger to me. He had just heard about me and said, "You would be perfect for me."

I needed to take care of myself and my family, but really I just staggered around, not knowing what I was wearing or even my name. Words passed over me. I was haunted by Bob's absence. Surrounded by hundreds of friends, I was utterly alone.

I remember the most comforting message I got during the time of Bob's illness. The French ambassador, Claude de Kemoularia, said, "Joanne, we are not going to talk about Bob. We will do that later.

Right now, we want to talk about *you*. How do you feel?" During Bob's whole illness, the only other people who ever asked how I felt was Robert Mosbacher, who called me daily, and the di Portanovas. They gave me the strength to get through the torture of those eighteen months, and they stood staunchly beside me after Bob's death.

Tears pour down my face today as I write about this. I didn't cry then. The pain was so awful at that time, I couldn't. But now I want to share what comforted me.

So many say, "If there's anything I can do . . ." Then there are those who don't ask, they just do. Instead of empty words, they gave me great comfort by doing.

Of course, food poured in. It looked like a delicatessen in the kitchen, just overwhelming amounts of food. I needed someone to take charge, and my friend Marilyn Wilhelm did, thank goodness. I remember her saying, "This is terrible; all of this food just sitting here. All of these people are here. Where are the silver trays? Take this; make it look beautiful."

People think they want to be alone when a loved one dies, but they don't. I did not think I could bear to see people, but it actually helped.

Every night my boys and my goddaughter Isabel, the daughter of the Count de Bourg-Bozas, would get movies, the funniest ones they could find. She and my kids were young, but they thought, "What can we do to help?" They *did* help. We didn't talk about the movies; we just laughed. It gave me time to come out of the shock.

In the meantime, I just slid along on the wave of love that came from those who sincerely cared about me and provided the material things that were really significant at the time. I had wonderful dinners brought by friends and I had my children, whom I loved, around me. These friends and family did the caring, necessary things to keep our lives going when I couldn't.

I remember thinking that I might need a full year to mourn Bob before I could ever appear in public, socially. I was repulsed by the notion of dating. I prepared for a quiet year of semi-isolation.

Also, I thought that no one would ever want me without Bob. I thought I would be forgotten as a "nobody," but at least one high-profile couple was watching from afar. I got an invitation from the Reagans for dinner at the White House in March of 1982 (about five months after Bob's death). From utter despondency I thought, "If the Reagans think it is time for me to go out a little — I shall go." I went without an escort. The press loved it, taking many photos, saying, "Joanne is back." As the shouting and the tumult died and I boarded the flight back to Houston from Washington, I became despondent again. I left my sable coat on the plane. It had survived barrels in Afghanistan, but not a widow's absentminded grief in America.

In an effort to cheer me up, my thoughtful friend Lorraine, now Lady Palmer, said, "You are going to London with me, and that's that!"

"No, I can't possibly," I told her.

But my mother packed my bag and they threw me on the plane. It turned out to be the best therapy in the world because I met so many new and exciting people who did not know I was a widow. No one asked me about Bob. It was wonderful not to have to relive his death every day.

God must have known I could not face the future without this reviving respite, which I described in a letter to Bob and Mary Keenan, friends from Houston.

Blenheim Palace

Dear Bob and Mary,

You have been so gallantly kind to help me through this terrible period and so kind to support me when gossip hurt me — thank you! I ran away to London because I simply could not stand that house another moment. Bob was everywhere and yet, nowhere. It began to dawn on me that he was never coming back, never going to be there . . . I felt as if I were being slowly lowered into a well and every day I was going deeper into a dark horrible place full of sadness and despair. I began to doubt myself as a person. My whole serenity was threatened. I have always felt so at home in Europe, so a part of my friends here. It was like coming home. I decided to leave in one day. I made no plans, called no one — just left. Christina and Emilio Pucci heard from their son that I was coming and came to chaperone me. All my friends called and set up dinners at their homes — why don't Americans realize how badly widows (I hate that word. It reminds me of black, creepy crawly things that go bump in the night) need to get out of sad surroundings? Anyway, I had dinner with Prince Charles and Princess Diana the night before they announced publicly the great event [that she was pregnant with their first child]. The president of Italy was there. He and [his wife] Mrs. Fanfani invited me to visit them in Rome. The lord mayor of London gave me a dinner at Mansion House. The Marlboroughs invited me here to Blenheim. The Duke and Duchess of Argyll invited me to shoot in Scotland at Inveraray Castle. Henry and Kathy Ford, George and Lita Livanos, all have asked me to come and stay in San Moritz.

Although I felt the stirring of new life and hope and the warmth of caring friends, I never finished or sent this letter. Black clouds still shrouded the sun.

I was accompanied to the small private dinner at the Italian ambassador's home for Prince Charles and Princess Diana by designer Emilio Pucci and his wife. Pucci was from a noble family dating back to the twelfth century and still lived in his palace like a king. Everyone's credentials *had* to be special on this evening.

Diana came in, radiant, smiling, and beautiful, wearing a magnificent gray satin embroidered dress with pearls. Charles was looking very pleased too. They walked around, holding hands, looking very much in love. This seemed to be a party of close friends, thus things were very casual as far as protocol was concerned. The women dipped a small curtsy and the men nodded, but it was nothing like the formal occasions where they had to appear regal every moment. They talked to everyone, including me, most cordially. It was a very special feeling to be in an informal setting with "the people's princess," an unrecorded moment in a life where virtually every moment was recorded by the press.

After dinner as we all stood in a group, they announced that they were expecting a baby — their first! Diana tilted her head as she was famous for doing and looked pink. Charles smiled proudly like any happy young father-to-be. It was a terribly sweet moment. This momentous announcement had not yet been revealed to the press. It came out the next morning, but we were the first "friends" to know. (Of course, I was not a real friend; I just happened to be there). Everyone felt honored with the news and shared genuine joie de vivre for the next generation of British monarchy.

It was a sparkling moment, but it died quickly upon my return home to Texas to face the grim reality of life without the only man who had ever understood me and valued me for who I *really* was. We had only nine years.

A short while after returning from England, I was jogging to get ready to go skiing (so that I wouldn't break my leg). When my unleashed dog hit me from behind, my leg twisted. All I could think of as I was falling was, "This leg is going to break." And it did — in three places. The doctors were not sure it would heal or ever be straight again. I was once more faced with being crippled for life.

As I was adjusting to the cast on my leg, the fog was beginning to lift over my new financial landscape in a world without Bob Herring. The scenery wasn't pretty. The most recent Houston energy bubble had burst just before Bob's death. My personal finances took a hit. I was solvent but not the sixth richest woman in Texas, as described in George Crile's book.

My only real assets were two pieces of real estate that took tens of thousands of dollars to operate but that I couldn't sell. I was responsible for my two boys, my mother, and retired nanny Reverend Stevens.

My longtime friend John Loeb became ambassador to Denmark and decided to have a great party to celebrate his arrival. It was to be the gathering of the year in Scandinavia. Even the Danish queen would be in attendance. The invitation arrived in February for the party in June. "I can sit here and feel sorry for myself, or I can go to all these marvelous places to which I am invited, crutches and all," I said. "If the crutches do not bother my host, they will not bother me." I accepted every invitation I got.

I was afforded these fabulous trips and events through the generosity of friends. As for my broken leg, though it was hard for me to learn to depend on others, even in the smallest ways, my son Robin quit his job and saved my life by accompanying and assisting me. He has saved me many times over the years, and I cannot think of him without a surge of gratitude. With the party in Denmark looming, however, I knew I had to learn to go on my own.

At about the same time, I was named to the list of Women of Distinction by Birmingham-Southern College in Birmingham, Alabama, in the company of some of the most fascinating women of our time: broadcast journalist Barbara Walters, actress Bette Davis, Helen Boehm of Boehm Porcelain, fashion designer Carolina Herrera, the Duchess of Bedford, Countess Anne d'Ornano, and the mayor of Deauville. I attended. However, I felt I shouldn't spend the money frivolously.

To my delight, the Houston Natural Gas Board offered to send me and Robin to Alabama in the company plane. Pierre Cardin then gave me a dress. I felt like Cinderella. God played fairy godfather, giving me my coach and my dress, waving His magic wand over everything. While I oftentimes still felt alone, He was always there making things work.

Friends began flying me around in private planes and surprised me with exactly what I needed (including crutches made from Lucite — they became my "ball crutches"). When Bob died, I had assumed life as I knew it was totally over. I had little money, no position, nothing to look forward to. Yet God provided for every need and even found noteworthy places for me to shine enough to find my self-worth, which had been so deeply buried under grief and despair.

On my way to John's party in Denmark, I stopped in London, with my sweet friend Lorraine, Lady Palmer, pushing me around as usual. We stayed with her friend Salah Hawila. He was very rich and wanted badly to enter the closed door of the British aristocracy. Lorraine suggested he host a party for us in Mark's, the city's poshest club.

Salah invited the cream of London society, and to my delight, all of them accepted. The blue-blooded guest list included the Duke and Duchess of Bedford, the Maharani of Jaipur, the Duke and Duchess of Argyll, the Duke of Marlborough, and a token Yankee, the American ambassador.

But there was one guest, Heini Thyssen, whom I had always found very attractive, and for whom I felt a small connection. To my surprise, it seemed the feeling was mutual. I asked him if he was going to John's party.

"I will if you go," he replied. Then laughingly I said, "Call John and say that you will accept only if you sit next to me." I was teasing, but he did just that.

Baron and Baroness Thyssen had a complex and shaky marriage. How shaky, I didn't realize until later. The baroness was present only at "important" occasions, and absent from all others. Still, everybody wanted the Thyssen family. They were treated like gods, and I was soon to see why. Heini was good-looking, tall, and slim, the very personification of the Teutonic heroes in Wagner's operas. He was so rich that he lived and was treated like a king. I could list what the family owned, but it would be easier to list what they did not own. Heini even had a factory and a lot in Houston that he had never seen — as well as the greatest private collection of art in the world.

Heini's sister Gaby (Baroness von Bentinck) was a great supporter of mine from the moment I met her. These older ladies are essential in this sort of society. They must support you, or you're out. I had a sponsor like this in every country. Without them, no woman with neither position nor husband would ever have made it.

The Duchess of Bedford put her arm around me and smiled knowingly. "I think you can get him if you want him," she said.

"Come with me to my villa in Lugano," Heini suggested. I accepted with alacrity.

I had enjoyed several visits to Blenheim Palace, but *this*... this was almost beyond fairy-tale dreams. His palace had been built by King Leopold of Belgium, the richest man in the world in his day.

We were surrounded by the world's greatest art — things seen only in art exhibitions or coffee table books. Even in bedrooms and bathrooms, there were world-famous Picassos or van Goghs. Any name, era, or field of art was right there in the room with you. On a later visit to Daylesford House, Heini's English mansion, I saw a silver tureen casually sitting on the dining room table. Heini had just paid a million pounds for it, the highest price ever paid for a piece of silver. Photographs of it had been in the newspapers and slick magazines. I remember looking at it, astonished that he actually lived with and used these famous museum pieces. In Lugano, he had his own private museum where he kept the "really" good stuff. My imagination failed me at what earthly treasures Heini considered to be more precious than these "everyday" priceless household items. There were guards everywhere to protect this "Ali Baba cave."

Of course, Heini entertained ceaselessly. One couple I well remember was Prince and Princess Thurn and Taxis. She was one smart cookie. He was a plump, balding, difficult man with "mixed proclivities," especially for men. She sat on his lap, kissed him on top of the head, and sang his praises to everyone to flatter him into "granting" her a child, a possible prince. She succeeded — she became pregnant.

The princess wore the most outrageous clothes, which amused the prince vastly. She kept him entertained and happy at every moment, though it wasn't easy. The moment he died, she changed her personality completely. She became a brilliant businesswoman, dignified and elegant.

While the prince was still alive, they begged me to come to Regensburg, their fabled palace in Germany. I could not go, however, because I was tied to Heini's "wishes," and his wishes were that I should stay with him. There was never a moment for anything that was not rigorously scheduled. The curator of the Rijksmuseum in the Netherlands visited. He had different guests every three days. As he had made a practice of marrying the most beautiful women in the world, he was constantly called by one former wife or another about unruly children. Children from his other marriages were all there too, jockeying for position. There was no stability anywhere; no foundation anywhere; no sense — just grandeur and high living and strict conformity.

Home began to seem far away and rather nice. Life with Heini was all so complicated. There was so much tension in the air that I thought maybe, just maybe, the cost was a bit too high. There was no room for long walks in the spring mornings or deep conversations at night about foreign policy or anything I found interesting.

Years before, I had said to his sister, my great friend Baroness von Bentinck, "I want to meet your brother."

"No, you don't," she said. Now I realized that she had a point.

Both Heini and Gaby were supremely caring and very much worth loving, but theirs was really another world, and I was not sure that I could bring happiness there or find any for myself.

We knew all of the same people, did many of the same things, and belonged loosely to the same "tribe." But I am first an American. They were very European. I missed my home and my children. Where would they have fit into this "mixed society"? There were too many misplaced children already.

God showed me the heights and the price that must be paid to be there. He showed me that the grass is not greener on the other side of the fence. He taught me not to sell my soul for money or high living. Once you have experienced it, you learn that you drink from one cup at a time. You can drink just as well from cracked crockery as you can from gold, and the cracked cup is much easier to care for. You don't cry if you break or lose it, and no one will kill you to get it.

I stopped yearning for great wealth with all its heavy burdens. It seemed clear to me that the palaces and princes own you, you do not own them. A prince can take a palace away with a snap of his fingers. Palaces require undying care. The glamour is all on the outside.

As the grandeur began to fade, I realized that there was no freedom there. Heini was king. I left without regret and went home happier than I had been in a long time. I was beginning to take charge of my life and enjoy it in whatever manner God chose. I didn't know it at the time, but I was learning to make it on my own. This was a big step — and I took it in a cast.

God did a thorough job in rehabilitating me. Back home, I suddenly found more invitations and men willing to escort me than I could handle in my still fragile condition. I was haunted by what I call flashbacks, sudden memories of beautiful moments of the life I shared with Bob Herring. They left me haggard and saddened almost beyond my ability to recover and go on. I sometimes dreamed that Bob was alive, and then I wakened to the sickening awareness that he would never be there again.

God had said I would be all right; thus, the kindness and attention from friends continued. God never fails us. He even sent Senator John Warner of Virginia (I was his first date after his divorce from Liz Taylor). This was recorded in the supermarket tabloids under the headline "John's Woman." My mother saw it in the beauty shop and practically fainted.

"How could you appear in such an article?" she said.

"Mother, they don't ask."

I was many things, but never merely someone's "woman."

I think maybe God broke my leg so that I would not have real problems "out there." "Out there" is what I call being single and a target for a roll in the hay in exchange for dinner. Men seemed to expect a return for the "luxury" of a plate of food and a cocktail. It is a horrible situation, which God knew I simply was not strong enough to handle at the moment.

Frankly, I was never strong enough to handle it. I almost stopped going out because I hated coming home to the inevitable fracas surrounding "payback" at the front door. Today, being available for sex and being single seem synonymous.

Fortunately my boys and mother lived with me, which gave me an excuse. After being refused, many dates never called again. These expectations are the bane of a woman's existence today. Even if you pay for your own dinner, men still seem to expect sexual favors at the end of the evening. I was too unwary and dumb to suggest picking up the dinner check myself as a deterrent to these racing hormones, but I would today in a New York minute if I were on the dating circuit. Now I'm on the friend circuit, of course, so it doesn't come up.

I needed someone I could trust, just a male friend with no interest in me other than friendship. A man with so many female distractions that he would never target a poor woman on crutches.

CHAPTER 21

Laughing Again . . .

Joanne Herring, Texas Rep. Charlie Wilson and Dodie Kazanjian

Musical Chairs

HAY-ADAMS HOTEL—"I wanted to get my friends entwined early," said Texas socialite **Joanne Herring** as she and **Dodie Kazanjian** tied a silver and red helium balloon to guests' wrists at their dinner dance honoring **Marine Commandant and Mrs. P. X. Kelley.** The ice-breaking balloons set the tone for the light-hearted mingling of celebrities and politicos, including **Eva Gabor, SEC Chmn. John Shad, Senators John Warner** and **Robert Kasten.** Herring, poured into a sexy St. Laurent gown, made the rounds on the dance floor with all the eligible men, as the other ladies, obeying her directions, asked the gentlemen on their left for a spin.

The disappearance of the super-hosts of the '70s save Orfila, and the dearth of lavishness leaves Washington wide open for a qualified host or hostess to inherit the "top berth." **Betty Beale,** The Washington Star's leading social columnist, states bluntly that the only personality on the horizon who could capture Washington's fancy would be Texas millionairess Joanne Herring. "If she lived here, she'd be IT," Betty remarked. "She has the know-how; she's bright, articulate; she has a feeling for royalty . . . but I don't think she has the desire."

with the Wildest Man in Texas

*C*ongressman Charlie Wilson had been on the periphery of my life for a long time. I did not realize how much or how often he was there until I sorted through old photos looking for those most pertinent to this book. He seemed to always be somewhere in the background. Wherever Bob Herring and I went — Houston; Washington, D.C.; New York — Charlie was there too.

I thought that Bob introduced us, but Charlie said no, that he had seen me many years before at KHOU, the television station that aired my show. He said he never forgot me.

I was so in love with Bob Herring that I never thought of another man while I was married to him. I certainly *noticed* Charlie; you would have to be dead not to! I knew — as we women often do — that he was attracted to me. But I was sure it was the same sort of admiration that I felt for him.

Not quite, as I was to find out.

After Bob died, Charlie sent me two dozen yellow roses on Valentine's Day. My heart was so bankrupt, I barely glanced at them and never thanked him. He couldn't understand this. He was Charlie Wilson, every girl's dream come true!

I had been told that I needed to get a Democrat if I wanted to make headway helping the Afghans fight the Russians. My Republican friends said they hadn't even been able to get three million dollars for Nicaragua to fight the Sandinista communists in our own hemisphere. "You've got to get a Democrat," they said. "What about Charlie?" He was on the two committees I needed, including the all-powerful House Appropriations Committee. The committees had the money — and after I gave him a call, I had Charlie.

If you didn't read the book or see the movie *Charlie Wilson's War*, maybe I should explain how it fits into this story. These are the bare facts ("bare" being the key word because that's how Charlie liked to play — bare, in the hot tub):

While I was toodling around the world collecting kings and fighting communists, Charlie was busy with Miss Universe, Willie Nelson, and his gang of guys who threw beer parties and salivated over stories of his conquests with *Playboy* pullouts. Charlie collected women like baseball cards. But Charlie was not just a playboy. He was a very serious and successful congressman. He had done significant things for Texas and was very admired by the top executives in the state for his acumen and his business accomplishments for free enterprise.

Charlie and I started spending time together regularly. He told me, as if it had happened years ago, about a ballerina whom he'd been dating. I thought it was a very romantic story, not dreaming it had *just* happened. She had said to him, "Pass or play." He passed to date me, a decision I wouldn't know about for some time, with consequences that played out at Charlie's funeral.

In the beginning I had several different people escorting me to parties. But suddenly it was always Charlie because he was always around. He was so around, there was no room for anyone else. He did not seem to mind staying in the back of the house. In fact, he did not seem to mind anything. My heart began to heal.

Charlie was in a lot of trouble over his lifestyle, which I did not understand because I never saw the troublesome parts of it. Some of the more questionable elements shown in the movie came before me, however, such as the belly dancer, who predated my arrival in Charlie's life by a year. I met the belly dancer during the filming of the movie, and I liked her. She was a sweet girl and deeply appreciative of Charlie. She hadn't seen the world before Charlie took her on that trip to the Middle East, and now she's an airline hostess and seeing lots of it.

There *was* one questionable element that came up early on. On our first date, Charlie and I joined friends at the Kennedy Center for an event. We had such a marvelous time, Charlie said, "It's too early [it was eleven o'clock] to go home. Let's go to my apartment. I have the record from *Cats* [the newest hit on Broadway], the best view of Washington, and champagne."

My friends and I accepted.

Charlie was *very* proud of his apartment. He had good taste, and even though it spelled s-t-u-d, it *did* have a spectacular view. There was just one discordant note: *the hot tub*. I shall never forget my dismay when my friends, some outstanding blue bloods who did not know Charlie, walked in to see the king-sized hot tub, significantly close to the king-sized bed. What would they think of me as they envisioned his hot-tub habitués? I wished myself on a deserted, unnamed island in the Bahamas. Charlie had no idea we were shocked, however; he was called "Good Time Charlie" for a good reason. I hurriedly explained to our friends that this was my first date with Charlie and I was ready for it to be my last.

But it wasn't. Charlie taught me to laugh again when I never thought I could.

Naturally, my interests in communism and the Afghans came up in our conversations. If Charlie wanted to be with me, he had to care too. He listened attentively...then gave me the same glazed look that I'm getting everywhere today. Still, he was around all the time, so he had to listen. The movie indicated that it was Dan Rather's newscast that introduced him to the issues in Afghanistan, but what *really* happened was that Charlie watched my son Robin King's documentary at my house in Houston and was shocked, saddened, and horrified along with the more than five hundred thousand people around the world whom Charles Fawcett showed it to privately.

The film had a great impact on him, but he had limited interest in Arab affairs. He supported Israel. Otherwise his world was the United States, his Texas constituents, and the good old boys with whom he played. Afghanistan was half a world away. Finally, however, thanks to Robin's documentary and my talking, he began to really listen. The facts that I presented made sense to him because he was smart. He began to see communism as the threat it was. This insignificant country began to seem real to him. As a Texan, he identified with the fighting spirit and bravery of these men railing for independence against tremendous odds, fighting for freedom, no matter what the cost. Soon Charlie became their greatest advocate. He wanted the good guys to win and was determined to help them.

But many things were evolving simultaneously. One night at dinner, Charlie got up, excused himself, and found a florist at eight in the evening. He bought every flower in the shop and came marching back with an arm full of flowers, followed by more in the arms of the waiters. He put them, three-deep, around the table. (While Charlie was surrounding me with flowers, labor leader Vernon Jordan was trying to play footsie with my friend Lorraine under the table! Lorraine, who became Lady Palmer, now lives in a one-hundred-room palace with a sterling silver staircase and dashing husband Lord Adrian.)

Maybe I fell in love with Charlie that night. In any case, from then on we were a team.

Around this time, in 1983, my cast, at last, came off. The doctors said they hoped it would be straight and strong. No one had seen this leg for eight months — the break had been a bad one. When my cast came off, Beau asked, "Which leg did you break? They look exactly the same." And they did! Talk about somebody up there...

New again, I could walk, dance, and ski, and I did, by the grace of God.

Charlie and I could now take walks together. We danced all night every night. One night Charlie kissed me, and I liked it. I liked it a lot!

"Go to the French air show with me. It's wonderful fun. We'll have a ball," he said.

British Aerospace had already invited me to the show, at which aircraft from all over the world are showcased and demonstrated, to discuss accepting a job as consultant, as I now had something to offer companies they were willing to pay for. My access to leaders in the Middle Eastern world was almost unmatched. Businessmen would pay me to make appointments for them, which I could get and they could not. I did not have to sell their companies, deals, or products, but simply open the doors. I did not have to use my friends. I only had to ask if they would give an appointment to a company interested in doing business with their country. I was always careful to tell my friends that I was being paid. This made them laugh, as this was expected in their world. People were paid for everything. Even the gatekeeper in the Middle East expects and needs a tip. I began to make real money *on my own*. The lessons I had spent my whole life learning were about to pay off when I was alone and needed them most. My toolbox was full of valuable tools.

"Yes!" I said to him. "Let's go to the air show."

Charlie asked for my passport. It stated that I was five years *older* than he. (I hadn't learned, as my friend Eva Gabor did, to have the date changed.) Ouch! This guy who liked really young chicks now had an older one. I sent the passport, noting, "I'm sorry about the stork," referring of course to the birthday stork, which had so rudely brought me home five years before Charlie. He wrote me the sweetest letter, saying that he was mad that I thought the stork mattered at all.

"I have adored you from the first moment we met and maybe

before," he wrote. "My crush has been an ill-kept secret. I miss you every moment we are apart. You are the light that dims all else."

We went to the show and it was perfect. We danced into the morning, slept for a few hours, then got up to see the dawn. We went to everything in Paris, and I did not see or miss any of my fancy friends. I lived in Charlie's world just as I had in Bob's. I did not know it, but I was looking for a shared life in which we would work as partners. But this was not God's plan, as I was to learn later.

Charlie and I were good together. People loved to have us at their parties in Paris — our photos appeared everywhere. My picture was taken even more than the young starlets'. Charlie was happy. I was happy.

When I flew to England on the Concorde, with all expenses paid by a London banker who wanted to discuss my being his consultant, Charlie and I called each other every few hours — we were now really involved, but not intimately.

People who knew Charlie couldn't believe it. This was a new Charlie, at least for the moment. He flew into Houston every weekend from Washington or I flew there. We talked at least six or seven times a day. The romance got so intense that we couldn't bear not talking — we spoke every fifteen minutes, like a couple of teenagers. At this point, our relationship still hadn't progressed past a kiss. (It did later — after he asked me to marry him.) We were having a glorious platonic time, laughing and playing like kids.

In the movie, they made so much of Charlie's shenanigans, they forgot to show how smart he was and how good he was at what he did. It saddened me that the smokescreen of his playboy antics obscured his serious legislative skills. When he was with me, the brilliant, competent Charlie came out and totally eclipsed the handsome, dashing clown. Still, every minute with Charlie was a riot of fun.

Being a Democrat, Charlie had previously accepted President Jimmy Carter's assertion that the Afghanistan situation was merely a "tribal" war. But at this point, Charlie had listened and understood all I had been saying about communism and its spread and its imminent danger to our country. He began to see that the world as we knew it was threatened by the Soviets' march into Afghanistan. What if Hitler had been stopped in Poland, or MacArthur had been allowed to win in Korea? Think how many lives would have been saved and we would not be facing nuclear bombs in North Korea today. The Soviet Union would never have become a superpower without the treasuries and slave labor of the millions in Eastern Europe. The Soviets had taken Cuba and Angola, and now they were in Chile and Nicaragua and El Salvador, as well.

We knew we must stop them in Afghanistan now, before they got the Strait of Hormuz and cut off our lifeline to Middle Eastern oil. Soviet control of the strait would have ended American life (and luxury) as we'd come to know it, so Charlie and I decided to stop the Soviet communists in Afghanistan.

We were now seriously working together to open doors to save Afghanistan (and Pakistan). We knew we had to get arms to the mujahideen immediately before it was too late for them to save themselves. This was crucial because Afghans would fight when others would surrender. The Soviets were killing Afghans by the hundreds daily, the Russian pilots strafing women, children, everything that moved. We visited as many experts as Charlie could garner meetings with, and he had the power to get to anyone. It was agreed that a World War II anti-aircraft gun, last made in Germany, was the only gun available to shoot down the murderous Hind helicopters. We hoped some could be found in a warehouse somewhere, but we didn't know where.

"We must find that gun," said Charlie. "Do you know any Germans?"

I did. I knew exactly the *right* German — Baron Bertrand Von Stohrer, an executive at Oerlikon-Bührle. He was a social giant, as handsome as a movie star, and president of Oerlikon, one of the largest arms producers in the world. He lived in Rome, and he was our man.

See how interestingly God works? The aristocratic contacts I made at parties provided exactly the right person at exactly the right time and place to provide exactly the right tools to begin to end global communism.

The smaller arms we needed had to come from an outside source as well. To protect Zia from invasion and to not involve the United States in a potential World War III, none of the arms could be marked "Made in the USA." We found what we needed in Egypt. Charlie knew the minister of defense, so we flew out to meet him.

The scene in the movie is a scream, but it's wrong (Hollywood used a bit of poetic license). In it, Charlie has a belly dancer seducing the Egyptian minister so that Egypt will buy Soviet-made arms from the Israeli patriot Zvi Rafiah to ship to the mujahideen in Afghanistan.

In actuality, I was the one who was there with Charlie, Zvi, and Egyptian defense minister Abu Ghazala — not the seductive belly dancer (she went the year before), or CIA agent Gust Avrakotos, for that matter. Zvi did sell the arms to the Egyptians, and the Saudi Arabians did pay for them and half the war. Did you know that the Saudis matched the United States dollar for dollar in that war *and* in Desert Storm? They have supported the United States over and over. It is not the Saudi government that causes trouble — it is terrorists like the late Osama bin Laden and his hoods. For helping us, the Saudi king has a price of millions on his head from some of his own countrymen (members of Al-Qaeda).

One morning my father stormed into the room and announced, "My daughter is an arms dealer!!"

"No, I'm not, Daddy," I replied. "Someone else is buying, someone else is selling, and someone else is paying. I'm just putting them together." He shook his head and sighed.

After the meeting with the Egyptians, we traveled to Rome to meet with Von Stohrer, but en route we stopped in Paris for a night. We couldn't help ourselves — we thought we were in love. It was

Charlie's birthday or near it. One of my French buddies, Count Pierre-Alain de Malleray, took us to a famous Russian restaurant where they played violins. We had the best table in the house. The musicians came to our table and played just for us...

We went to a disco, and right in the middle of the dance floor, Charlie stopped, looked at me, and said, "I love you. Marry me. We can do anything together." Once again a man was telling me that the sky was the limit. The sky still seemed the limit the next morning as we boarded a plane for Rome to meet Von Stohrer and arrange the sale. It was adventure, unending adventure.

Finally, everything was signed, sealed, and hopefully on its way to being delivered by Von Stohrer.

Oerlikon had the guns, and Von Stohrer arranged everything. Now we had to get the weapons into the mountains of Afghanistan. They were heavy, though, and trucks could not carry them because there were no roads. We cornered the world market on mules, and the weapons were quickly en route.

In Egypt, we arranged for the machine guns and other arms to be available in Israel and Egypt, arranged for the Saudi payments, and convinced the Israelis and Egyptians that they could trust each other enough to complete this covert action. This was really something special, as it was against the law in both countries to even fly from one country to the other. The only way to travel from one to the other was by private plane because each country still considered the other an enemy, despite President Carter's Camp David accords. Our passports had to leave Israel unmarked for us to enter Egypt.

In Israel we visited Zvi, whose lovely Jewish wife, at Charlie's request, took me to many of the Christian shrines. Charlie had such a sweet side. He thought of things like this even in the midst of such turmoil.

We had the guns. Now we had to get the votes for the U.S. share of the funding.

It was a covert operation... but it wasn't *that* covert. This initiative involved millions of dollars, and Congress had to know about it and vote for it. Thank God that's the American way. So many people played a significant role. For instance, when the vote came up at the crucial moment in the Senate, there were two Republican senators who were undecided: Pete Wilson of California and Ted Stevens of Alaska.

John Tower, who was chairman of the Senate Armed Services Committee, was working feverishly to help, but he had not been able to get these two significant senators to commit. Charlie and I decided to give them the dinner of their lives in Washington, D.C.

I called a friend in London the day before. I knew I had to have a man of enormous stature and integrity to make our case, someone the senators would respect enough to really listen to and who could earn their vote.

"You've got to come to this dinner," I said to Lord Robert Cranborne, junior minister of defense. He was the heir to the Marquess of Salisbury, a portentous position in the English monarchy. The marquess precedes the queen at the opening of Parliament or during a coronation.

"Joanne, I can't come. I have appointments," he protested.

"Robert," I said, "you've got to! Take the Concorde and fly back the next day. You can do it. You have to do it. Everything depends on you. They will listen to you."

He came at his own (great) expense.

The fact that this great man would come on the Concorde for an overnight visit to talk to these two key senators made a difference. He really cared about stopping Soviet world domination. His brother had been killed in Afghanistan by the Soviets for photographing their atrocities. Robert thought supporting the Afghans was essential not just for the United States, but for the world, and his lucid argument turned the tide with these essential senators. They were great patriots, but they just weren't sure about our getting involved in Afghanistan. Robert was a huge asset in gaining their understanding — and their votes.

It didn't hurt a bit at this dinner that I served Cristal rosé, the world's finest champagne. Cristal was known of, but Cristal rosé was little known and impossible to buy. I called the Cristal vineyards in France and cornered the market. I would buy the world's supply to use for moments like these. It was created in 1876 for Czar Alexander II of Russia, who ruled that the bottles had to be clear instead of the typical green to prevent a bomb being placed inside. It was the most prized item in the world at the time, something most people had just read about. It was supposed to be as delicate on the tongue as nectar of the gods and cost a fortune because it was so rare. I kept it under my bed. Toasting the end of Soviet communism with the champagne of Russian czars was an ironic bit of history that made each sip more sweet.

The night of the dinner, I carried a Louis Vuitton bag filled with six bottles of Cristal rosé — one each for Charlie, me, Stevens, Wilson, and the marquess, the only guests. The reserve bottle was for me and Charlie if the dinner went well.

Naturally, it wasn't the champagne that swung the votes. These were brilliant men. They would never have voted for anything unless they truly believed it was important to America and the world. It was a pivotal moment in the fight. The next day the motion carried. The mujahideen in Afghanistan would be supported.

During our trip around the world (France, Austria, Egypt, Israel, Pakistan, and the Venice film festival), Charlie and I were always a sensation as a couple. Wherever we went in Venice, crowds of people would follow us — they thought we were movie stars. At a restaurant as they snapped our pictures and asked for autographs, Charlie grinned and said, "You sign 'Zsa Zsa Gabor' and I'll sign 'Gary Cooper.' If they want to think we're movie stars, let's give them movie stars. Make 'em happy." So we did. Together we twinkled. But when you twinkle too much, you begin to burn.

CHAPTER 22

When a multinational corporation needs help in Pakistan, it naturally turns to a woman with the looks of a fifties movie star, the wiles of a Southern belle, and the title of...

Honorary Consul

By Sandy Sheehy

The champagne reception preceding last November's opening of the "Treasure Houses of Britain" exhibit at Washington's National Gallery was one of the hottest invitations of the 1985 social season. That opening, after all, was bringing Prince Charles and Princess Di to these once-colonial shores; and they, in turn, were drawing more of the nation's far-flung rich and powerful to Washington than an inaugural ball.

Despite the crush of celebrities, the image that dominated the front page of the *Washington Post* "Style" section on Saturday, November 2, was that of Houston's curvaceous blonde honorary consul for Morocco and Pakistan, Joanne King Herring Davis, offering her hand and a radiant smile to a wordly-looking gentleman in a tuxedo. Seven years earlier, Sally Quinn—the Boswell of capital society—had introduced her to the *Washington Post*'s readers as Houston's Scarlett O'Hara. And like the heroine of *Gone with the Wind*, who tore down her velvet drapes to make a ball gown, Joanne exuded a blend of charm and inventiveness that evening. The dress she'd bought for the occasion hadn't arrived from New York, so she was wearing her grandmother's scoop-necked black evening gown, dating from the turn of the century, when hourglass figures like Joanne's were the height of fashion. The chatty article quoted a Washington wag praising the lush view the mezzanine afforded of her décolletage below.

She was dazzling, with her heart-shaped

(Above) In 1980, Pakistani President Zia-ul-Haq asked Joanne King Herring to be his honorary consul general. (Right) Getting comfortable in the home designed for her new husband, Lloyd Davis.

face, bow mouth, upturned nose, and the contrast between her warm brown eyes and tumble of honey-colored curls. But there were plenty of beautiful, strikingly dressed women at the party, many of them considerably younger than Joanne, in her mid-fifties. (Although she looks fortyish and doesn't like to discuss her age, the Houston Social Directory lists her as a member of the University of Texas Class of 1950.)

"For some reason, the article focused a lot on me," she says in an amused tone. "That was so ridiculous, because I wasn't a stately home, and I'm not *somebody* in Washington."

Truth be told, Joanne Herring Davis frequently *is* somebody in Washington, where she entertains the likes of Henry Kissinger

Bye-Bye, Charlie

and Prince Bandor, the Saudi foreign minister, at the Regent and the Hay Adams (her favorite capital hotel, since the ballroom looks across Pennsylvania Avenue at the White House). She's also somebody in New York, in Karachi, in Rabat, in Abu Dhabi—in fact, much of the world. But the world doesn't know what to make of her. In Washington, they look down her dress. In Moslem countries, they address her as "sir" (in Arabic, all feminine honorifics refer to a woman as So-and-So's wife, daughter, or girlfriend). The recently remarried widow of late Houston Natural Gas Company Chairman Robert Herring, she continues to function independently and with considerable clout in a culture where women are virtual nonentities.

Even her home town, Houston, has a tough time figuring Joanne out. Last summer, Rosellen Brown, a professor in the University of Houston's creative writing program and author of *Tender Mercies* and *Civil Wars*, encountered her at the Moscow hotel where the Soviet government had lodged them both. The novelist was visiting refuseniks, Russian Jews who've been denied exit visas. Joanne was winding up her honeymoon with her third husband, lighting and electronics entrepreneur Lloyd Davis, after two weeks of sleeping in yurts (igloo-like portable huts) in the wilds of Mongolia.

"I must say, she didn't look like a Moscow woman, for sure," Rosellen says. "In her tight black pants and angora sweater and high heels, she certainly didn't blend in."

The next time Rosellen encountered Joanne Herring Davis was in mid-September at a benefit for the National Endowment for the Arts. Joanne chaired the dinner at the Four Seasons Hotel; the novelist, who'd received two NEA grants, was the keynote speaker. Rosellen described the Soviet Union's shackling of creative expression and the impoverishment of its writers and artists. By comparison, she told the audience,

the situation of their American counterparts was blissful. When Rosellen sat down, Joanne said that she agreed. Furthermore, she observed, people in the U.S.S.R. had to endure a deplorable lack of fresh vegetables: She'd begun to wonder if she'd ever see another fresh tomato.

"A lot of people were very amused and suggested we should travel in tandem," Rosellen says. "Either she'd be my straight man or I'd be hers. I'm not sure which."

Yet the same woman who can speak with equal zeal about freedom of expression and availability of fresh produce can also help an American multinational corporation deflect a lawsuit by the Pakistani government and get cabinet ministers to return her phone calls.

"The image I seem to create is so different from what I am that it really leaves me in a state of shock," Joanne says.

To her dismay, the image is often one of a frivolous socialite for whom the realm of world affairs is just an exclusive party circuit.

"I decided that people would either like me as I was, or not like me."

241

"What happens at a party is that people can come up and talk to each other," she says, displaying acute insight into the serious purpose of entertaining. This helps explain why she's such a hit in Washington, where parties are the field where the power game is played. "Nothing they say is binding. It is totally unofficial. Bob Herring used to do more business at parties in two minutes than he ever did at offices."

For Robert Herring (a sober-looking executive who sometimes sported a *Forbes* tie with "Capitalist Tool" printed across it in a tiny repeat pattern) everything was business, even his honeymoon—in Saudi Arabia. "Wasn't that romantic?" Joanne asks mock-seriously. With his vivacious bride in tow, Herring received invitations to the palace for dinner; when she stayed home, the Saudi royal family saw him at the office.

"She was as big an asset to Bob Herring as his money, his home, and his airplane were to her," says the *Houston Chronicle*'s Maxine Mesinger, who's been keeping tabs on the local rich since the mid-fifties.

In 1960, Joanne threw the party that established Houston's oil-rich as an elite that could laugh at itself. She was married to a real estate developer named Robert King, and her hair was its natural brunette. King wanted to give his wife the most creative birthday bash the Bayou City had ever seen. It was billed as a Roman Bacchanal. It turned out to be the ultimate toga party.

"We never *dreamed* it would have such repercussions," Joanne says, rolling her eyes to the ceiling. "This is the whole story of my life, this Roman party."

The Kings invited about fifty of their closest friends to attend the party and to participate in it. They were Old Houston—people whose names grace buildings in the city's fine arts complexes and on university campuses. Everyone had to come in costume; everyone had a part to play. There were even rehearsals. A Ballet Russe choreographer coached the "gladiators" and "slave girls" in appropriate dances.

One lunch hour, the businessmen/gladiators were practicing their line dance in the Kings' living room while workmen spruced up the exterior of the house. "There was this painter looking in, and there we were doing these funny dances," Joanne recalls. Craning her neck around her right arm, extended to hold an imaginary roller, she continues, "He was painting and doing this. And Claude Williams [then a general contractor, now a painter himself—in oils and acrylics] looked up and said. 'You know, that's what causes communism. That poor devil's out there working, and we're in here dancing at noon in our underwear.'"

So much effort was going into the soiree that Joan Fleming, whom Joanne describes as "*very* Junior League," suggested that the Kings invite *Life* to document it. The magazine often took pictures for its regular "Life Goes to a Party" department but seldom used them, Joan explained; it would be a great way to have some professional photographs to giggle over in years to come. Even when *Life* accepted, no one thought the party would see the light of print. Apart from the epic splash wildcatter Glenn McCarthy had made when he opened the Shamrock Hotel, national coverage of Houston had been confined to the business pages.

Everyone showed up at the Kings' sprawling Tanglewood château in costume, ready to play the parts. The gladiators danced. The slave girls were auctioned off. Little Nubian slaves—members of a troop of ten-year-old black Boy Scouts—refilled the silver goblets raised by the reclining revelers. Thanks to cleverly employed fire-

(Left) Joanne poses before the mansion of her father's family, built in Mississippi in 1812. The house now rests on the banks of the Brazos River. (Above) King Hussein of Jordan attended Joanne's party before going off to dine with Vice President Bush.

works, the burning of the Christian looked terribly realistic. Except for the glare of the arc lights, it was just an average evening at Nero's palace.

Life captured it all, and to everyone's surprise, they printed it: Nancy Robbins sitting in a fountain with her legs exposed, Alfred Glassell lounging on a mattress covered in black satin, John Blaffer as Bacchus lifting a crystal goblet to lead the revelry, Susan Nelms drinking out of a boat, Patrick Nicholson bicycling home in his toga, Joanne herself being thrown into a pool. Not about to be scooped by the national press, the Houston papers appeared uninvited and ran the story the next day on the front page.

"As I remember the early days in Houston, two events occurred," says Claude Williams. "One was the opening of the Shamrock, and the other was Joanne's party."

"Houston was *so* shocked," Joanne says, imitating an expression of wide-eyed disapproval. "They thought it was *the* most decadent, awful, incomprehensible, tasteless affair that anybody had ever had. But it was really just a lot of fun. Nobody even got drunk." Of course not; they didn't have time.

Part of what makes Joanne such a celebrated hostess is just this penchant for getting the guests involved in the action.

"I was the first person to move people at dinners," she says. "It got to be such a big thing that the *New York Times* did a write-up on it." Asking the men to change tables after the soup and again before dessert may be just the thing to enliven a little River Oaks dinner for thirty. But what about playing musical chairs at a formal Washington banquet, where strict protocol dictates who may sit next to whom?

In 1983, when Saudi Arabia sent, for the first time, a member of the royal family to be Ambassador to the United States, Prince Bandor (now foreign minister) asked Joanne to introduce him to Washington. When word got out that she was planning a dinner for 116 in the ambassador's honor, she began receiving cautionary advice from powerful friends.

She recalls Senator John Tower phoning the morning of the party and saying, "Every cabinet minister will be here tonight. You've got to behave yourself. I know how you like to move people, but you can't do that in Washington. I care about you, and I don't want you talked about tomorrow because you did something that hasn't been done."

Joanne says she had every intention of following this well-intended counsel, but then, between the fish and the entree, "Something inside of me said, 'Move them.'" She stepped up to the microphone and announced, "Every man, pick up his wine glass and move two tables to the right."

This bold party ploy may have raised a few carefully waxed eyebrows, but it had the desired effect. "It was the biggest success that ever happened," she reports exuberantly. "Everybody said that they'd never had such fun. They all got to sit next to Henry Kissinger and Caspar Weinberger and Barbara Walters."

Let Joanne's detractors snicker about the dinner in 1977 for which she converted the party room of her Frenchified River Oaks home into a seraglio straight out of the *Arabian Nights* to help Jordan's King Hussein and Saudi Arabia's Prince Saud feel at home. Despite the attentions of Houston's most beautiful socialites, King Hussein stayed but briefly, pleading a dinner engagement with George Bush. Prince Saud also retired disappointingly early. But even Pearl Mesta had her off nights, and one smash hit in Washington, however unconventional, can make up for any number of social fizzles back home.

Convention has never carried much weight with Joanne. She doesn't take herself seriously, so why should she pay attention to other people's rules?

"One day I decided that I had to be like everybody else, and I wore the cashmere sweater and the little pearls," she says. "Then I got tired of wearing the cashmere sweater and the little pearls, and I decided that people would either like me as I was, which was doing what I really felt like doing, or not like me."

Nonchalant though this may sound, she hates being criticized, especially in print. She goes ahead and does what she wants, she says. "Then I'm mad when somebody writes about it, and I'm very *unjustifiably* represented," she continues with a perceptive laugh. "I think it comes from my father always encouraging me that anything you did that was fun was okay and my mother saying you had to have good taste and obey the rules."

Joanne's father was William "Bull" Johnson, who became Texas A&M's first all-America quarterback although he weighed just 155 pounds at the time. Her mother is a Dallas-born Southern gentlewoman with Georgia roots. Mrs. Johnson, Joanne says, has always believed that there are certain things that ladies do and certain things that they don't do, and that that distinction is terribly important. "In the South after the Civil War, they didn't have anything but manners," she explains.

"You never see my mother when she is not perfectly dressed," she continues. "If we go out to Sam's Barbecue, my mother is turned out. We went to Kenya on safari, and she wore a full-length mink coat."

To hear Joanne describe her childhood, she grew up as the poorest little girl in River Oaks. Granted, she lived in the fifth house built in that exclusive subdivision—a colonial that stood on what's now the site of the mammoth modernist mansion built for Prince Abdhul Rakman on Kirby Drive. And granted, her father's family owned a grand house that they had built in 1812 in Mississippi. After the Civil War, they had moved it to Texas by riverboat. (Joanne has since had it cut into three pieces and trucked from Westheimer to the banks of the Brazos River.) But on those frequent occasions when her grandmother, who restricted herself to two servants, gave seated dinners for eighty, Joanne had to pitch in.

"I set more tables, cooked more cookies," she says. "Nobody was more of a scullery maid than I was. Then, I was expected to dress up and sing for the guests."

Her deprivation may have been relative, but it was painful nonetheless. "I grew up with what you might call the Big Rich of Houston, and I wasn't," Joanne says. "They all had beautiful dresses from Neiman-Marcus, and mine came from the local dressmaker. I was *with* the group that made their debut, but my parents decided that I didn't need a debut, so I didn't have one."

What she did have were a lot of unusual and seemingly contradictory experiences. Her father insisted that she be brave; her mother insisted that she be a lady. When a water moccasin wrapped itself around his daughter's leg, Bull Johnson demanded that she locate an appropriate weapon and kill it herself; she did it in with a hoe. When seven-year-old Joanne read that the zoo was seeking a home for a newborn tiger cub, he encouraged her to plan how she'd care for it; if she could persuade the zoo director to give her the cub, she could have it. "Fortunately for my mother, the cub died," she says.

What mattered to Mrs. Johnson was not that her daughter had the courage to get back on a half-broke horse that had thrown her, but that she had the courage at the age of twelve to approach such socially prominent party chaperones as Mrs. Morgan Davis, wife of the then-chairman of Humble Oil, and make polite conversation.

"I grew up where we had artichokes and butter knives at lunch, because my mother said, 'This is the way people live,'" Joanne says. "Once, when I was two years old, I picked up a finger bowl and drank out of it, and I think it left a scar on her."

She continues matter-of-factly, "Being an only child, I had to please everybody or I didn't have very much. I had a perfume bottle to play with, dolls, toys, but I never had very many people."

But her biggest pain came from another quarter: She was dyslexic.

"I was always considered very dumb," she says. "The terrible thing about dyslexia is what the teachers do to you and the students do to you." One handwriting teacher, for example, kept sending her to the blackboard, although she knew Joanne couldn't form the letters correctly. But another teacher spotted her problem in second grade and discussed it with her mother, who worked patiently with Joanne until she learned to read. Joanne continued to have trouble with math. "Then, when I turned thirteen, I became very popular, and it didn't matter if you were dumb," she says with a shrug. "I rolled up my hair one day."

With the encouragement of her high school principal, Joanne made the National Honor Society; but even now, she remains hypersensitive about her intelligence. She bridles when people mistake her associative thought patterns and nonlinear logic for stupidity. Yet she persists in hopping from topic to topic with blithe enthusiasm. That's because her apparent flightiness is effective. It charms; it disarms; it helps get her what she wants. Like Scarlett O'Hara, Joanne is a survivor. And she's not above using all her wiles to ensure that she has fun doing it.

Another major weapon in her arsenal is her clear understanding of enlightened self-interest, so important to everything from charity fundraising to international diplomacy. For instance, when an American multinational corporation, whose name she declines to disclose, ran afoul of the Pakistani government, which threatened suit, Honorary Consul General Joanne offered to intervene. She let President Zia know that the company would rather donate a substantial sum to Pakistan to finish its railroad than spend a similar amount on lawyers. The gambit worked.

"You have to look at the other person's problem and find a solution that's useful to them as well as to your client," she says. "It's a matter of saying, 'I don't ask you for anything unless I can give you something back.' You do this on a [charity] ball, business, anything."

By her late thirties, Joanne had chaired most of Houston's major balls and fund drives (there were fewer of them then) and was ready to tackle something bigger. In 1963, to raise money for her grandmother's favorite cause, the Women's Christian Mission, she appeared on television to publicize the charity's good works. She was an instant hit.

"All I had to do was tell these lurid tales, because it was just like something out of *True Confessions*," she admits. "What had happened to those women and what had sent them to the Women's Christian Mission was just terrible."

Channel 11 was so impressed that they asked her to host her own show. Despite her natural talent for tear-jerking, Joanne was far from a polished media personality. "Everyone was in a state of shock, I was so bad," she says of her first weeks on the air. "There's no way to describe it. I was awful. Everybody told me how *wonderful* the woman before me was. She was so professional."

But persistence and personality pulled her through. She moved from Channel 11 to Channel 2, where her spot on "The News at Noon" evolved into "The Joanne King Show," which captured a whopping 50 percent of Houston's lunchtime viewers. Her approach was highly personal. When her sons Beau and Robin (now twenty-eight and twenty-three) celebrated birthdays or suffered childhood diseases, she shared the experiences with her audience.

"If I had a problem, I assumed other people had it," she explains. "I would try to find somebody who could describe it and give an answer. I never put anything on that didn't have an answer, because why frustrate people?"

"I cannot analyze her appeal; I can just say she had a lot of it," says Ray Miller, who as then-news director at Channel 2 was Joanne's immediate boss. "Women especially liked what she did."

While she always cooperated with whatever the station was trying to do, he says, "I don't think she knocked herself out on it—except that, in a sense, she was working all the time. She was always 'on.' She wasn't one person when you were talking to her in your office and another on the air. She charmed me, so I'm certainly not surprised that she charms Washington and the National Trust and whoever else gets in her way."

To make Prince Saud of Saudi Arabia feel at home, Joanne converted her River Oaks party room into an Arabian seraglio.

Joanne began transferring that charm into the international arena in 1964, when she and late real estate tycoon R.E. "Bob" Smith staged the city's first successful Consular Ball. For the previous thirteen years, the Port of Houston had hosted the occasion and picked up the tab, but nobody came. In the second largest port in the country, the business leaders and the international set didn't mingle.

"Houston is important to a lot of countries and they send us their best," Joanne says. "And the thing was, nobody knew them. Our main objective was to be sure that the important business people of Houston knew the exciting, important representatives of our worldwide community."

To ensure a good turnout, Joanne asked the prominent couples in town not only to buy a table and invite their most stimulating friends, but to ask a consul to join them. She suggested that it might be a good idea for the host couples to throw little dinners for their adopted diplomats in the weeks preceding the ball. And she arranged a solemn ceremony at which the Houstonians so honored received official-looking sashes in colors of their consuls' countries. Everyone was delighted to accept—from Cadillac dealer W.W. Bland and his wife Lorraine to General Maurice and Winifred Hirsch. From that point on, Houston's Consular Ball has been one of *the* social events of the year.

"When we first did that ball, I never *dreamed* I'd become a consul myself," Joanne says. But she did. Less than a decade later, she became honorary consul for Pakistan, assisting Pakistanis living or visiting here, helping Houstonians obtain visas to Pakistan, and generally representing that country's commercial interests. In 1978, the King of Morocco asked her to accept a similar position with his government. Joanne is the only public official he has appointed personally.

"It was a big shock to me," she says. After she and Bob Herring had met with the monarch and discussed world affairs for two hours, the king's chief of protocol appeared at their hotel. "He said, 'His Majesty wants *you*—not Bob Herring—to be consul,'" she says. After checking with her existing client, Pakistan, she accepted.

"The reason I wanted to do it for those two countries is that one is on the Strait of Hormuz [through which much of the Mideast's oil flows] and one is on the Strait of Gibraltar," she explains. "So in working for them, I feel I'm working for my own country, too."

Joanne first earned the consular plates which decorate her white Cadillac in the early seventies, when she was appointed honorary consul by Pakistan's then-President Bhutto. After military strongman General Zia-ul-Haq staged a successful coup and shocked world opinion by executing his democratically elected predecessor, he not only asked Joanne to continue her post, but promoted her to honorary consul general in 1980.

"I work directly with the president in Pakistan, and he has taken a great interest in the people—anything for the poor," she says. "He's a much-maligned man." But can a frankly undemocratic, right-wing ruler be sincere about helping his country's poor? He can, she says, see that they eat better and have roofs over their heads. "That's all they care about," she insists. "They're not worried about whether they have a democracy or whether they can vote."

The sentiment may sound like an expedient rationalization, but it's consistent with her firmly rooted faith in the salubrious social potential of grass-roots free enterprise. Joanne is an unabashed cheerleader for capitalism.

"I looked at these two countries, and I said, 'What can I give them?'" she asks rhetorically. "I can give them parties in Houston. I can get drunk sailors out of jail. I can send dead bodies home—all of which I do. *Or* I can contribute something that they really need: money. *Where* do they need money? In the poorer sector. I want *badly* to export free enterprise. If we don't export free enterprise, then we can't blame Third World countries for listening to other voices in other rooms."

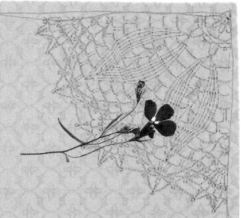

By the time we got home to Texas, we were both tired — and maybe just a little tired of each other. We were stars that shined together, but only in places where there was no previous baggage. At home, there were two different camps of friends and associates, and the twain did not meet. We ran into the schism again and again. Our worlds were simply too different.

His friends did not like me. They called me "Princess T&T." None of them could ever see his attraction to what they described as an "older woman" when he could go out with Miss Universe. With me around, they had no fun at all. There was no cursing, no ribald jokes, not much beer, and certainly no drunken Charlie to pal around with. I just couldn't make it with the good ol' boys. I cramped their style, and they wanted me gone.

My friends were shaking their proper heads, frantic. Charlie did not fit in their world. "I hope Joanne doesn't want to bring that Charlie Wilson," they all whispered to each other when they invited me to weekends away. "We don't know what we will do if she does."

They could never understand my interest in anyone who would *want* to go out with a twenty-five-year-old or a Miss Universe. But mostly, they thought he drank too much.

How, after Bob Herring, could I be interested in this carousing drunk? (He wasn't really a carousing drunk and I wasn't a prissy and fun-squashing snob, but perception counts.) Basically Charlie liked to go out and drink and brag with the boys. It was not living the antics that he enjoyed so much. It was sharing them with the guys who, openmouthed, lived vicariously through his adventures. Charlie could tell a story better than anyone I ever knew.

But he had this sweet, romantic side. One day he said, "Do you remember the first time I held your hand?" He told me the name of the movie and the exact moment when he took my hand. You couldn't help but love him. My friends knew nothing of these moments, though. Our friends weren't the only obstacle, however. Fun and games were fine, but both of us were feeling uncertain about our being married. We saw that being together all that time did not bring us closer as it had for Bob and me and would later for Charlie and his wife, Barbara.

So after two whirlwind years, our romance crumbled like a stale cookie.

I never saw Charlie drunk but once, and I did not contribute to his campaigns.

I gave him a fund-raiser at my home, inviting heads of banks, Exxon, Chevron, and everyone I knew that he did not. Charlie had many outstanding contributors who liked and admired him, but there were plenty of others who did not. I hoped to help them get to know the real Charlie. He was so overwhelmed by this contingent of skeptics in my home that he got drunk and fell into his plate.

It's very hard to explain Charlie. He had many facets. George Crile wrote, "Very few were aware of the depths of [his] frequent depressions....No matter what his inner mood, whenever the public door opened, the darkness disappeared, replaced by the bigger-than-life, can-do Texan." Charlie was living with the masks of comedy and tragedy in each hand, ready to lift into place whichever face the moment called for.

The weekend after we returned from Europe, he explained that he had other obligations to fulfill and might not always be available.

In fact he was going to Florida for a New Year's Eve date (he had promised long ago and was "obligated").

When I looked surprised, he explained that I would have to be like the other girls now and expect that. "Expect what?" I thought. "Be like the other girls, indeed! I am not part of a relay team, Mr. Wilson. I run my own races, thank you. Go run yours!"

He did. He went to Florida and I went to Jamaica. Thank goodness I had somewhere to go. It's hard to save face sitting at home.

Contrary to what people thought, he did not flirt with other women when he was with me. He gave me his entire attention. But when the romance cooled, he liked very much having other dessert plates waiting for him on the table. But I was not simply another dish on the buffet line.

As he galloped into the center ring with his plumed ponies, I left the circus like a popped balloon, and it hurt.

I had the craziest experience of my life in Jamaica. Remember, God has His plans, and He likes to laugh.

I had been invited by the distinguished Mandell J. Ourisman family of Washington, D.C., which had provided most of the furniture for Jackie Kennedy's White House and chandeliers to the State Department. They were Washington social lions, and they had the most glamorous house in Jamaica. Among the houseguests while I was there were "Lucky" Roosevelt, Reagan's chief of protocol, and her distinguished husband, Archie. There were parties every night. I went with my bruised ego and my suitcase and proceeded to have a Demi Moore/Susan Sarandon moment.

Charlie was off chasing young girls, so the Lord decided to help me through this by having young men chase me! It shook everybody. These were the young titans of the new cyberworld who had made millions overnight. They had yachts, private planes, and houses on the beach. They were sought after by every hostess. Understand, they were not chasing me with honorable intentions. They were only interested in a fling. "So what?" I thought. It was very good for my ego. At every party I attended I was surrounded by this elite young group, all vying for my attention. These were not gigolos. They had more money than they could possibly spend. It was a revelation and a resurrection for me.

Of course, these guys were rather like children. The only thing they desperately wanted was what they couldn't have. On New Year's Eve, one jumped the fence, ran through three guard dogs, and came in the window. Fortunately, I had studied kickboxing.

Their attentions did not end in Jamaica. One Brad Pitt look-alike followed me to Washington. I enjoyed flagrantly flaunting him in front of Charlie. "What's good for the goose is good for the gander, you rat," I thought.

But "Brad's" idea of healthy living was "a roll in the hay keeps the doctor away." With that in mind, he burst into my hotel room, pretending to be room service. I literally had to jump over two beds, grab the desk chair like a lion tamer, and force him out. Leaning against the door, I heard the lion say, "I'll return." To myself I said, "I'll return too . . . to sanity."

On the next plane, I was out of there!

Charlie and the guys continued to call, but the price of all this high livin', sportin' life was just too high.

I got a call one day from the CEO of Ling-Temco-Vought, a big conglomerate. One of his companies had underbid a job rebuilding the Pakistani railroad. They couldn't finish it, so they left an unfinished railroad, tools, and equipment strewn all over Pakistan. Naturally Pakistan threatened to sue — big-time. The CEO said, "I was told you were the only person in the world who could fix this. Can you?" Remembering my lessons in corporate action and thinking, I did the math and figured that ten million dollars would probably finish the railroad.

"How much do you think it will take to finish the job?" I asked.

"About ten million," he said.

I thought, "Bull's-eye!" I could do this.

Out loud I suggested, "You will never win a lawsuit with a government in its own country. It will cost millions and take years. This will hurt the price of your stock. Why don't you give the Pakistanis the ten million and let them finish the railroad and go home free?"

He mused, then said, "I'll do that!"

I called President Zia, and the CEO and I went to Pakistan and finished the deal in two days. I left rich! I couldn't believe I actually got paid to do this. As usual, as I walked into the room, I said, "Mr. President, I am being paid for this." I wanted to be clear and aboveboard with him always. This was the first time I was paid.

I had fabulous invitations in London, so I decided to celebrate my success. On the way, the plane stopped to refuel in Dubai. Before Dubai became the grand citadel of finance, it was merely a great shopping stop. Everything on earth was for sale on the cheap.

I debarked from the plane "just to look." Is there such a thing? Not in my lexicon. I always find some enticing bargain for which I suddenly have a desperate and immediate need. I simply *must* buy it. After all, I might never pass this way again. I believe this is called "impulse buying." I considered it Texas frugality. So I bought something "divine" at a price so low it was "a shame" to leave it.

It was a watch. I thought it very elegant. Its broad gold band resembled a stylish bracelet rather than a watch, and the workings were indiscernible at its center. I was quite proud of it, as I had never seen anything quite like it. I thought it would be the perfect accessory when I attended the opening of Parliament in London. It almost got me locked in the Tower of London.

The Hall in the Palace of Westminster is quite small and invitations are extremely limited and very much prized. I had given great thought to my ensemble — my Chanel suit that Coco herself had chosen and given to me in 1969. "These colors will be perfect for you," she said. It was a purplish tweed — very subtle. "I want you to have this to remember me," she said (as if I could ever forget).

I was divine, or so I thought that crisp winter day in 1984 at the opening of Parliament. My lordly host was sitting with the other aristocrats in their ermine-trimmed robes, their consorts in tiaras.

Oh, such elegance! No one does it like the Brits. They know how to create moments of magnificence. Each new session of Parliament features the royal procession in all their finery traveling from Buckingham Palace to the Houses of Parliament by state coach, which, of course, is gold.

Inside, the royal family members, led by the queen and Prince Philip, glided down the aisle with only a red velvet rope to separate them from the guests. They were closely followed by Princess Diana and Prince Charles, Prince Andrew, Prince Edward, and Princess Anne, then the Duke and Duchess of Kent, followed by the Prince and Princess Michael of Kent (my special friend). It was a passing parade of utter grandeur, which, due to security, is no longer possible. The space is so narrow that one could touch these gloriously costumed and storied personages if one dared. The queen wore her crown and the robes especially made for just such pomp and circumstance.

It was a storied, privileged moment...until the solemn stillness was suddenly broken by "Oh, give me a home where the buffalo roam, where the deer and the antelope play..."

"Home on the Range," the world's corniest and best-known western song, was inexplicably filling the rarified air of the Houses of Parliament. Everyone's eyes widened in utter disbelief, then horror. Everyone looked at everyone in insulted outrage. You could just imagine what they were thinking: *"How could anyone possibly, possibly dare...*It was simply *not* to be borne! An outrage, never to be forgiven and never to be forgotten. Off with the heads of the perpetrators, and soon please!"

The queen herself was directly in front of us at that moment. Even she, who is never at a loss, could not help glancing in the direction of this offending noise. This could *not* be happening at the opening of Parliament. *It just could not.*

I joined the crowd in looking around disapprovingly. I, too, was mortally offended, seeking the culprit. Alas, all horrified gazes were fixed upon me.

Great balls of fire! It was me! The watch! It crooned away, and, horror of horrors, I did not know how to stop it. I desperately punched everything in sight, but there was nothing in sight to punch. The watch simply had no buttons anywhere. I could not slink out unobtrusively because there were so many around me. Obviously silence was not an option.

Suddenly the crowd melted around me, and a way was opened for me to leave. No one wanted to be seen anywhere near me.

The second chorus of "Home on the Range" began to play as I fled. If looks could kill, this book in your hands would never have been penned.

I made it outside with my watch still singing — but my composure was in tatters. "Fortunately," I thought, "no one knows me." Otherwise, I would have made Britain's "most wanted" list for sure.

Three gentlemen ran out behind me. The British are so wonderfully kind. They took my hands, patted my back, and tried to comfort me by saying ludicrous things like, "No one really noticed"; "It happens all the time"; "It made that stuffy old ceremony bearable."

Their best words were, "We will take you home. Where are you staying?"

"Claridge's," I sniffed. I knew one of them a little, but I really would not have cared if they had been Jack the Ripper and his brothers. I wanted away from there.

There was a brief moment of silence. Biting their lips, they looked at me. I looked at them. And then we were unable to contain our laughter. They literally doubled over, almost hysterical.

"Where in the world did you get that? Why choose that awful tune?" one said between gasps. I couldn't answer through peals of laughter.

The British are gallant, so fortunately the story did not circulate... and neither did the watch.

Execution was the only solution.

"...and the skies are not cloudy all day..." played cheerfully as we threw the shining offender into the murky water of the Thames. I like to believe that at that moment, in her royal finery in front of Parliament, the queen felt a twinge of a smile.

My next trip to England was a dream come true.

I sometimes have trouble sleeping at night. I wrestle with the day's unfinished problems and think of the same things, over and over.

"This has got to stop," I said as I saw circles forming under my eyes, but what could I do? I decided to pull a black shade over unpleasant thoughts and think of something wonderful, something that could never happen...a dream that could not come true and never would...a total fantasy. It worked. I thought of never-never land and went to sleep.

What was my never-never land, the thing that could never happen?

When Prince Philip married Elizabeth, the soon-to-be queen of England, he was considered the perfect fairy-tale prince — six foot four, blond, blue-eyed, and slim, with perfect military bearing. He was known to be smart, full of new ideas, educated, and charming. Every woman in the world was a little in love with his image. No matter how many handsome men, movie stars, or princes came and went, he was *my* dream of what a prince should be.

"I shall dream of waltzing with Prince Philip at a private party at Buckingham Palace," I thought. Never in my life did I dream that would ever come true.

I was chair of a benefit to restore the Old Vic Theatre in London.

Prince Talal of Saudi Arabia accompanied me to the event and said, "Joanne, how much money do you want to raise?"

"About a hundred thousand dollars," I said.

He sat down and wrote me a check for the entire amount!

The royal family was very grateful and invited me to a small private party given by Prince Philip. There were only fourteen people invited, most of whom I knew well.

It helped that I had met the prince's best friend and aide and spent a few evenings at Annabelle's, London's most exclusive club, with him. He probably had a lot to do with my invitation, and because of him, I would get to have a more intimate chat with His Highness than was usually permitted on these occasions.

The night of the party, off I went, thrilled and excited, hardly breathing. I was actually going to meet the (literal) prince of my dreams who had helped me drift off to sleep so often. As I entered the palace grounds, I passed the famous Buckingham Palace guards, who are known for never changing their expressions. It has become a game for tourists to entice them to change expression. To my knowledge they never have. They have endured water thrown in their faces and all manner of indignities, but never once have they lost their composure. They keep their pact to remain stoic out of respect to their sovereign majesty. They are legends.

I drove proudly into the courtyard of the palace, feeling very elegant and very grand — only to find that I was not expected! A puzzled gentleman (the butler to the royal family) came to the car, bowed gracefully, and said very gently and kindly, "Madam, I rather think the party is tomorrow night."

On the way out, the stoic guards lost their storied calm and laughed. For a moment I was nonplussed; then I laughed too. I returned to Claridge's and in the bar I met my friends Heini Thyssen and Armand Hammer (who also loved rollicking with the royals), where I regaled them with my misadventures.

Cinderella was too anxious... but at least I hadn't left a glass slipper. I tried again the next night after my dress rehearsal: same dress, same car, same entrance. The guards recognized me and smiled in welcome. I could tell they wished me well. The butler came personally to get me. It seemed the whole night was smiling.

I floated up to the private quarters of the royal family, ready to meet the prince of my dreams. I felt the warmth of friends all around me. I was presented to the other guests, most of whom I knew very well and who had come to England just for this party. Armand and Heini were there, as was the former king Constantine of Greece.

At last his aide led me to the prince, who bowed elegantly and smiled. He was all I ever dreamed he would be. By now you know that I like to play, especially with significant people. We chatted for a while, and then I said, "Do you know that you are my fantasy?" His eyes opened wide and he turned quite pink! I quickly explained my dream sequence and how I put myself to sleep dreaming about the impossibility of waltzing with him at Buckingham Palace.

Standing tall and straight he said, "By all means, let us waltz." And we did!

The next day his aide called and said that the prince had thoroughly enjoyed the evening. "I did not think anyone could make him blush," he said. "He loved every minute of it."

Ah, the end of dreams. There was nothing else impossible to dream about.

God so enjoyed all of my misdemeanors that He decided to give me every small thing I could ever want. I felt sad. I had no wish to become a friend of the prince. He was a one-night stand in fairyland, but I do miss my dream...

When I returned to reality, Charlie and I were able to help each other once more. Charlie and I wanted to thank the Saudis for their much-needed financial support in the war. We decided that a

Washington, D.C., party was in order, only this time, I threw the party on my own — not with Charlie or Bob Herring. This time, it was just me.

Everyone wanted to meet the new Saudi ambassador, Prince Bandar. He was a jet pilot, a famous wit, and a towering force in the Arab world. However, it was not so easy to honor him. Like most Middle Eastern royals, he liked to entertain at home and rarely accepted invitations elsewhere. He was very reclusive. In fact, one powerful senator had a dinner in his honor, and the prince failed to show up.

Just getting him to come to a party in his honor was a tall order, but tall orders are a bit of a specialty for us Texans.

The press said that the guest list for that party has never been duplicated. They should know — they covered them all for years to come. We had all of President Reagan's cabinet, the chairman of the Joint Chiefs of Staff, and the commandants of the army, the navy, and the marines. We had the most significant ambassadors of the day and important congressmen and senators — all in one room on this one night. People couldn't believe it.

The *New York Times* sent its top writer, Charlotte Curtis, to cover the party. Then Diana McLellan, the oh-so-fun columnist for the *Washington Times*, wrote another article that I thought so witty I couldn't choose between the two. For the first time these ladies did not write the caustic comments that they were famous for.

I want to share them with you because they are a true history of the time, written as it unfolded.

When you read them, I hope you'll chuckle and feel that you were there.

Why was the party significant? It established me as a single woman able to operate in Washington by myself. For the first time in my life, I was established as a person on my own, not Bob King's wife or Bob Herring's wife or Charlie's woman of choice. I was me. I was a person who could think, who could talk, who could analyze, who could actually get things done on my own without a man.

A Feast, Texas-Sized

Special to The New York Times

WASHINGTON — When Secretary of Energy Donald P. Hodel first saw the elaborately decorated 100-foot dinner table, it looked so long he thought he was seeing a shorter table reflected in a mirror. Secretary of Defense Caspar W. Weinberger said it reminded him of some Napoleonic banquet. James A. Baker 3d, the President's chief of staff, just smiled. He is as much a Texan as the hostess who ordered up the single narrow table for 110 guests. He knew he was in for the stuff of Texas legend.

"Joanne and I went to kindergarten together," Mr. Baker said. "We've known each other all our lives. She's a bright, imaginative, wonderful girl."

Joanne is Joanne King Herring, one of Houston's seemingly endless supply of beautiful blonde heiresses, the honorary consul general of Morocco and Pakistan and a habitual visitor in the courts of the Middle East.

Her friend Prince Bandar bin Sultan is Saudi Arabia's Ambassador to the United States. She wanted him to meet the right people. So she borrowed the vast mezzanine of the Hay-Adams Hotel last week and threw him the sort of extravaganza most Americans know, if they know at all, only from fiction, the movies and television.

Her party was a black-tie Arabian Nights feast with an eclectic menu, brass animals and bright, sequined tablecloths from the third world, mariachis ("because I'm a Texan") and a seating plan requiring each man to change his place three times.

"You are the entertainment," she told guests over the pomegranate sherbet.

Mrs. Herring used a microphone to give her marching orders. Whatever else she said from her place at the middle of the table was lost, drowned in a hubbub of voices, punctuated by what may have been a moan of protest. After the lamb, when she issued her first set of orders, the men — including bewildered Senators, self-made oil tycoons and Joint Chiefs generals trained to act decisively in a crisis — glanced beseechingly at their neighbors, asked if anyone knew where they were to go, stood up, moved timidly to the right and sat down again.

"I'm not sure this is where I belong," one man said, approaching a woman he hoped was a new dinner partner, "but my name is James Lyon."

Mr. Lyon, a banker, was part of the giant Texas contingent that included Baron and Baroness Enrico di Portanova of the Cullen clan, Robert Mosbacher and Carolyn Skelly. Mr. Lyon was barely into his Salade de Nuit Arabian (watercress with grapes) when Mrs. Herring called for another move. He was replaced in the course of the evening by Robert H. Lilac, who flew fighter planes with the Saudi Ambassador; Senator Pete Wilson of California, and Lawrence S. Eagle-burger from the State Department. Senator Edward Zorinsky of Nebraska passed by, a stoical look on his face.

Selwa Roosevelt, the Chief of Protocol, smiled throughout. Carter Brown, director of the National Gallery moved precisely. Several women were enchanted to discover themselves momentarily beside Henry Kissinger. The second move put Prince Bandar next Barbara Walters, whose side he refused to leave.

The Prince sat though the third move and the arrival of glass goblets layered with mangoes, vanilla ice cream and clouds of pink cotton candy. The guests attacked the dessert with the speedy relish they'd given previous courses.

"Stop! Stop!" Mrs. Herring cried. "Don't eat the dessert! You have to have it flambéed!" The ever-diplomatic Mr. Eagleburger, who had re-

There were 110 guests — all at one 100-foot table

moved his cotton candy to a saucer, reassembled his dessert. Waiters flamed it and the other desserts with burning brandy (inadvertently torching Lee Thaw's souvenir fortune scroll), purposely melting each into what the hostess called a "Taste of Texas." Mrs. Herring said the hotel planned to add her sweet to its regular menu. Seeing all that firepower made Mr. Lilac a touch nervous.

"It could be dangerous," he said. "My wife's hair caught fire at Bandar's. He didn't hesitate a minute. He put her in the swimming pool."

Mrs. Herring toasted the Prince and his diamond-bedecked wife, Princess Haifa al-Faisal, King Fahd's niece, and said they'd become friends when her late husband, Robert Herring, a natural-gas tycoon, did so much business in the Middle East. The Prince, a nephew of the King's, thanked her and toasted President Reagan.

Senator John G. Tower of Texas responded with the toast to the Saudi King. Shortly thereafter, the party began to disband.

"I'm a serious person," the hostess had contended, reiterating a familiar theme because some Easterners seemed to misunderstand her. "I want to be a catalyst. Somebody who brings people who have to work together really together. So they know each other. I didn't really intend to become another Washington hostess."

But of course that's exactly what she became: Another overnight sensation simply by laying on a big-name spectacular that's still the talk of usually staid Washington.

DIANA HEARS

This was a pure "la di da" gossip column but helped to entice important Texas people to dress up come & listen... They came They listened

BRING ON THE BLINKERS . . . Well! Washington hasn't goggled at anything *this* glittery since the Shah's poor ambassador, Ardeshir Zahedi, shuffled off to Switzerland. Picture it, please: A sequinned tablecloth dazzling all along a single long dinner-table for 110. Gold candelabra and Moroccan elephants twinkling. Also twinkling: The spanking-new Saudi ambassador, Prince Bandar bin-Sultan and his Princess Haifa al-Faisal. Megatwinkling: Hostess Joanne Herring, dripping with Bulgari diamonds and silhouetted against the White House outside the Hay-Adams window. The munchies: Divine fishy little things in pastry cockleshells, pomegranite sorbet, lamb, salad with black grapes and, *quelle grande finale*, a yummy plop of mango and ice cream topped with cotton candy, which was set afire — can you stand it? — before serving. The only *really* familiar things at the soiree, darlings, were the dear old mugs lined along the table: The Caspar Weinbergers, Jim Bakers, John Towers; Barbara Walters and Henry Kissinger sans Nancy (she was stricken with something); not to mention the Senators Heinz, Pell, Zorinsky, and Cohen; the Bill French Smiths; the J. Carter Browns; and a smattering of diamond-drenched Houstonians and stray ambassadors. A fun note: Every couple of courses each man was forced to hop up, grab his napkin and wineglass, and slide smartly five places over, so he could plop down and tell the same jokes to new ladies. (Many crashed *en route*, but it was all so hooty that even the Prince, who wasn't supposed to, leapt up and slid over too.) Everyone got a Japanese horoscope. (Cap Weinberger's a Snake, Jim Baker a Sheep, Barbara Walters a Dragon and Henry the K a Boar. But you knew that.) The best fun of all came when Joanne Herring, who'd paid for it all, toasted the Prince, and talked about how terribly alike Texans and Saudis are. "We're both really simple people, from simple country," she said. "A lot of sand, and a lot of oil. Now if we can only find some way to make money off the sand." They all adored it. This has been your night on the town. Now settle down, please, and get on with the gossip.

This put me in the position of being sought after by the biggest companies in the world — and they wanted to pay me high figures as a consultant. They needed my help for the access I had to consequential world figures. This was a time when I was being valued like a man in a man's world. They were not interested in me and my slinky dresses or my dancing ability or my conversational expertise. They were interested in my ability to analyze and to put together business deals. You must remember that I lived in an era when women were classified as society figures, secretaries, glamour girls, "wives of," and volunteers — no matter what their education, expertise, intellect, or ability. I was thought of as a stellar, productive volunteer who could get things done that others could not. I was respected and admired. But *nobody* had ever offered to pay me for my expertise — except the Pakistani general who offered to bribe me and the Pakistani women who wanted to use me to make money. You can't imagine what a window these legitimate offers opened in my life. In astonishment, I thought, "Maybe, just maybe, I could legitimately be called 'sir.'"

The night of the party I wore my 1972 black gown with the fur bottom that I wore in the show in Spain with Charlie. Charlie put his hands on my shoulders and said reprovingly, "That is the same dress I've seen before."

"What do you mean?"

"It's high-necked, long-sleeved, and clingy. To hell with the dress. I love you. Let's try again."

"Charlie, darling, it's too late. And I don't want to spend every day in the gym! I want a real life with someone who loves me for who I am, not how I look." (Charlie had once said, "Please don't get fat.")

"But I do love you for those reasons," Charlie declared. "The only real problem is you scare me."

"Charlie, you're too much."

CHAPTER 23

Down the Rabbit Hole

Herring-Davis wedding truly a glamorous affair

The Houston Post/Tues., August 13, 1985

SUPER PEOPLE — The Nassau wedding of Houston's glamorous Honorary Consul to Pakistan and Morocco **Joanne Herring** and millionaire **Lloyd Davis** was attended by several Houstonians, a beautiful affair where everyone wore white. The bride and groom now are sailing through the Bahamas aboard their yacht, The Wave Dancer. It was described to me by one of the wedding guests as "a four-bedroom, three-bath boat as big as a split-level ranch house." The newlyweds had only to walk down their private pier in order to board.

But back to details of the entire event, starting off with the black-tie dinner party held the night before at the posh Lyford Cay Club. There, several guests offered light-hearted toasts, and our town's **Jack Blanton** — with wife **Laura Lee** — stole the limelight with his great humor. Close on his heels with her sparkling personality was Joanne's mother, **Maelan Johnson.**

Some of the biggies in the party included **Prince Caniar Pahlavi,** nephew of the late **Shah of Iran; Barbara** and **Gerald Hines, L.F.** and **Eleanor McCollum** and her actress-daughter **Virginia Kiser** (you've seen her on Dallas); **Louise** and Dr. **Denton Cooley, Jenard** and **Gail Gross** and their daughter **Dawn, John** and **Brenda Duncan, Lorraine McMurrey** and Dr. **Chehlaoui Riad, Robert** and **Georgette Mosbacher,** Joanne's aide **Steven Charlston,** and Dr. **William Walker** and wife **Mary.** Publicist **Barry Horn** was the dinner's host.

IT WAS HELD IN Lloyd's home, and naturally the guests wandered around the pool area. It was in that area that Robert Mosbacher became the evening's minor casualty: He turned his ankle on one of the stones that made up the pool's patio. Not to worry; Mary Walker tore napkins into strips, and her mom Louise bandaged it right on the spot. With such wonderful attention, Robert seemed very pleased about the whole incident.

The wedding was held at 5 in the afternoon and was attended by the aforementioned guests plus the children of both Joanne and Lloyd. The children circled the bride and groom at the altar. The ceremony was reported to be so sincere and moving it resulted in several guests having to dab away tears of happiness. Joanne wore a white handmade tea-length dress from Paris with a peach satin bow at the waist. Her shoes were peach-toned. So were some of the ribbons on her white portrait hat. Lloyd's trousers and shirt were of white linen.

After the ceremony, there was a calypso dinner dance at his home, and all of the food served was Bahamian. It included the good old reliable island standbys of conch fritters and eggplants stuffed with seafood. There was lots of bubbly, as one might imagine.

AFTER THEIR CRUISE, Joanne and Lloyd will dock at Fort Lauderdale, where they'll catch a plane to Rome, where they'll spend a few days with **Baron Ricky Di Portanova** and **Baroness Sandra** before going on to the northern Italy resort villa of the **Count** and **Countess Pecci-Blount**. After their honeymoon, Joanne and Lloyd will live here.

Joanne Herring to wed millionaire Lloyd Davis

SUPER PEOPLE — **Joanne Herring,** Houston's glamorous honorary consul to Pakistan and Morocco, is packing for a trip to the Bahamas where on Aug. 10 she'll marry millionaire **Lloyd Davis.** Yes, despite her constant globe-trotting and being linked romantically with such handsome gents as Virginia's Sen. **John Warner** and Texas' U.S. Rep. **Charles Wilson** and Mideast oil sheiks, she's marrying the "boy next door," so to speak. Lloyd is a Houstonian and her longtime friend. They began dating last December

**HERRING:
Wedding bells**

and right away knew it was the real thing.

In the biz world, he has made it big as head of Fisk Electric and even bigger with that firm's worldwide telephone communications division.

Their blending will take place in the posh Lyford Cay Club near Nassau. It is decidedly British in flavor, and membership is tough to come by. Lloyd and Joanne are both members. Lyford Cay is a high-priced resort area of about 250 private homes, owned by some of the world's wealthiest. Lloyd owns a home there, and until last year, so did Joanne. She sold hers to the **Sheik of Kuwait** after he'd knocked on her door and asked if she'd part with it.

Almost all of the people attending their very small wedding will be members of their families. Although between them they probably know three-fourths of the "in" people of the world, they want their marriage vows to be very private. I'm with them. I believe that's the way it *should* be.

THE GUESTS will include her children **Beau** and **Robin King,** and **Robbie, Carolina, Randy, Laura** and **Diane Herring;** and his son and daughter-in-law **Ken** and **Mary Davis,** and daughters and sons-in-law **Susan** and **John Johnson** and **Terry** and **Bruce Harrison.** Additionally, there'll be Joanne's goddaughter **Isabel Ferreros** and husband **Enrique.** Isabel is the daughter of the **Count de Bourg-Bozas.**

The wedding invitations were handpainted by Houston artist **Rachel Britt** and feature watercolors of a Bahamian hibiscus. Joanne and Lloyd will headquarter here in his lovely home off Woodway, close to where Vice President **George Bush** and wife **Barbara** resided before moving to D.C.

A honeymoon around the world in six weeks

STACY MEIER

Houston socialite **Joanne Herring's** recent nuptials in the Bahamas were certainly in keeping with her reputation for extravagance.

The night before her Aug. 10 wedding to Houston millionaire **Lloyd K. Davis** in exclusive Lyford Cay, Joanne and 92 wedding guests danced at the Lyford Cay Club. The merrymaking continued into the following day, which was capped off with a chapel wedding, where the guests all wore white. Among them were Prince **Camiar Pahlavi** (the nephew of the late Shah of Iran), Galleria developer **Gerald Hines** and heart surgeon **Denton Cooley**.

The wedding was the third for both parties. Joanne and Lloyd, an independent investor who is "into everything," have known each other for many years, according to Houston fashion personality **Barry Horn**. The couple fell in love while in the Bahamas, he says.

Since the wedding, the newlyweds have embarked on a six-week honeymoon that sounds like something from the movies: nine days sailing the Atlantic on Davis' yacht Wave Dancer, a few days in Rome visiting Baron **Enrico** and Baroness **Sandra di Portanova**, a few more days in northern Italy seeing Count and Countess Pecci-Blount, and some time exploring Moscow, Siberia and Mongolia.

Mongolia?

"The reason they picked those exotic places," explains Horn, "is that those are the only places on the globe neither have ever been to."

Are you ready for this? **Joanne Herring** and **Lloyd Davis**, who'll marry in Lyford Cay in the Bahamas Aug. 10, have decided on their honeymoon destination — Russia, Siberia and Mongolia. They say those are the only places they have never been. To each his own, but the fact that neither has been there should tell them something! They do plan a few days of cruising the Bahamas in Lloyd's yacht ...

*C*harlie was thrilled with the success of our evening on the night of the Bandar party. He looked at me very seriously and said, "Do you want to try again?"

I looked at him as someone wonderful and very special and said, "No."

That chapter of my life was ended. Perhaps for the moment he wanted to rekindle the flame, but in reality, he liked his life of chasing girls and drinking beer with the guys. We both needed to move on.

But there was one more unexpected chapter. Many years later, but before he finally married, Charlie had a heart attack. He came to Houston for treatment. "Please come," he said. "I really must see you."

I was married at the time, and I was also afraid of my husband Lloyd's jealousy.

"Please," said Charlie. "This may be the last time I see you."

Of course I went.

Charlie took my hand, looked at me seriously, and said, "Let's try again."

I kissed him on the cheek and said, "What do you mean? Charlie, I'm married! It's too late."

"I was crazy," he said, referring to the girls he had wanted to date. "But so were you! We can make it this time. Give us a chance."

I squeezed his hand and walked away. Memories can play tricks on us, letting us remember only the good while we forget the bad.

Ours had been a good, productive chapter in each others' lives. We had trudged through some very trying times, through the hails of bullets from all manner of enemy fire. He will always have a special place in my heart. I hope he saved a place for me in his.

⁓

I was happy with my life as it was. After the Afghanistan adventure with Charlie, I began working, taking on the consultancy of several major corporations. Mainly I was traveling around the world at other people's expense, staying in their marvelous châteaus and island retreats. I was always packing to go somewhere and often couldn't remember where I had been the week before.

Returning me to reality, my mother said, "You need to get married." Today parents say, "Get a job." My other-generation mother thought jobs were for others. In her book, marriage was easier. (It isn't.) My mother looked at my successful life alone as meaningless. The clock was ticking. I was fifty-five.

She had noticed me taking on the responsibility of maintaining my excruciatingly expensive house full of family and staff and a constant stream of houseguests. She realized that this could not continue forever, and she was concerned. At the time I was not lacking in husband contenders, but she knew the day was not far off when the cupboard would be bare. I quaked at the thought and began to think seriously that she might have a point.

Soon afterward, I got a call from multimillionaire Lloyd Davis. He had just sold his private electric company and his telephone company. No one ever thought that anyone could challenge AT&T. Lloyd broke the monopoly by starting a cell phone company, which became Sprint.

He had the toys: a plane, a house in the Bahamas, and a yacht. Each husband had given me something significant. Bob King had given me a private railroad car that had belonged to the Vanderbilt family. It was a magnificently decorated and restored dream. The only thing was — it cost as much to run as a jet plane. (It ended up getting stolen and stripped of its beautiful furnishings. I gave the husk that was left to charity.)

Bob Herring brought into my life the use of the company plane. We used it for business only, but we always combined business and pleasure. With a plane you could have dinner in New York and wake up in Paris for breakfast, which left Bob still fresh enough to do business.

Lloyd had a plane, too, and a yacht. He was slim, attractive, and much sought after by women. He built a house in the Lyford Cay Club outside Nassau, with his yacht parked outside. He was the talk of the club. They called him "the bachelor." (There were twelve rich widows for every man on the island, and young girls flocked around.)

He wanted his Bahamian housewarming done properly to ensure his place in this close-knit upper-echelon enclave. It was known as one of the most snobbish clubs in the world.

He knew *Town and Country* had done an article on the club. The magazine had used me as its centerfold, so he invited me to serve as hostess for his housewarming. I thought this was a great idea. I packed up my Louis Vuitton bag and everything chic I could find, and tripped out to his private plane feeling quite at home. The party was a big success, and Lloyd was thrilled.

The next day, we took a group out on his yacht. Most of the ladies refused to swim so they wouldn't "ruin their hair." I dived into the water, not caring, which impressed Lloyd immensely. He fell hard.

I was invited to the Winter Ball, at which Jacqueline Kennedy was hostess. Lloyd accompanied me. We danced all night and had a glorious time.

When Lloyd read that Slim Aarons, a celebrity photographer covering the event, said, "Joanne walked in behind Raquel Welch and all the photographers were elbowing each other to get a shot of Joanne," he was thrilled and bought all the photos.

When he asked me to marry him, Lloyd said, "I know you have a big emerald. [Bob King had given me the stunning emerald.] I know you have a big diamond [the "working" diamond that Bob Herring gave me]. I want to give you the biggest, most beautiful ruby in the world."

Buying a big ruby is very difficult. A law established by the kings of Siam and Burma declared that any ruby over six carats belonged to the king. Thus, when any fine ruby was discovered, the dealers cut it so that it would not exceed six carats. Lloyd somehow snared a flawless fifteen-carat stone that was fit for a king. I deeply appreciate the lovely things that Lloyd did for me.

Most of our friends were happy for us, but not all. Two who knew him well said, "Joanne, be careful. He has a dark side." I remember thinking, "Oh, it will be different with me."

Our hand-painted wedding invitations of Bahamian hibiscus requested that everyone wear white. Later, a Neiman Marcus employee said that the store had never had so many requests for white ensembles in its history. The church was filled with guests wearing white; they were as beautiful as the decorations.

People magazine, the television program *Lifestyles of the Rich and Famous*, and many other media outlets wanted to cover the wedding. We said no press, but the press covered it anyway by interviewing the returning guests.

Lloyd liked buying me clothes and chose my wedding dress. It was white lace with a big lace hat with ribbons, bows, and ruffles, my signature look — which, after all these years, really bores me to death.

The wedding was held in the Chapel by the Sea in Lyford Cay. People came for three days of frivolity, and then Lloyd and I left on a storybook honeymoon — a week on his yacht, called *Wave Dancer*, touring the Caribbean Islands.

Then we flew to Russia. It hadn't been long since I had waged war against the Soviets. But Lloyd vowed to do things I hadn't done with my other husbands. He suggested Russia since neither of us had ever been, and as it turned out, I *loved* the Russian people.

At this point Russia was still under Soviet control, and only tour groups were allowed to visit. Our tour was through Rice University. The scholarly people on our tour thought they were going on an intellectual journey. They even hired a professor to instruct us in Russian history and the Soviet Union. They had no idea they would end up dancing with Russian strangers in a Moscow hotel and later in a disco yurt in the middle of the Gobi desert with the young people from the Moravian Ballet.

Lloyd was a great dancer, I loved to dance, and the ballet loved dancing with us. As for those staying in the hotel with us, we shook Moscow up by cutting in on the local people and dancing with them too. By the end of the evening everyone in our group, plus the Russian diners, were laughing and dancing with each other, even though no one could understand a word anyone was saying. Think Tower of Babel and bubbly. It was hilarious.

Our tour group hired an entire car on the Siberian Express to travel from Mongolia through Siberia and back to Moscow. There was no fruit on the train and, really, very little edible food — except caviar. You could have as much Beluga caviar as you could eat. We ate it on eggs for breakfast. We ate it alone and with pretty much everything else. It was divine — for a while.

But we yearned for fruit. We saw some glorious melons rattling down the street on a horse-drawn cart. We followed the cart to the market, rushed to the vendor, and said, "Oh, what beautiful melons!" This darling man picked three, handed them to me, and said in broken English, "My gift to you, beautiful lady." We tried desperately to pay him, but he absolutely refused payment.

We later learned that those melons cost a fortune, as they were rarely available and had to be shipped thousands of miles. This dear man had given us a gift that I will cherish always. I call moments like these jewels for the heart.

The Russians were wonderful people; they were simply enslaved. They knew it, and they yearned for the freedom of life in America, just like the Afghans and everybody else in the world.

The Soviet officials knew very well who I was and put three KGB agents on the train posing as tourist guides. They accompanied us everywhere, but they didn't know a thing about the tourist sites we visited or about Russian history.

One morning I looked at them and I asked point-blank, "Are you KGB?"

"Yes," they said. "We have been sent to see that you are safe," not exactly a believable excuse.

They were very reserved and careful until they saw me relate to their people. The Russian people liked me, and I liked them, which softened the agents' animosity. They realized I couldn't be *all* bad. Once they began to soften, they told us more than they realized about life under communism. The Berlin Wall had not yet come down, and they were still under the full weight of their ponderous government-controlled world, so different from our free capitalistic country.

The female KGB agent told us she was thrilled because her parents, an upper-class couple, were at last going to be able to afford a cheap Russian car. They had saved for thirty years, and finally it was going to be possible. Why did they have to wait so long? The Soviets did not allow access to banks or lending agencies; thus, you could not make a down payment on a large purchase and pay off the rest monthly. These hardworking people had to save their money until they had every penny, not just for the car itself, but also for the taxes and licenses and other requirements that the communists slapped on a weary populace.

Imagine being relatively financially secure yet having to wait thirty years for a car or a house. Our KGB "hosts" thought the story was wonderful. We, on the other hand, were appalled and saddened that this was the only sign of greatness they saw in their government, which had been created supposedly for the people.

Returning home from our honeymoon, Lloyd and I seemed ready to settle into a storybook marriage. I thought I would be happy. After all, a columnist had written, "I hear that when Lloyd proposed to Joanne, he said: 'My goal — for the rest of my life — is to see that you have a marvelous time every day.'" And for a time, the days did not disappoint.

Lloyd had a 120,000-acre ranch in Rhodesia, which gave him access to the world's most legendary gamekeepers. One of these men suggested that his son, a handsome twenty-year-old named Jim who reminded me of my son Beau, take us into an area where tourists were not allowed.

One night, we were sitting around the campfire, telling stories, and Jim began discussing elephants — his life's work and that of three generations of his family.

"Elephant families are so devoted to one another," Jim explained, "that if one of them is killed by accident or necessity, the rest of the family might grieve themselves to death."

Just a few days prior to our conversation, a tourist had been picked up by an elephant's trunk, thrown down, and trampled to death. "What do you think happened with the woman who was killed last week?" I asked.

"That's rare," Jim assured us. He speculated the woman had done something out of ignorance that threatened the animal.

"Bull elephants look intimidating," said our young guide, "but they are not particularly dangerous — unless there are females with babies. Then they will quickly kill you. They protect their young just like humans. Otherwise, they are so gentle you can walk among them."

My eyes widened. "Have you done that?"

He grinned cockily. "Yes."

"Could *we* do that?" I asked.

"Uh, sure," he said, looking dismayed.

"Let's do it!" I said. "Could we go tomorrow?"

"Well...I guess so...," Jim agreed slowly.

My horrified husband, silent until now, sat up straight and said in a strangled tone, "You can't mean that."

"He says he does it all the time," I said.

"He said he had *done* it. He did not say 'all the time.'"

"He says they're not dangerous," I continued. "Think of the adventure! Few people in the world have an opportunity like this."

The next morning, my husband and I joined Jim and the gun bearer — the man whose job it was to protect wayward tourists should something go wrong in the bush. We loaded into a Land Rover.

Before long, we found a group of seven bull elephants calmly standing in a copse of trees across from an open field filled with knee-high grass.

"Let's go," I said excitedly.

Still a good distance from the elephants, Jim warned us. "We will walk single file and I will lead the way," he said. "Do not talk. Do not make a sound. Do exactly what I do and be very calm. You must not threaten them at all. That's when they're dangerous."

Single file, we waded slowly and silently through the knee-high grass toward the enormous black bulls. They looked like tanks. Jim was at the front, and I was right behind him, followed by my husband and the gun bearer. Soon we were close enough to see every fold and crease in their skin, sniff their earthy smell, and hear them chewing. Jim and I were in so deep, we had an elephant on either side of us and could almost touch them. Then my husband saw a heart-stopping sight.

He lightly touched my back. "There are females...with babies," he quietly hissed at me. Sure enough, through a screen of green leaves off to the side we saw a group of mothers and babies.

"Back...up...slowly...," Jim whispered to me. I whispered the same to my husband — who didn't have to whisper anything to our poor, petrified gun bearer. Silently, in single file, we gingerly stepped backwards, slowly, slowly, one step at a time. Then, to quote my husband, we ran like hell.

Still, as my daddy had taught me, fearlessness usually worked in my favor. My adventures with Lloyd were magical, and we did have some fun times, especially dancing.

But things change. Or maybe they just become clear. Lloyd missed his ten thousand employees and had to give orders to somebody. I was all there was, so the orders fell on me.

Lloyd was wonderful to me in so many ways. We traveled all over the world on incredible trips. He gave me wonderful gifts, including beautiful dresses and jewelry that I still wear.

Everything was fine...as long as no one else was included. The minute we got married, he didn't want me to even talk to anybody. He monitored every phone call. We had very few friends. He really wanted just to be with me, so we had very little life outside the house or away from each other.

During the painful parts of my marriage, I needed something to distract me. I was fortunate to have a monumental task to throw myself into: the family's house modeled after Mount Vernon. I was still working on the house when Bob Herring died and when I started dating Charlie Wilson. (Bob died before it was anywhere near finished.) I showed it to Charlie and could never understand his lack of enthusiasm. The first thing Charlie said when I told him I was going to marry again was, "Has he seen Mount Vernon?" That house gave me a purpose during the twenty long years of my marriage to Lloyd. Thank the Lord! Just as I had worked on TV to save my marriage to Bob King, I now tried to save my marriage to Lloyd by throwing myself into the house restoration.

I look at dilapidated buildings and see them rehabilitated. Every time we see an old building, Beau says, "Look, Mama, there's your

Christmas present. I can get it cheap!" Then he dissolves into laughter.

It took five horrendous years, but finally, Robin and I got the house restored. It is beautiful, has been in many slick magazines...and is more expensive to maintain than the International Space Station. It now belongs to my son Robin, who purchased the house when he was twenty-nine. Thank God he is young.

Unfortunately, this diversion could not change the truth about my marriage to Lloyd. We just were not suited.

It is still difficult for me to talk about this part of my life. Desiree Lyon, author, foundation head, and my best friend, saw the situation with clarity.

"I watched helplessly as you transformed from a confident, vivacious woman to a withdrawn, depressed waif," she says. "Lloyd was always known to be difficult, but over time he became more so. You were the major target of his attacks. He placed on you the full weight of his personal happiness. You tried, but I could tell it drained you completely. Your friends attempted to divert your attention from him, but he seemed to consider this a threat. I know you felt that people would not understand the real situation and that you stayed out of obligation. When he wrote those letters to your friends saying that you had departed because you wanted to travel and that he could not because he was sick...well, people realized he was not sick. We just wanted you to have a life too!"

The situation with Lloyd occurred so gradually, I didn't realize what was happening at the time. Lloyd and I were simply not supposed to be together. Our life goals were too different.

I am sure he did not realize that he was being controlling, but my friends did and felt sad. After twenty years of marriage, Lloyd decided to move to an assisted-living facility. He thought that withdrawing all of his money would be an incentive for me to move with him. But it played no part whatsoever.

I was done. I had tried and tried, but I couldn't anymore. I wanted to stay in the condominium where we had lived, and I wanted my life back. Lloyd became even more difficult and began to threaten me with financial ruin.

"Lloyd," I said, "let me buy anything that you think that I owe you. I do not want to go to a lawyer. I do not want a financial settlement." I hate the hatred that springs from dividing money and belongings. (Bob King and I didn't use a lawyer either.)

Lloyd threatened a lawsuit, but I paid him for everything. I paid for my Jaguar. I paid for our place at the Huntingdon in Houston (I had paid for three-fourths of it anyway). I bought my way out. I didn't want to fight him. I walked out without asking for anything.

Not a single person ever asked me why I left Lloyd. Nobody said, "I'm so sorry about you and Lloyd. What happened?" They knew.

I felt like a used car left on the lot, but suddenly people who hadn't paid me any attention for *years* reappeared in my life. I had been hurt by their absence, and only now was I to learn that they had *tried* to be there but had never been allowed.

My life bloomed. I walked into the sunshine of a new life, which God had planned very well. It took me out of the rabbit hole and into the light.

A year after our divorce, I received a handwritten letter from Lloyd. It meant so much to me. Maybe I had paid, too, for his many kindnesses by making him happy.

3/13/06

Dear Joanne,

For the first time in my life I now find that I have nothing to do of importance and nothing to look forward to — mostly idle time for reflection. Physically and financially I'm in good shape. My mind is in good shape but I realize I need some sort of stimulation.

After much thought, it dawns on me that our years together were the most satisfying and exciting of my life. So, what I'm getting ready to do is to record many highlights of those years which I can enjoy (and you, too) in future ones. This will be the most enjoyable endeavor I could do.

Love,

Lloyd

Lloyd's letter meant so much to me. I had given him the best I had. He had been happy and had no regrets. He said our time together were the best years of his life. We had shared many happy moments and he had felt rewarded. I had paid my dues, and I was free.

Money would not be flowing freely down the river of my life, but I had enough that I had earned myself when I was a consultant to major companies, and I had land that I had bought from Bob King when we divorced. I had made enough to support myself for the rest of my life if I invested carefully. Darling Beau invested some of it in his deals, which made lots of money, so I was neither alone nor broke.

Swarms of friends, and even some gentlemen, returned, but more than anything I wanted to be free to be me, to do the things I wanted to do, when I wanted to do them: spend my money; drive my car; dress up or not. For the first time in my life someone was not telling me what I should do, how I should live, what I should eat, or any of the whens, whats, whys, shoulds, and oughts that had governed every decision I had ever made. What was good for somebody else had hovered over my life and dictated everything I did — until now.

A whole new life unfolded. Mine was suddenly the life of a woman who, for the first time, was happy to live alone. Now there was no special man in my life. I was happy. There is a time in life for everything. I've been married three times — enough for anybody. Now... now I like my dog. When I became single, God saw to it again that I had not been totally forgotten. George Crile published his book, *Charlie Wilson's War*. And I found myself right in the center of the movie it inspired!

CHAPTER 24

Red-Carpet Ready

The Telegraph

Charlie Wilson's War: Meet Charlie's better half

Girls on film: Julia Roberts in
Charlie Wilson's War

Mark Palmer
12:01AM GMT 21 Jan 2008

Joanne Herring, the millionaire hostess who helped a womanising American congressman fight the Soviet-Afghan war, tells Mark Palmer the truth about their relationship

'That bit was just so ridiculous," says Joanne Herring, the wheeler-dealing Texan multi-millionaire played by Julia Roberts in the acclaimed movie Charlie Wilson's War. "The truth is, I've never had a double martini in my life."

This particular "ridiculous" bit comes early in the film when Herring hosts a cocktail party for the great and the good - and the weird - in her Houston mansion to raise money for the mujahideen locked in battle against the Soviet Union in Afghanistan. Congressman Charlie Wilson (Tom Hanks) has been invited along to the bash, and no sooner has he charged his glass than Herring has persuaded him to go upstairs and inspect her boudoir - not that Wilson needs much persuasion.

The next scene shows Wilson enjoying a restorative bath after completing his inspection, while Herring, his sexual predator, touches up her make-up before rejoining guests downstairs for another round of cocktails and canapés.

THE WOMAN WHO WAGED *CHARLIE WILSON'S WAR* LENDS HER SKILLS TO RED CROSS WOMEN LEADERS

Think like a man, but act like a woman. That's Joanne Herring's advice for women. And while she's aware it's a similar sentiment expressed in a current bestseller title, it's been the blueprint for her life. She is now lending her leadership and drive to the Greater Houston Area Red Cross as the Honorary Chair of the Tiffany Circle Society of Women Leaders.

Tiffany Circle is a nationwide leadership network of women leaders and philanthropists who want to impact lives and make a real difference in their communities through their local Red Cross chapter. An annual gift at the Tiffany level supports local Red Cross services and allows women to become catalysts for change in our community.

Herring's name is usually preceded by the words 'Houston socialite.' While it's accurate, it belies the grit and intelligence that have made her a force to be reckoned with. The book and movie, *Charlie Wilson's War*, catapulted her image from socialite to global political player. It revealed her pivotal role in the 1980s, working with U.S. Representative Charlie Wilson, to secure government funding for the Afghan rebels fighting to drive out the Soviet Union.

Herring says her strength and determination are the hallmarks of Texas women. "It's almost genetic. When you think about what it was like 100 years ago…the Comanches, mosquitoes, floods and hurricanes. They learned to survive. And Texas was settled by people from the Old South, educated but poor. Women would be reciting Shakespeare as they were carrying water. They could do what was necessary."

She relates to strong women and is excited about providing her leadership to the Tiffany Circle, a group of accomplished women. She recently met several of the members. "I admired every one of them. They aren't just trying to play the game. They're sincere."

Joanne Herring invites
you and a guest
to a
Private Screening
of

CHARLIE WILSON'S WAR

Mr. and Mrs. John Schiller
invite you to a
Pre-Screening
reception

Wednesday December 19, 2007
5:30PM-7PM
River Oaks Country Club
1600 River Oaks Boulevard

7PM Red Carpet arrivals
8 PM Screening at
Edwards Greenway Grand Palace 24
3839 Weslayan St
Houston

Black Tie

To confirm your tickets, you must RSVP to
mparker2008@comcast.net or call 713-666-0280

Tickets to the Private Screening will be at Will Call and
must be picked up at the theatre with a valid photo ID

NO RECORDING
This screening will be monitored for unauthorized recording. By attending, you agree not to bring any audio or video recording device into the theater (audio recording devices for credentialed press excepted) and consent to a physical search of your belongings and person. Any attempted use of recording devices will result in your immediate removal from the theater, forfeiture of the device, and may subject you to criminal and civil liability. Universal Pictures retains ownership of this invitation, which is being provided to you for your p... and may not be transferred, sold or bartered by you to any other person or entity.

* Please allow additional time for heightened security. You can assist us by leaving all non-essential bags at home or in y... versal Pictures thanks you for your cooperation.

This invitation is absolutely
Non-transferable

$\mathcal{E}$verybody wants to know what it's like at a movie premiere and what you wear. The invitations for *Charlie Wilson's War* suggested "business attire," which makes it difficult to shine. At a premiere, you're expected to *shine*. I wore a cream-colored satin designer top that was twenty years old and redone but still beautiful.

Universal had given me only twenty tickets to the December 2007

280

premiere. James Hackett, chairman and CEO of Anadarko Petroleum, offered his plane to fly me and my guests to the event. When a company lets you use its plane, the CEO pays for everyone personally, so this was quite a gift!

The night before the premiere in Los Angeles, Kelley and Robert Day gave a beautiful dinner. They have one of the largest private foundations in the United States and are always doing generous things. She is beautiful, he is elegant, their home is a Hollywood palace, and their parties are famous.

They invited many key people in the Los Angeles society world. One guest, Vicci Walters, was so rich that when husband Raoul bought her their house in Beverly Hills, he added a stable and riding trails by buying the houses around them at about twenty-plus million dollars each. They bought Cher's home as a guest house! When he made Vicci the CEO of his company, she said she knew so little about business that she thought CEO meant "cocktails on every occasion." Fun friends!

On the big day I visited the Kazanjians, old friends and the exclusive jewelers who've provided many of my best pieces, including my "working" diamond. They also own a tiara made for the queen of England. Madonna wore it for her wedding and I wore it when I was guest of honor at the consular where I was escorted by the grandson of the last kaiser. They said I might wear anything they had for the movie premiere. I tried on everything and chose an emerald necklace. Oh, joy!

I chose the emeralds because I had to think of a sound bite to give the media. *Entertainment Tonight* had come to Houston to film me and was now putting me on the air regularly. On the day of the premiere they were filming my friends and me as we tried on stunning jewels at the Kazanjians' brunch. *ET* is the highest-rated entertainment news show on television, and Universal Studios expected me to promote the film. So I promoted.

I had to think of something snappy to say that the producers would like. When they asked me what I was wearing, I said, "Emeralds, of course. They're green, the color of money." Not exactly me — but *Entertainment Tonight* loved it. Remember, you must play the game.

I had planned to just pop in at a gathering of my friends, then head back to the hotel to rest before the premiere that evening. My friends were so much fun and so excited for me, though, that I couldn't break away. I remember retreating to the hall to rest my Manolo Blahniks.

It had been like that for months before the movie came out. I gave newspaper and magazine interviews daily, sometimes three or four a day. The networks came too. It was exciting and exhausting. After twenty years of being trapped in a marriage, it was like being reborn.

Having my special friends and children there at the premiere was the best part of the whole exciting moment. My friend Mickey Rosemarin, the owner of Tootsies, Houston's top dress shop, had paid for makeup artist Heidi Schultz's plane ticket and hotel to come to the premiere to make me "red-carpet ready." She worked on me gratis so that I would have everything that Julia Roberts had. This type of treatment was not provided by Universal but by my dear and caring friends.

I was touched when I read Heidi quoted in the *Houston Chronicle*: "It's not always about the money. Joanne is full of grace and very kind. I think if she thought she could help you, she'd go to the end of the world. Especially if she thinks you're truthful."

I finally got to go back to the Four Seasons to dress.

We went to the premiere in a "green machine," an electric car that traveled thirty miles an hour — period. The driver was Russian, ironically, couldn't speak English, and had no idea where the premiere was to be held. Unfortunately, neither did we! We traveled to San Diego and back looking for it before we arrived at the theater...late!

I had missed walking in with Charlie, Julia, and Tom, which was too bad, but I had my sons, who looked devastatingly handsome; Beau's lovely wife, Stanisse; Robin's girlfriend, Miss Rodeo Texas runner-up Lacey Spitzenburger; and my best friend, Larry Brookshire.

Larry is my dearest male friend. Life would be awful without him! When journalists coyly ask about my relationship with the handsome, megarich, debonair Larry I laugh and tell them, "If you don't have a brother, you get to pick one. He is it for me."

When somebody asked him what he did at the movie premiere, he said, "I held the coats."

I was so glad Charlie was able to be there too. He had had a heart transplant only a few months before. In fact, a cardiologist accompanied him from his home in Lufkin, Texas. I told reporters, "His recovery makes me so happy. I would have hated it if Charlie had missed it. This is his moment." And it was.

The movie had great publicity and was followed with such interest that the media and paparazzi were there en masse. As I walked through the hundreds of lights from photographers' cameras, I wondered if I could make it down that red carpet. I was blinded by the flashbulbs and couldn't see a thing.

"Joanne," they called, "look here...look here." I have never experienced anything as difficult as that walk. I lost all sense of time, space, and balance. I just prayed I wouldn't fall down!

At the end of that seemingly endless stroll, there were about ten small stages, about eight feet square, set up for the television commentators. They looked a mile high. Now completely blind, I thought, "Am I supposed to leap up on those things like a ballet dancer, look dazzling, and speak to someone I cannot see?" I was almost speechless by now. Even in LA, December is still winter for a

Texas girl, and I was very cold and tired, stiff and almost stuttering as I tried to say something interesting to each without knocking the commentator off the crowded platform. Robin's girlfriend clutched his arm to keep from falling too. The scene was as much fun as hiccups on a trampoline.

Once we were inside, Robin, Beau, Stanisse, and I were seated right behind Julia. Tom was there as well.

I had never seen the new script or a foot of the movie before it began, but I held my breath and thought positively. As the lights dimmed, the movie's infamous opening scene of Charlie Wilson in a hot tub appeared. As soon as it began, I started to cry. I couldn't stop. The tension from the months of anguish about how my life would be portrayed had left me weary and wondering if I would be able to survive another unkind scenario.

Through my tears, I realized that the film was great! It was intelligent, funny, and brilliantly executed.

Praise the Lord! He had done it again!

The point of movie premieres is to attract the press and to thank those who worked on the movie. The party after the Hollywood premiere was a huge gathering of people, a thank-you to the technicians and the many other people who play crucial parts in making a film. There were two tents: one for the cast and crew and another for the guests. Naturally, no matter how elegant the party, everybody wanted to be in with the stars.

Buffets had been set up in every corner, covered with delicacies, everything from lamb chops and asparagus to chocolate soufflé and champagne (though not Cristal...even Universal has a budget). Lacking doggie bags, some guests were stuffing goodies into their coats.

Gary Goetzman, Tom's business partner, appeared like a vision from heaven and introduced me to his beautiful wife, whose influence you could see in the film. Gary, who has the lean elegance of a leading man and is equally charming, took us to Tom, who graciously talked to everyone for as long as they wanted. I saw all of "Charlie's angels," the women who had worked in Charlie's office and who had gotten a bad rap in the film. Charlie didn't attend the party, though; after the film, he immediately boarded a plane to Houston with his doctor.

As for Julia, she was amazing. She was everything I should have been and more. I decided to clean up my act and be more like Julia playing me than me! "I'm thrilled," I told the reporters after the premiere. "I told Julia Roberts that I loved the way she portrayed me. She was so sweet, and just radiated."

She said to me, "I'm so glad you liked it. I did so hope you would."

James Baker, the former secretary of state and treasury secretary, had come with his lovely wife, Susan, to see their daughter the talented Mary Bonner Baker play one of Charlie's angels.

Amy Adams, who played Charlie's administrative assistant, had swished down the carpet behind me in a tight-fighting long red dress. She looked marvelous, but "business attire" was left in the envelope with the invitation. Smart girl. Maybe that is a lesson: when it's your moment, take it.

In truth, I didn't know where I belonged at this gathering. I felt shy, like a little girl from Texas surrounded by big stars. Strangely enough, though, some people *did* want to meet me.

Aaron Sorkin, who wrote the revised script, is a word master. The sparkling repartee is so well written and so wisely witty that even I, who knew the story so well, enjoyed his imaginative words dancing over the pages.

"Oh, I really wanted to meet you," Aaron said. Though miles apart politically, we became friends immediately. I later saw him on the History Channel talking about this movie. His comments about me were so kind. Before we met, he had thought of me as a kind of Jezebel who used my Christianity as a ploy to promote myself. Now he seemed to understand the real me.

I was most impressed with Philip Seymour Hoffman, who had

portrayed intelligence agent Gust Avrakotos, a fat, fiftyish, balding brunette. When he told me, "I've been dying to meet you," I looked at him in utter disbelief, first that he would care to meet me and second because he was young, blond, and very attractive. I barely recognized him!

Attorney Dick DeGuerin told columnists, "I loved the movie. She didn't say one bad word. But I wasn't bluffing. We were going to sue!"

Fast-forward to our Houston premiere, by invitation only, we didn't have a single star...but we had more fun than we had in Hollywood. It seemed the entire city wanted a peek at the way Tinsel Town had depicted our tale. There was fighting over the tickets! We had a thousand tickets and that wasn't nearly enough. We even had to ration family.

Beautiful Kristi Schiller and her CEO husband gave a party beforehand at the River Oaks Country Club. One shouldn't mention money, but the club told Posey Parker that it ended up costing thousands because of all of the people who crashed! The club couldn't handle it, but the wonderful Schillers didn't even frown.

Our town toppled Hollywood for sheer glamour. Everyone wore black tie, and Houston news anchor Jan Carson interviewed guests on the red carpet. The mayor of Houston, Bill White, spoke. He and his famous writer wife, Andrea, bless them, actually cut short a trip to Argentina to attend the premiere. Forgive me if I feel proud of my city and its people. They looked gorgeous — Texas women are, you know — and their husbands are hot stuff too.

We couldn't help but laugh as we sat in the movie theater in our black tie and formal finery, munching on popcorn and sipping Coca-Colas. I wore my red sequined dress, which, much like my working diamond, is worn to make a statement. Tonight I was supposed to be a movie star, and so I dressed the part.

We didn't know it then, but the film was to be nominated for five Golden Globes: Best Motion Picture, Best Performance by an Actor

(Tom Hanks), Best Performance by an Actor in a Supporting Role (Philip Seymour Hoffman), Best Performance by an Actress in a Supporting Role (Julia Roberts), and Best Screenplay (Aaron Sorkin). Philip Seymour Hoffman was nominated for an Academy Award as well.

Prompted by suggestions from the press, people began to ask if by supplying weapons to Afghan warriors, we had armed the Al-Qaeda terrorists. The short answer is no. A Stinger missile has a shelf life of only five years. Whatever weapons have been or ever will be aimed at the West by Islamic radicals didn't come from "Charlie Wilson's War."

My larger response is this: You cannot predict future wars. You can only fight the enemy you face at the time. Who were our allies in World War II? The Soviets. We spent billions in aid rebuilding their nation and were still not able to avoid the Cold War. The charge linking me to 9/11 was particularly hurtful. All the work I did to arm the Afghan people against the Soviets was done with my heart. For years, I sacrificed everything to defeat the Soviets and to save Afghanistan. And now *I* was being blamed for attacks against my homeland. I was willing to give my life to *protect* my country, not destroy it.

We wanted to stop the Soviets from controlling Afghanistan, and we did. Or, as Charlie put it in his interview for the movie's DVD, "[It] ended with the Soviet Army with their tail between their legs, in 1989, marching out of Afghanistan, a defeated army." Charlie and I tried desperately to convince the U.S. Congress to spend a fraction of the covert war's budget on rebuilding the country — to no avail. Thankfully, this was alluded to in the film.

I was so grateful to the Lord. He had interceded. He turned the movie, which could have been a disaster for me personally, into a glorious experience. God never ever lets us go down too far before He steps in. Still, a couple of (fictional) scenes from the movie continue to haunt me: the martini and the hot tub.

Since the movie came out, I have been invited to speak at various functions. In one case, I was making a speech to a group of outstanding businessmen who were taking me very seriously. The host, a devout Muslim, approached me and said, "I have never been in a liquor store in my life. I have never served liquor in my house. But I went myself to the liquor store to buy the ingredients to make you the perfect martini with two olives." With a flourish, his eyes sparkling with delight that he could give me such an appropriate gift, he served the drink in an oversized martini glass.

I looked at him blankly.

"From the movie! It's your martini with two olives!" he explained.

He had gone to so much trouble and had put so much thought into his gesture that I would have drunk the martini if I could have still made my speech afterward. But though his disappointment was sad to see, I had to confess that I rarely drink, and never martinis.

Incidents like this prove to me that even the minor scenes from the movie were treated as gospel by movie audiences. So to put to rights another piece of movie fiction, I must tell you that I *never* in my whole life called anybody a "slut," especially "Charlie's angels" (the women who worked in Charlie's office). They were ladies — all of them, and they were precious to me, real friends. Not one ever stepped out of line or had a fling with the boss or any of his friends. They observed Charlie's love life from afar, and Charlie, no matter how tempted, would never have played fast and loose in the office. He was too smart.

Charlie would not have picked up a constituent's daughter, either, as the movie claims. Why commit political suicide with the guys who voted for you when there are always other choice ladies to court?

I do not want to dwell too much on Hollywood license because it really is necessary. To write a script from a nearly six-hundred-page book is a feat, but some things have to be implied through pictures or in speech that's measured in seconds. That's why they included Julia's famous scene in the bikini — they said they wanted to imply that I could still compete with Miss Universe. Mostly, the filmmakers wanted to make a movie about a serious subject that could make us laugh — and they succeeded.

I am so glad that Charlie got to be there at the premiere. When he had his heart transplant, I knew that the future was not certain. Dr. Michael DeBakey, who had done the operation and who was in my mind the greatest genius I've ever met, said that very few people who receive a heart transplant live beyond two years. I felt the clock ticking at the premiere, less than one year after Charlie's transplant, and a tremendous sadness crept over me.

On February 10, 2010, I received the call that Charlie Wilson had passed away.

Nothing prepares you for when the door closes and someone you loved is actually gone. As I prepared to say my good-byes, Congressman Jerry Lewis called. He had served with Charlie on the Ways and Means Committee and had been a very real bipartisan hero. A Republican from California, he supported Charlie, a Democrat, right down the line in his fight for Afghanistan funding in the 1980s. In fact, his gorgeous wife, Arlene, was responsible for Tom Hanks and Tom's partner, Gary Goetzman, even *knowing* about the book *Charlie Wilson's War.*

The evening of the day Charlie Wilson was laid to rest in Arlington National Cemetery, Jerry Lewis and the whole Appropriations Committee wanted to honor Charlie with a celebration on Capitol Hill with his special friends and members of Congress. Jerry and Arlene called me personally from Washington to invite me. I thought it was a touching salute and I certainly wanted to be among his grieving and admiring friends.

Grace Nelson, the beautiful wife of Senator Bill Nelson (D-FL), went with me. She and her husband had arranged a meeting with the Senate Select Committee on Intelligence, whose members had graciously agreed to stay after work to meet with me to talk about Afghanistan. This was important, something I had dreamed of having an opportunity to do, but I was not going to let anything interfere with honoring Charlie. They understood and arranged their schedules to help me meet all my commitments.

My friend Paul Erickson (who had arranged for me to speak in Washington on the same platform with Glenn Beck, Ann Coulter, Laura Ingraham, and Newt Gingrich) gallantly offered to go back to the hotel to get our Afghanistan plan paperwork to present to the committee.

When we entered, I was immediately surrounded by friends, and we hugged and remembered the "Charlie-isms" that made him so much fun. It was a warm, wonderful moment.

I will always remember Charlie as a patriot and admire him as a great man of strength. George Crile mentions many times in his book that Charlie desperately needed me at that time in his life to bring out the greatness that was in him. The truth is, after grieving my lost husband and casting about for my life's direction, I needed him too.

We had been soul mates in our desire to save our country. Together we had united Washington in a bipartisan effort. As long as I live, I will cherish that in my heart — to see senators, congressmen, cabinet secretaries, the CIA, and all caring governmental officials in power actually working together without grabbing a television mike and telling everyone what they were doing. This *was* a true covert operation. Thirty years later, not one of them had tried to take credit. To me it was the greatest expression of patriotism I had ever witnessed. I was sorry more attention was not given to Jerry Lewis and the Republicans who fought so valiantly beside Charlie and Gust and me. I begged George Crile to mention Ronald Reagan, George H.W. Bush, Jim Baker, Secretary of Defense Caspar Weinberger, CIA director Bill Casey, and others in *Charlie Wilson's War*, but he chose not to. Make no mistake — it was Charlie who got the money.

It *was* Charlie's war. He won it. But he could not have done it without the Republicans.

Afghanistan would be threatened again with totalitarianism, this time under the mask of religion, and plunged back into war. But this time I would have to fight without Charlie.

CHAPTER 25

STAR

BELLE OF THE COLD WAR

Houstonians thought they knew Joanne Herring, former TV talk show hostess, philanthropist and jet-setter. Turns out, there was a side to Herring few people knew — she played a small but pivotal role in ending the Cold War.

JOANNE HERRING

FRANÇOISE DUHAMEL

JULIA ROBERTS

CLARISSA CONTRERAS PHOTO ILLUSTRATION : CHRONICLE   KAREN WARREN PHOTO : CHRONICLE
STAR QUALITY: The part of Joanne Herring will be played by Julia Roberts in the upcoming film *Charlie Wilson's War.*

Afghanistan...
Again

When the premieres were over, I was tired — tired of the press, tired of the process, and tired of me and my past. It was time for me to relax in my hammock, listen to the mockingbird that sings in the night, and enjoy being with my grandchildren and my dog.

This was not to be. Daily e-mails, calls, and letters poured in begging for help for Afghanistan. "Surely you want to help?" No, I didn't. I was like Scarlett running from the hospital, sobbing and saying, "I can't take any more pain." I couldn't bear to think about the children with no arms, the result of the Soviet butterfly bombs, which looked like toys and attracted children, and which the *New York Times* kept saying never existed. Whenever I think of them I shiver and want to roll up and die of the pain I saw all around me in Afghanistan, endured with more courage by this gallant, forgotten people than most Americans are ever required to feel.

So what am I doing in Afghanistan *again*? It is all the fault of Esther Coopersmith, doyenne of Washington society, and Caroline Firestone. However Caroline, the daughter of a railroad magnate and widow of businessman and philanthropist Leonard Firestone, was the main culprit. She has dedicated her life and fortune to saving Afghanistan. A selfless, beautiful woman and a fearless advocate, she's a Democrat, and I love her, but I may never forgive her for pulling me back to Afghanistan.

She pulled me back in with this story: A father, weeping, explained to her during one of her trips to Afghanistan that he had to sell his son to keep his other children (all sixteen of them) from starving. He told her he was selling him to a Muslim boys' school, where the child, fifteen, would have plenty to eat and be educated. The father understood that he would never see his son again, and this broke his heart, but he did it so his other children could live. After the father left, the person telling the story to Caroline turned to the buyer, who she suspected was not a mullah (teacher), and said, "What are you really going to do with the boy?"

"I am going to sell him for his eyes," said the man, a trafficker of human organs.

When Caroline told me this story, I said, "No parent should ever have to make that choice."

I went back into Afghanistan with everything I had — which, frankly, wasn't much.

All of the things that got me in the doors of power before were now gone. It had been more than twenty years since the whoop-de-do happened with Charlie and Afghanistan, and two decades is a long time in Washington. Most players' memories are short, so I am a has-been, hardly in a position to push a plan to save a country.

"Do you know anyone or anything about Afghanistan today?" inquired my buddy Posey Parker, who selflessly joins me in everything.

"I knew a dead ambassador who was said to be a crook on the side," I replied.

That wasn't very helpful, so I needed to reach into my toolbox again. What is happening there? What do the people of Afghanistan need? What do I have that can help?

First I needed to find out why, even with money pouring into Afghanistan, nothing is changing. The Taliban is attempting to reform and has found some support there, and I needed to know why.

Well, if you're hungry, the Taliban might give you food. If your child needs an operation, they get it for you. When choosing a government, which one would you pick? If my family members were starving, I would choose the one that feeds them.

But then, too late, these needy people would realize that they have opened the door to the Taliban again. Too late they'd realize that they paid for necessities with their freedom.

How can we eat our dinner tonight remembering that father and the ghastly fate of his son? Still, what can we do? Charlie had asked Congress for money for just one school in the movie, and even his friends turned him down.

If the United States had implemented a Marshall Plan in Afghanistan (similar to the one that rebuilt Europe after World War II) after the Afghans defeated the Soviets in the 1980s, terrorism might never have gained a foothold in Afghanistan and Pakistan.

For the last thirty years of my life, I have been involved with the Afghans, a people not dissimilar to our own when George Washington was alive. The difference is that they don't have what we had in fledgling America — strong and stable allies. We sent weapons to help the Afghans defeat the Soviet Union in the 1980s, but once the Soviets were expelled, we just left. We forget that not one American died liberating Afghanistan. The Afghans did it all. The Soviets, the greatest war machine in history, were defeated by a fierce local population living in a nation the size of Texas. And, at their moment of triumph and rebuilding, we cut off their aid. Afghanistan was a ruined nation that had won an enormous strategic victory for the United States, and we left them with no means of repairing or defending themselves. The people were starving, wounded, and dying.

So in 2009, I founded the Marshall Plan Charities — a Texas-based nonprofit corporation dedicated to "winning the peace" in war-torn Afghanistan. I like to think that MPC is uniquely positioned to complement the ongoing U.S. military operation in Afghanistan by rapidly and effectively redeveloping normal, healthy civilian life in hundreds of Afghan villages. I believe that through civilian aid we can transform totalitarian dictatorships into democratic allies.

An Afghan civilian population with clean water, sustainable food sources, basic health care, modern schools, and real jobs has no need for Taliban poppy fields or U.S. military protection. If the U.S. military operation in Afghanistan is to be deemed a success, we — America — must provide Afghan civilians with the basic tools of civilization so that a culture of self-reliance can permanently supplant a hopeless return to dependence upon a fundamentalist dictatorship. In the process, we can spare the world a breeding ground and staging area for international terrorism.

It is my conviction that Afghan villages can be restored only by following the Marshall Plan Charities' holistic model of simultaneously introducing clean water, food, health care, schools, and jobs.

Toward this end, for two years Posey Parker and I researched nonprofit aid organizations to find the most capable and most devoted to restoring this bleeding country, which Congress so callously abandoned in the 1980s. We have begun to assemble a series of private, nongovernmental organizations that have agreed to work together to provide these civil essentials — village by village rather than project by project.

We are about to combine — for the first time — the collective work of such NGOs as the Afghan school-building organization Central Asia Institute and former Goldman Sachs CEO Connie Duckworth's Arzu (which produces everything from carpets for export to fuel for village fireplaces). Dr. Steven Kwon's revolutionary soybeans (one bean yields forty-five new beans — enough for food, replanting, and export), which he acquired through his Nutrition and Education International organization, will be given even higher levels of support in MPC villages.

After 9/11 we asked the Afghans to fight the Taliban with us. All of the terrorists were training there, turning out leaders for more and bigger terrorist attacks. The Afghans fought to the death with us again.

Did we thank or help them? *No!* How would you feel if you were they? Would you trust us? Now they have nothing. They are literally starving. The water is bad. There are no jobs. Some 90 percent are illiterate. They have no vaccines. Malaria and dysentery are epidemic.

We could change the health of the whole country by helping them grow food and by cleaning up their water. Think: a polio vaccine costs fifty cents, a mosquito net $1.50. Yet few are available in Afghanistan.

That's it, then. We have to feed and educate the Afghan people, give them water and jobs, and provide them with basic health care. There are nonprofit organizations that are doing it and have been doing it so successfully that they are being targeted and killed — not by the Afghan people but by the terrorists. Each nonprofit specializes in one of the five living essentials the villages must have: food, water, education, medical care, and jobs, simultaneously, to survive and get strong enough to fight for themselves.

The country is full of good, yet overwhelmed, charitable organizations, each of them struggling to raise money to solve all of these problems themselves instead of focusing on their specialty. MPC is an umbrella organization for these nonprofits so that they can focus on the one thing they do best.

I care about the Afghan people. But I also care about our country and the ramifications for America of failure in Afghanistan. I want our troops to come home. We are not the world's policemen. The blood of our children is too precious. Why should our troops risk their lives on missions for which they were not intended? They do not speak the language and do not know the customs as MPC organizations do. More than 80 percent of the MPC's workers will be Afghans. Why is that important? Because the terrorists brag that they do not care about winning the war. They brag that when the troops leave, they will come back. Our MPC organizations will not leave because most of them are Afghan based; they're already home.

Afghanistan is a subject no one ever wants to discuss because it seems so complex and hopeless. This war is half a world away — and yet right next door because, hard though it is to believe, it threatens our country. My ongoing work on behalf of Afghanistan is about stopping terrorism there. I want this for our country, our troops, and the Afghans. We need the friendship and help of the Afghan people to stop the terrorists. We must win the peace in Afghanistan or the terrorists will reassert control there. The repercussions to neighboring Pakistan — and eventually to the United States again — are too terrible to imagine.

If Afghanistan falls back under Taliban control, a fundamentalist Islamic state will have been reestablished on the border of Pakistan — at a time when Pakistan itself is under severe threat from fundamentalist elements within its own borders. The lawlessness of the so-called tribal regions nestled between Pakistan and Afghanistan would spread throughout Pakistan. An Islamic fundamentalist coup in Pakistan would place a fully functional nuclear arsenal in the hands of religious forces intent on the destruction of the United States. These are the stakes. Any misstep or loss of will now exposes my country to inconceivable horrors.

Please do not confuse the Afghan people with the Taliban. Before the Taliban and sharia law came, the Afghans had a viable country — poor but free. It was known as the fruit basket of the Middle East, providing fruit, wheat, and produce. The women were not tortured and enslaved. The girls went to school.

When I speak on Afghanistan, our men and women in uniform often approach me. Sometimes they've lost a limb or their sight or had their faces marred. Almost always, they tell me about how they want to go back and help the people of Afghanistan. They really love the Afghan people. Our troops who are over there fighting this war believe in what we're doing — and they've come to believe in the people they're protecting.

Our young fighting men and women in Afghanistan are exceptional. They give me hope for our country's future. When I hear about their enormous sacrifices, I want to bring them home for good. But even they temper their desire for home with the desire to succeed in their original mission.

As I write these final words in my memoir, I just received exciting news: our first Marshall Plan Charities operations have begun in Herat Province. Soybeans have arrived for planting, fresh water has been tapped, a school is being built, and a clinic will soon be open in a village dedicated to our holistic development model. American military forces friendly to our effort are enthused. This glowing testimonial was just received from an Afghan provincial leader: "Had Mrs. Herring been able to help us after the Soviets left, our country would not have been poisoned by fanatical ideologues — our people would have been educated and we would have an independent, progressive nation and government." You can find me at joanne@joanneherring.com and Facebook if you'd like to be a part of this new Genesis story!

I fervently wish that I could write that our troops were already home, no longer needed because the Afghan people are standing on their own, no longer enslaved by religious or terrorist thugs. But I know now that that day is coming. This is God's plan and I know we're going to win.

I will use diplomacy and diamonds or whatever charms and strength I have left to fight this last battle. The story of true freedom in Afghanistan is still being written. But change is in the wind, the fragrance of hope is in the air, the stirrings of new life and success are being felt.

The will to win is as strong as the certainty of a new dawn. Pray with us; stay with us. Tomorrow is just around the corner. Right will succeed; just you wait and see.

Afterword

*W*hile I was in the midst of writing this book, David Adickes, the famous sculptor, artist, and philosopher, walked into my office and said, "What really interests me about your life is that it's the story of a woman in Houston, Texas, who recognized the Soviet threat and did something about it. Others saw it, but the Soviets' formidable strength and the threat of a World War III silenced them into constant negotiations and endless debates. That one woman could arouse Congress and foreign heads of state to acknowledge the threat and to set in motion the defeat of the greatest war machine in history is not only a miracle but a fascinating story that changed the world."

The essence of this memoir is that small people can make a big difference. The seed of the assurance that we could stop the Soviets and that we must stop them now was planted in me here in Houston, Texas. (God uses small people to do big things — remember David and Goliath?) I had no idea how to stop them; I just knew it had to be done. I was a fifty-year-old widow with few financial assets and many responsibilities. Yet I was determined to do what I could. And if I could do that, imagine what you can do.

They say if you want to make God laugh, tell Him your plans. In my life, I tried hard to tell Him. When His laughter died down, He directed me in ways that I — and a lot of the world — could scarcely imagine. I'm as surprised as anyone at the seemingly fictional turns my life has taken.

I was the only woman at that time to earn the title of "honorary man" in the Muslim world — a title that allowed this little dyslexic girl from Texas to be named a consul to Pakistan at the moment when the tide of the Cold War turned in neighboring Afghanistan — when all I really wanted to do was to sing on Broadway.

The world has been as close as my private jet one day while my children would have starved without the gift of deer meat from friends the next. I've been married three times (two times too many) and widowed once (one time too many). I was the first woman to host a daily television show when women were "too dumb" to do it and nobody could spell "Oprah." I've danced with kings and almost died of grief.

The passage of time has allowed me to see how every chapter in my life was built on the one before. And I don't mean that in the cloying, "we all learn things" wise-grandmother-aphorisms kind of way. I mean that I would not have survived each new act in my life without some brutal lesson or astounding coincidence from the act before.

As I've said in these pages, my life has had a pattern. Every ten years, I've experienced an overwhelming tragedy. Ten glorious years and — wham! — something ghastly. But each decade's debacle taught me something that I would desperately need in order to take the next step in life. And each seemingly coincidental event or brush with greatness would later open a door to opportunities that I could scarcely have orchestrated or even dreamed.

And with every step in my life, there has been drama, always drama. My son Beau once told me, "Mother, I used to feel sorry for you for living in a hurricane, but you like living in a hurricane!" Well, I can't say that's true, but really strong winds no longer faze me.

The Lord has given me the tools that I would need to climb the mountains of sadness and disappointment that He has placed before me — and to save me as I tumbled down the other side. Everything we learn or experience becomes a tool in our life's toolbox. I implore you to recognize those in yours. Otherwise, they'll sit uselessly in the box as you continue to make the same life mistakes — all for the lack of the right tool.

This was not meant to be a how-to book. The libraries are full of those. This is a book about what *not* to do. I may have been blessed to have achieved a few things in my life, but surely there are less painful ways to succeed. So give this book to your children and say firmly, "Read this book. Don't do a thing in it and you'll be fine. Well, okay, maybe a few things."

As someone who's lived a bit of history and (they say) made some along the way, I'm fascinated and frustrated by the world's habit of repeating some of its worst mistakes. I was seated next to Henry Kissinger at a dinner at the Iranian embassy and he offered me an important insight.

Henry was secretary of state at the time — witty, sophisticated and brilliant — and everyone wanted to hear what he had to say about anything. He told me that one reason people don't heed the lessons of history is that they don't understand the eras that preceded their own.

For instance, if you've lived all of your life since the collapse of the Soviet Union, it's hard to understand the Cold War or what all the fuss was about in *Charlie Wilson's War.* And if you don't understand why Afghanistan was a tipping point in the greatest threat against America in the 1980s, you probably won't understand why Afghanistan is the tipping point in the greatest threat against America today.

So I started to write about the eras I've lived through in the hopes that you would understand perceptions at those times to better cope with whatever you face today. Too often we use today's thinking to analyze history and are horrified at our country's past poor judgment. But the times and knowledge were different then — and will be different in the future. Only people remain the same, doing the same things over and over — just in different clothes. (And more often than not, it's all about power and money.)

So I've told you the story of my life and the history I've lived through until now. You don't want to read the dry statistics so well covered elsewhere. People *live* history, and the decisions they make are sometimes as much about whom they love (and what they wear) as they are about war and peace. This, then, was intended to be a romp through history, a gossipy memo about people, places, and things.

I talked with you like a friend. I strayed, like friends do when they talk. When a thought occured to me, I told you a story. Nobody sits down with a friend and tells them their whole life without stopping, right? You'd quickly have a phone call to take or would use me as a sleeping pill.

At the end of the tales of men and marriage, of royal dinners and yachts, of exotic parties and congressional intrigue, I'm at war again in Afghanistan. As much as I love the Afghan people and as dedicated as I am to improving their lives, I'm working again in that corner of the world to save America from terrorism. My new war is for my children and grandchildren — and for yours.

And I'll make mistakes, as I have before. I try to be good and to obey the rules, but I've often failed. If you've stumbled too, take heart! Walk with the Lord and He'll pick you up as He's done with me. If you see yourself on these pages, use my disappointments and failures to avoid them in your own life.

I've learned not to worry if people laugh at me for my mistakes. I laugh with them. If you can laugh at yourself, your friends will cheer you. And when you admit your mistakes, you disarm your enemies.

Maybe you can look at my life and learn.

God looks at my life and laughs!

Index

Permissions

P. 2:   Shelby Hodge, "Dinner Abuzz over Film Role," *Houston Chronicle* (October 13, 2003), section D. Reprinted by permission.

P. 3:   *Charlie Wilson's War* feature film, still photo. Courtesy of Universal Studios Licensing LLC.

P. 5:   Review of *Charlie Wilson's War: The Extraordinary Story of the Largest Covert Operation in History, Publishers Weekly* (May 26, 2003). Reprint by permission.

Pp. 5, 4:   Cover image and page snapshot from *Charlie Wilson's War*, copyright © 2003 by George Crile. Used by permission of Grove/Atlantic, Inc.

P. 14:   Shelby Hodge, "Cross-Century Garb Highlights Sixth Annual Plantation Ball," *Houston Chronicle*. Reprinted by permission.

P. 15:   "Trotter Great-Great-Granddaughter Returns to Ancestoral…" Reprinted by permission of the Clarke County Tribune, Quitman, MS.

Pp. 20–21:   River Oaks Country Club Estates, Heritage Society Map Collection MC012, Harris County Archives, Houston, Texas 77002.

P. 28:   Cover of *H Texas* (Fall 2009), featuring Warner Roberts, "25 Most Beautiful." Reprinted by permission of Gittings Photography, copyright H Texas magazine.

P. 118:   Maxine Mesinger, "People by Maxine," *Houston Chronicle* (February 25, 1982). Reprinted by permission.

P. 118:   Maxine Mesinger, "Big City Beat," *Houston Chronicle* (October 14, 1986). Reprinted by permission.

Pp. 126–127:   Suzy Says column, "Joanne Rounds Up 'Tout' Paris," *Houston Chronicle* (July 26, 1974). Reprinted by permission.

Pp. 128–129:   Susan Watters, "Filming Another French Connection," *Women's Wear Daily* (August 16,1976), page 14. (Including photos.) Reprinted by permission of Susan Watters.

P. 129:   "She Snoops to Conquer," *Houston Chronicle* (August 30, 1972). Reprinted by permission.

P. 140:   Maxine Mesinger, "Have Tongue, Will Tattle," "Friday Flashes," "Houston Natural Gas Prexy," "Memos from Max," and "Count Alain de Taillach, who has homes in Paris…," *Houston Chronicle*. Reprinted by permission.

P. 152:   "Partyline: Suzy Reports from New York," *Houston Chronicle*. Reprinted by permission.

P. 152:   Eugenia Sheppard, "Around the Town," *New York Post* (May 13, 1976). Reprinted by permission.

P. 153:   "84 or No, Rose Kennedy Cuts a Mean Dance Beat," *Houston Chronicle* (March 16, 1975). Reprinted by permission.

P. 153:   Betty Beale, "Benefit Premiere," *Victoria Advocate* (March 16, 1975). Reprinted by permission.

P. 155:   Judy Lunn, "Would-Be Hosts Scrap for Honor," *Houston Post*. Reprinted by permission.

P. 155:   Susan Watters, "The Saga Continues," Eyeview, from *Women's Wear Daily* (December 9, 1982), page 28. (Including a photo of Joanne Herring by Guy Delort.) Reprinted by permission of Susan Watters.

P. 156:   Betty Beale, "Word from Washington," from *Washington Star* (January 27, 1980). Reprinted by permission.

P. 156:   "Joanne Herring's List of Honors," *Houston Chronicle* (December 5, 1979), section 4, page 4. Reprinted by permission.

P. 157:   Amy Penn, "Around the Town," *New York Post* (January 21, 1985). Reprinted by permission.

P. 158   Photo of Eva Gabor, Gen. Paul X. Kelley, Barbara Kelley, and Joanne Herring. Reprinted by permission of Bill Cunningham.

P. 158:   France-Michele Adler, "Parties Where the Guests Change with the Courses," *New York Post* (July 22, 1984). Reprinted by permission.

P. 159:   "Fan" quote, W (September 21–28, 1984). Reprinted by permission of Condé Nast.

P. 159:   Susan Watters, Eye…Eye…Eye…column from *Women's Wear Daily* (May 9, 1977), page 4. (Including a photo of King Hussein, Joanne Herring, Joan Schnitzer, and Luciana Avedon.) Reprinted by permission of Susan Watters.

P. 170 (photo):   Photograph of Joanne and Bob Herring, *Fortune*. ©1980 Bob Gomel.

P. 170:   Excerpt from "The Right Honorable Businessman," from *Fortune* magazine, May 19, 1980 © 1980 Time Inc. Used under license. *Fortune* magazine and Time Inc. are not affiliated with, and do not endorse, products or services of Licensee.

P. 180:   Marge Crumbaker, "Moroccan Royalty to Sit In on 'Desert Song,'" *Houston Post*, (October 15, 1986). Reprinted by permission.

P. 196:   Eugenia Sheppard, "Around the Town," *New York Post* (May 28, 1982). Reprinted by permission.

P. 196:   Liz Smith, People, *New York Daily News* (May 23, 1982). © Tribune Media Services, Inc. All Rights Reserved. Reprinted with permission.

Pp. 240–246:   Sandy Sheehy, "Honorary Consul," *Ultra Magazine* (February 1986). Reprinted by permission of Sandy Sheehy, author of *Texas Big Rich* and *Connecting: The Enduring Power of Female Friendship*.

P. 258:   "A Feast, Texas-Sized," from the *New York Times*, February 7, 1984 © 1984 The New York Times. All rights reserved. Used by permission and protected by the copyright laws of the United States. The printing, copying, redistribution, or retransmission of this content without express written permission is prohibited.

P. 259:   Diana McLellan, Diana Hears column, *Washington Times* (February 2, 1984). Copyright © 1984 The Washington Times LLC. This reprint does not constitute or imply any endorsement or sponsorship of any product, service, company, or organization.

P. 262:   Marge Crumbaker, "Herring-Davis Wedding Truly a Glamorous Affair," *Houston Post* (August 13, 1985). Reprinted by permission.

P. 263:   Marge Crumbaker, "Joanne Herring to Wed Millionaire Lloyd Davis," *Houston Post* (July 12, 1985). Reprinted by permission.

P. 264:   Stacy Meier, "A Honeymoon around the World in Six Weeks," *Dallas Morning News* (August 19, 1985). Reprinted by permission of reference editor.

P. 278:   "Charlie Wilson's War: Meet Charlie's Better Half," *Telegraph* (January 2008). © Telegraph Media Group Limited 2008. Reprinted by permission.

P. 279:   "The Woman Who Waged Charlie Wilson's War Lends Her Skills to Red Cross Women Leaders." Houston Red Cross press release. Reprinted by permission of Red Cross of Greater Houston.

P. 280:   Invitation from Mr. and Mrs. John Schiller to prescreening reception of *Charlie Wilson's War*. Reprinted by permission.

P. 292:   "Belle of the Cold War," *Houston Chronicle*. Reprinted by permission.